Your Values, My Values

(2000)

Your Values, My Values

Multicultural Services in Developmental Disabilities

by

Lilah Morton Pengra, Ph.D.
Multicultural Consulting Services
Buffalo Gap, South Dakota

·P·A·U·L·H·
BROOKES
PUBLISHING Co.

Baltimore • London • Toronto • Sydney

Paul H. Brookes Publishing Co.
Post Office Box 10624
Baltimore, Maryland 21285-0624

www.brookespublishing.com

Typeset by Eastern Composition, Binghamton, New York.
Manufactured in the United States of America by
Versa Press, East Peoria, Illinois.

All of the case stories in this book are composites of the author's actual experiences. In all instances, names have been changed; in some instances, identifying details have been altered to protect confidentiality.

Library of Congress Cataloging-in-Publication Data

Pengra, Lilah Morton, 1946–
    Your values, my values : multicultural services in developmental disabilities / by
    Lilah Morton Pengra.
      p.   cm.
    ISBN 1-55766-448-X
    1. Developmentally disabled—Services for—United States. 2. Multi-
culturalism—United States. 3. Social values—United States. I. Title.
HV1570.5.U65 P45 2000
362.19'68—dc21

                                                             99-044975

British Library Cataloguing in Publication data are available from the British Library.

Contents

In memory of my father, Robert Innes Morton, who taught me curiosity as well as the scientific skills of careful observation and interpretation

and

In honor of my mother, Virginia Mergy Morton, who showed me, through her years as teacher, social worker, and community volunteer, the importance of helping others

About the Author

Lilah Morton Pengra, Ph.D., Cultural Specialist, Multicultural Consulting Services, Post Office Box 126, Buffalo Gap, SD 57722

Dr. Pengra earned her doctorate in anthropology in 1975 from the University of Wisconsin–Madison, with special interest areas in sociolinguistics and American ethnic groups. She has taught anthropology for South Dakota School of Mines and Technology and transcultural nursing for South Dakota State University. Her practice of anthropology in the human services included 5 years as the director of an agency serving adults with developmental disabilities.

Dr. Pengra works as a cultural specialist. Her activities include giving workshops to promote multicultural competence, consulting with teams to design assessments for specific cultural differences, and assisting agencies to develop cultural diversity policies and procedures.

Preface

Missionaries have a calling. Scientists have intellectual curiosity. Missionaries seek to change the people they meet. Scientists try to measure data without changing them. Missionaries may become emotionally involved with their converts. Scientists are supposed to remain detached. Thus, years ago when a colleague told me I was more missionary than scientist, I was offended. Now I proudly claim I am both.

When I was an undergraduate, applied anthropology was not well accepted, nor had I discovered it as my calling. Using information and theories from anthropology to help people control what happens to them smacked too much of social work and not enough of science. In addition, social workers were suspect if they became interested in the cultural backgrounds of their clients. One summer prior to entering graduate school, I interned as a social worker in a program for Mexican American migrant farm laborers. The experience convinced me to continue in anthropology rather than switch to social work because it appeared to me that many problems were related to cultural differences. I was most concerned when cultural differences occasionally were targeted for eradication. It was then that I developed my proselytizing fervor. I wanted to teach anthropology to social workers to help them understand that their actions might unintentionally threaten rather than empower their clients.

I was not alone, of course, in identifying the importance of culture in social work as well as in nursing, teaching, counseling, and other helping relationships. Eventually, professionals had access to cultural anthologies written especially for them. Typically these books had a chapter on each of several different groups in the United States recognized as having a distinct culture. These books were criticized by scientific purists as being the "cookbook" approach to culture and by helping professionals as promulgating stereotypes. Gradually, however, these anthologies have become more sophisticated and are excellent references.

In combination with other resources, these cultural anthologies were an important part of the reading I assigned when teaching applied anthropology and transcultural nursing, courses I blithely taught for several years before I had the opportunity to practice what I preached. For 5 years I was the director of an agency providing both residential and vocational services for adults with developmental disabilities in a small community near an Indian reservation in rural South Dakota. I hope some of my former students are smiling as they read this because I quickly discovered how much more difficult it is to provide culturally sensitive services than it is to argue that they are needed.

The difficulty was not because people had developmental disabilities. Because culture is learned, some people question whether people with developmental disabilities learn culture the way others do and, if so, whether they learn normal or defective variants of it. In addition, the people I worked with had experienced far more abuse, poverty, and physical and mental illnesses than others in the community had. Many had also lived in institutions for significant periods of their lives. It would not be unreasonable to find that the effects of these experiences lessened the impact of culture on their behavior. In fact, I was constantly surprised by how much more often culture was a factor in influencing behavior than even I, the anthropologist dedicated to finding cultural explanations, had expected. Although not all problems were related to culture, this book is about those that were.

The difficulty I did face initially was how to use general descriptions of the culture of a distinct group, such as the Lakota who live on the reservation close to where I worked, to understand the actions of an individual. The solution was to shift from culture as the object of study to the values of a particular person. This also solved the dilemma of how to provide culturally sensitive services to a person whose cultural background was less marked (e.g., Norwegian American, Polish American) or not generally recognized as different (e.g., cultural variations associated with social class and rural versus urban locations).

Because I am suggesting that services should be based on the values of each person, it seems reasonable to call them *values-based services*. In the field of developmental disabilities, services that support normalization, self-determination, and inclusion are also called *values based*. In my mind, these are Values with a capital *V*, the overarching values that guide agency-centered goals and decisions. The approach used in this book is a person-centered extension of this usage—in other words, values with a lowercase *v*. What norms does this particular person embrace? What values does she consider in determining her own behavior? In what ways does she want to be included in the community?

This book addresses how to answer these and similar questions by using several approaches and techniques, including one that I developed. My technique provides a baseline for placing functional behavior assessments in cultural context and elicits cultural variations in meaning that lead to misunderstanding when not shared. This technique, as well as the other recommended approaches, draws on a view of culture as composed of schemas—that is, mental models people have of the meaning of actions and objects.

Part I of this book introduces the idea that everyone has values, including people with developmental disabilities (Chapter 1), and that these values give meaning to behavior through the schemas people have learned (Chapter 2). Chapter 3 describes the American schema of how people are classified to predict their behavior. Chapters 2 and 3 together provide a detailed introduction to schema theory and how it can pinpoint cross-cultural miscommunication. Because the relationship between theory and practice presents a chicken-and-egg quandary, the reader is encouraged to read these chapters for general content the first time and come back to them for a more detailed understanding of schema theory, if needed, after reading examples of its application in later chapters.

Part II illustrates several uses of the technique of schema analysis. Chapter 4 relates how an assessment of the meaning of theft was created and used to design culturally sensitive services for a woman with a penchant for taking things others owned. Comparing her assessment results with the results of others similar to her in ethnicity and social class enabled her team to distinguish between actions that differed because of her values and behavior that occurred because she needed to learn additional social and functional skills. Chapter 5 shows that contrasting  sets of beliefs about causality, time, and the relationship between individuals and society are found in conjunction with different decision-making strategies. Competence is thus a consequence of the fit between a person's decision-making values and the environment created by the beliefs and values of those around him, accounting for the success or failure of some community placements. Chapter 6 completes the exploration of the uses of schema analysis by applying it to the difficult decisions teams must make about how and when to intervene if behavior is disordered or considered abnormal.

Part III explores the environment created by the American values of privacy, independence, and equality. When people with developmental disabilities are stripped of their privacy and controlled by others,  they are relegated to a marginal and devalued status in American society and prevented from living in terms of their own values. Disability, therefore, is created by how people are limited by others rather than by their own physical and mental impairments. Chapters 7 and 8 make recommendations for increasing each service receiver's privacy and independence by building on her definitions of what these values mean. Chapter 9 analyzes how values about intelligence are embedded in the class structure of the United States and communicated subtly through language. Although some suggestions are tendered for changing attitudes, the pervasiveness of the schema of intelligence mitigates against equal status for people with developmental disabilities.

Part IV is a summary of the main themes of the book and a final glimpse of the people who challenged me to think more clearly about how culture affects everyone. Because changing names does not ensure confidentiality in a small town, real incidents are presented throughout the book as part of the lives of composite characters, each of whom is a combination of three or more people I know. Sex, age, medical conditions, and the particulars of place and time for some incidents are also altered when possible. If this book were based on interviews rather than on my work experiences, participants would have some control over what words and activities are attributed to them. However, all descriptions and interpretations are from my point of view, based only on memory and not on actual interviews.

In not including others' views I risk having my presentation criticized as an unacceptable assertion of power, particularly power over service receivers whose only voice is through my narration. I am not claiming that my memories are an accurate depiction of what happened or that my interpretations are objective. In fact, quite the contrary is true. My position throughout the book is that every person has a worldview that guides what she observes and how she interprets events, objects, activities, and ideas. Humans can, however, through communication, observation, shared experience, and even empathy, learn enough about another's view to see many things as that person sees them.

I chose to write a first-person account about this process because I want to convey a less scientifically detached, more ethically engaged form of knowledge that might resonate with the reader's own experience as a service provider, whether as a family member, volunteer advocate, paid staff member, or professional consultant. In all of these relationships, providing services confers power, but that power can be exercised responsibly by balancing careful external inquiry with caring internal reflection. I hope that my techniques and ideas will assist the reader in this endeavor and that I have achieved it myself in *Your Values, My Values: Multicultural Services in Developmental Disabilities*.

For the Reader

In this book people are referred to alternately as Indian, Lakota, or Native American; as black or African American; and as white, Anglo, or non-Indian because individuals have their own preferences about how to refer to themselves as well as how to label other people, and those choices continue to change. Events that occurred in the past are described in the terms that were current at the time they occurred. Using a variety of ethnic labels as well as alternating usage of *he/his* and *she/her* is intended to draw attention to the diversity of American society. With apologies to the citizens of Canada and Mexico, *American* is used to refer to the residents of the United States rather than of North America. No disrespect is intended by any term.

The terms *service provider* and *service receiver* are used to accentuate the relationship between two people rather than to draw attention to whether either person has been labeled as having a developmental disability. *Service provider* is also intended as a cover term for any person providing assistance and support, whether as a family member, teacher, advocate, helping professional, or interested citizen. The suggestions and theories offered in this book apply to any service relationship, such as the relationship between doctor and patient, teacher and student, or social worker and client; thus, *service receiver* is not intended as a euphemism for a person with a developmental disability but as a term that includes any person receiving services in any type of service system. When the discussion only applies to relationships with people with developmental disabilities, and that is not obvious from the context, then the term *developmental disabilities* is used.

In anthropology, to report an observation made by the researcher while she was using the method of participant/observation, the first person is used. Therefore, I use *I* in passages in this book when describing events I remember because I participated in them and often kept notes of my experiences. Certain quotes are italicized for three reasons: to denote words that were spoken to me or in my presence to distinguish them from other quotes (not in italics) that are exchanges reported to me or that are examples of things people might have said, to draw attention to the spoken words as verbatim utterances that the reader might interpret differently than I did, and to differentiate passages in which I am sharing conclusions I reached based on personal experience from sections in which I am explicating current theories that might further elucidate those experiences. I use *we/us* when I am recalling a decision or action I participated in as part of a team or other group or when I am presenting my ideas and feelings as reasonably representative of the thoughts of other service providers.

Although abuse, depression and other mental illnesses, potentially illegal behavior, and other difficulties are mentioned in conjunction with the life stories of composite characters in this book, a relationship between any particular kind of problem and an ethnic or social group should not be inferred. In all cases, service providers and receivers described in this book are composite characters based on three or more real people I encountered during my work as director of an agency providing residential and vocational supports to adults with developmental disabilities. Therefore, no character in this book is a real person.

Acknowledgments

My sister, Jane Weede, and my good friend, Rebecca Schweitzer, read early drafts and listened to me patiently as I honed my thinking. The ideas are mine, but they made me feel that sharing them in a book was a task worth doing.

Literally hundreds of family members, friends, and their friends and families volunteered to sort and label various versions of the assessment tools included in this book. In particular, I want to thank the Women's Network of Rapid City, The Tuesday Group, and my lifelong friend, Brenda Melton.

I am indebted to the editors and staff of Paul H. Brookes Publishing Co.; the interlibrary loan librarians at the South Dakota State Library; and the Buffalo Gap postmaster, Loretta Schroth, for performing their jobs with efficiency, kindness, and interest in my project that went beyond what was required of them.

To the service receivers and providers I knew at the agency where I worked, especially to those with whom I have maintained friendships after leaving, I appreciate having shared the good times, the joyous moments, and the successful changes as well as the bad times. I have learned from each one of you and from all of our experiences together.

Finally, my love goes to my husband, Roy Pengra, who coped with equanimity when a 2-year project stretched to 6 years, who kept his promise not to read any drafts, and who celebrated and commiserated with me as needed, both when I was employed as a helping professional and when I was writing this book.

Part I

PRINCIPLES OF
VALUES-BASED SERVICES

The main postulate of values-based services is that services to people with developmental disabilities should be designed in terms of values. This postulate is developed through three themes introduced in Part I. The first theme, which begins in Chapter 1 and is carried throughout the book, is that adults with developmental disabilities have their own values and that they share these values with others who have similar class and ethnic backgrounds.

Chapter 2 introduces the second theme: Values give meaning to behavior. That is, behavior that appears to be similar for two people can have different meanings based on each person's values. To respond to the behavior of adults with developmental disabilities appropriately, the service provider must first interpret the meaning of the behavior relative to the person's values.

Because providers of services to adults with developmental disabilities are generally more familiar with the paradigm of behavioral science, both Chapters 2 and 3 provide a basic introduction and illustration of one approach from cognitive science. Chapter 2 focuses on

how groups of people construct their world view by outlining definitions and beliefs significant to them and by guiding behavior through
norms and values, a construct called a schema. Chapter 3 illustrates this
approach by describing one schema, an individualist person schema,
and how it constructs the middle-class American view of cultural differences.

Chapter 3 initiates a third theme: There is a middle ground between human universals and individual uniqueness. Providing services
in terms of values shared with others of similar social background does
not stereotype people. Instead, it decreases prejudice by enabling service providers to look beyond the assumptions and judgments built into
their own world views to provide culturally sensitive supports based on
interpretations significant to the service receiver.

Everyone Has Values

"I cut my hair."

Yes, I could see that. Only "cut" was not the word I would use. "Hacked" or "chopped" would be more appropriate. Her beautiful hair hung in uneven lengths, with one tuft sticking out at the side. As I looked at Gloria sitting in my office at the developmental disabilities agency where I worked, I remembered the first time I had seen her hair. It had been matted with lice and ringworm and sticky with drainage from an infected eye and infected ears. She had been placed here by Indian Health Services because she had been neglected and abused since the recent death of her primary caregiver and protector. She had come so far since that terrible day 2 years ago when I first met her, when her eyes were flat black walls of anger and the planes of her face rigid with fear. Now, she sat relaxed and assured, comfortable with the rightness of her action. Finally, my anthropological training kicked in.

"Did Martin die?"

I knew that some Lakota women, like Gloria, express grief at the death of a loved one by using a knife to cut off hanks of hair and sometimes even to slash their arms and legs with parallel lines of cuts (Powers, 1986; St. Pierre, 1991). This behavior, which a person who is not Native American might see as odd, excessive, or even abnormal, is seen as normal and is even expected in traditional Lakota culture.

Martin's death would be difficult for Gloria. He was from the same reservation as she and had moved to this off-reservation community to receive medical treatment at the Veterans' Hospital. Gloria met him not long after she moved out of a group home into an apartment of her own. He became her apartment mate, her friend, and her lover. They were inseparable.

"No. He die Sunday."

This was Thursday. Gloria was telling me that Martin was going to die on Sunday. I wondered whether this was one of the times I should gently redirect her to a more socially accepted response. Maybe I should try to explain, based on my supposedly more knowledgeable understanding of the world, that death is not predictable; the "right" way to approach the death of a loved one is to wait for it to happen and then cope.

This time I didn't have to wait for my anthropological self to surface. The response she needed and the only response I should offer as a helping professional intent on creating support services based on the values of the people using the supports—an approach I call values-based services—was obvious.

"Do you want Donna to help you pack and drive you home for the funeral?"

I do not have the right to question what Gloria knows to be true. My role as director of the agency providing values-based services to Gloria was to help her to do what she knew she needed to do, not to judge or question her or act as if my understanding of the world is the correct one and superior to hers. Gloria has the right to live her life by her own values.

Donna, Gloria's community living coach, helped Gloria buy groceries for the wake, drove her to the reservation where the funeral was held, and picked her up 5 days later. And, yes, Martin did die on Sunday.

THE MAIN POSTULATE OF VALUES-BASED SERVICES

The main postulate of values-based services is that services should be designed in terms of the service receiver's values. Writers in other fields (e.g., nursing [Leininger, 1970], health care [Kleinman, 1980], policy science [Boone, 1991], mental health services [Pedersen, 1988], social work [Burgest, 1982], and education [Ross-Gordon, Martin, & Briscoe, 1990]) have long advocated that this principle should govern service provision because values-based services support pluralism and increase positive outcomes, including an enhanced quality of life.

Pluralism and Value Differences

Twenty-five years ago, when I lived in Alabama, I was the chair of a group working to decrease racism and sexism at our workplace. One day, we were waiting for our meeting to start when a visibly irritated white woman remarked that these meetings would be more successful if the black participants could just get there on time. She had very carefully used the term *black* rather than *Negro* to show that she was not prejudiced. To ease the tension that immediately arose, I turned the conversation to cultural differences in the ways that meetings are conducted, the issues that are considered to be important, and the way that time is perceived. Several opinions were expressed, but her next comment stands out in my memory.

"They're just late because that's a way of showing they're different from us."

Being fresh out of graduate school, I went into my teacher mode and admitted that impression management of symbols of ethnic affiliation might be involved. Being late, wearing a dashiki, or wearing one's hair in an Afro could be a way of consciously saying, "I'm black and proud of it." But still, I continued, one should not lose sight of differences in values—values that give very different meanings to similar types of behavior, such as arrival time at a meeting. To decrease racism and embrace pluralism, I explained, we first have to understand each others' values. She cut me short.

"Values, nothing. If they just started getting ready earlier, they'd be on time."

The woman's response rejected the premise that values give meaning to behavior. Her view of behavior as simply the enactment of a set of skills that are unaffected by values allowed her to judge the behavior of others in terms of her own values. Her evaluation might lead to misunderstanding and prejudice if she thought, "They are late for my meeting because they are disrespectful and disorganized," and worse, to racism, if she concluded, "They are late for my meeting because they are lazy and irresponsible."

⅄ Values define how the world ought to be. They are the measures by which people distinguish right from wrong and judge themselves and others. If values are shared, these judgments maintain social order. When they are not shared, in order for society to muddle along, we must either embrace pluralism so that differences are tolerated, or we must legislate and enforce whose values will prevail.

People do not always realize when their values are in conflict with those held by others. Americans, in particular, generally assume that their values are shared (Bower, 1997) and proceed to apply them to others. Consequently, the non-Indian social worker at Indian Health Services who arranged for Gloria to receive support services off the reservation judged that it was more important for Gloria to be cared for than it was for her to live in her home community with members of her own ethnic group—a conclusion that would be rejected by most Lakota social workers. An interdisciplinary team member who concluded that Martin was exploiting Gloria by living off her disability check thought that the team should be protecting Gloria from this relationship. Other team members considered the joy and companionship the relationship brought her as more important than the impact on her finances.

Unlike Gloria's situation, if team members have similar cultural backgrounds, then fewer conflicts may arise because key values might be more fully shared. However, conflicts will likely still occur because values vary relative to ethnicity, class, religion, education, job, geographic location, age, gender, political persuasion, and life experiences, creating the potential for much misunderstanding and prejudice. Values-based services provide a way to support pluralism and decrease prejudice in the complex multicultural context of the United States.

Positive Outcomes and Implicit Values

Professionals in the fields of nursing (Leininger, 1979), education (Eddy & Partridge, 1987), and mental health (McGoldrick, Pearce, & Giordano, 1982) have realized that cultural differences and, therefore, differences in values between a teacher and a student, a nurse and a patient, or a counselor and a client are sometimes the reason for miscommunication, failed programs, and dissatisfaction with services. For example, a classroom research project (Garbarino & Kostelny, 1992) found that African American students were not responding to leading questions, a style used by white teachers to create success by asking for information that the child already knows. The children assumed that the questions were not worth answering because, in their experience at home, parents questioned them only to elicit new information.

Arriving at a meeting or asking questions are functional skills, but they are guided by values just as much as responding to death is. The rules of how a person ought to behave are also used to observe, respond to, and judge the behavior of others. However, people are so accustomed to interacting automatically with rules that are out of awareness that reading behavioral cues for values different from their own is as difficult as learning a foreign language. Just as people do not think about the rules of grammar when speaking, they usually do not consciously think about their values. They just act in ways that feel natural and right (Stewart & Bennett, 1991; Strauss & Quinn, 1994).

Some values are explicit. People can identify and discuss values such as independence, autonomy, or honesty. Other values are implicit and are so self-evident that they are not recognized as values. Implicit values are the "unspoken assumptions about the nature of ultimate reality" (Douglas, 1973, p. 173)—the "tenets . . . comprising one large realm of the given and undeniable, a catalog of in-the-grain-of-nature realities . . . what anyone with common sense knows" (Geertz, 1983, pp. 76–77). They are usually the most fundamental of a person's values (Borofsky, 1994; LeVine, 1984).

For example, Dundes (1968) pointed out how "three thinking" permeates American thinking: three meals per day, three primary colors, three little pigs, third time's a charm, give me three good reasons, three colors on flags and traffic lights, and on and on and on. This pattern reflects a feeling that for some things, two is not enough; four feels like overkill; and three is just right.

For many Native American, West African, and Southeast Asian groups, four feels right. For the Lakota (LaPointe, 1976), there are four directions, four sacred colors, four fingers on each hand, four kinds of things that breathe (crawling things, flying things, four-legged and two-legged walking things), four things above the earth (sun, moon, sky, and stars), and on and on and on *and on.*

Three thinkers can feel uneasy when things go on "too long," just as four thinkers can feel shortchanged when only three items are included; essentially, there are right and wrong ways to think, even when we are unaware of the rules. As Powers (1985) noted, three and four are sacred numbers in Euro-American and Lakota cultures, respectively.

Common-sense implicit values may appear to be trivial on the surface, but they actually encapsulate fundamental differences in how people view their worlds.

Using implicit values to design services increases the chance of positive outcomes. For example, when we asked the physician to prescribe Gloria's medications on a four rather than three times per day routine, it made it easier for Gloria to remember to take them and increased her compliance.

Although the most striking value differences may be associated with people from linguistically or racially distinct populations (e.g., Hispanic, African American), spatially segregated neighborhoods (e.g., Italian Americans living in Little Italy, Chinese Americans living in Chinatown), or newly immigrated ethnic groups (e.g., Vietnamese), many other value differences persist in the United States. Less striking, but nonetheless important, value differences can be identified for German American Jews in New York, Irish American Catholics in Boston, Norwegian American Lutherans in the Dakotas, Greek American Orthodox in Ohio, English American Episcopalians in Savannah, Mormons in Utah, and so on throughout the United States. Ethnicity, as part of personal identity and as the source of different values, persists; values learned early are highly resistant to change, embedded as they are in family roles and child-rearing practices (Alba, 1990; Ortner, 1984; Spiro, 1955).

Professionals sometimes mistakenly attribute conflicts in values to lack of cooperation or personality defects (Aponte, Rivers, & Wohl, 1995). Not being aware of value differences can lead to interactions that make service receivers feel belittled. In contrast, values-based services communicate to the service receiver that her ideas are right and, by extension, she is validated as a competent person. She is in control not only of what she chooses to do but also of how she does it. Having one's values acknowledged, feeling competent, and behaving in personally valued ways lead to greater satisfaction and an enhanced quality of life.

Quality of life "is a multidimensional construct in which culturally consensual values and shared attitudes are reflected" (Schalock, 1996, p. 126). It has been equated with happiness, satisfaction, living up to one's full potential, and having access to the kinds of opportunities that others have (Taylor, 1994). Supporting explicit values, especially those that are widely shared throughout the United States, has been shown to increase satisfaction with services (Hughes, Hwang, Kim, Eisenman, &

Killian, 1995). For example, satisfaction surveys in group homes with different levels of restriction showed that residents were more satisfied with their autonomy when a greater degree of autonomy was supported by residential service providers (Jacobson, Burchard, Ackerman, & Yoe, 1991).

Values-based services push this concept one step further by requiring that the values to be supported are the service receiver's values. Two people may share a broad explicit value, such as autonomy, but differ in the specific way it is enacted in behavior (i.e., they may have different implicit values). Identifying a person's implicit values and incorporating them into services may take skill and sensitivity because the differences are subtle, and the service provider's own ways, whatever they may be, seem to him to be simple common sense. But making the effort to discover and build on the service receiver's implicit values increases positive outcomes for that person and enhances his quality of life.

VALUES-BASED SERVICE PROVISION FOR GLORIA

"She just reached up and turned off both her hearing aids. Lilah, what was I supposed to do? We couldn't just finish her IHP without her."

Brenda, Gloria's case manager, and Donna, Gloria's community living coach, sat in my office looking for an answer to a problem that might have no solution. They had just come from a team meeting regarding Gloria's needs for the coming year and were charged with the responsibility of writing an individual habilitation plan (IHP) describing the services she would receive from us to meet those needs. Brenda was working very hard to implement values-based services and had quickly found that talking about it and actually doing it were two different things.

Understanding Value Differences

Because values-based services depend on identifying and understanding value differences, I turned to Donna for her interpretation of Gloria's behavior. She is Native American—Lakota, like Gloria—and has an especially close relationship with Gloria. Donna has been my guide in helping me understand our cultural differences. I have become familiar with the explicit values of Lakota culture through reading ethnographies, histories, and autobiographies and attending workshops. Still, there are times when I don't have the deep down, in the gut, "I know this is right, but I can't put it into words why" kind of understanding that Donna has about her values; nor does she have that kind of understanding about mine. We have struggled on many occasions to put into words our cultural differences.

"I think she's telling us to mind our own business."

That's not too hard for me to accept. I value privacy and could understand that Gloria might rate some of the topics at her team meeting as too private to discuss. By my own values, I would think so, too. However, Donna was struggling to get me to see things a different way.

"No, not mind your own business like this is private, but mind your own business because I can take care of myself."

Well, okay, I can handle that, too. I value doing things for myself and not asking for help. Independence might be even more important to a person with a disability than it is to me if she had previously been treated as not able to take care of herself, as unequal to others. But Donna did not like this interpretation either. We may use the same words, but sometimes we mean different things:

"I can't put it into words. She means independence, equality, not being controlled by others, and a kind of privacy to make her own decisions. But not how you describe them. She turned off her hearing aids because you don't have the right to tell her what to do or how to do it, even if she needs help to do it."

Donna's explanation reminded me of Good Tracks' description of the value of noninterference:

Many human relations unavoidably involve some influencing, meddling, and even coercion or force. Indians feel, however, that Anglos carry these elements to an extreme. . . . In native Indian society, however, no interference or meddling of any kind is allowed or tolerated, even when it is to keep the other person from doing something foolish or dangerous. When an Anglo is moved to be his brother's keeper and that brother is an Indian, therefore, almost everything he says or does seems rude, ill-mannered, or hostile. . . . But if the Indian told the Anglo that he was being intrusive, the Indian would himself be interfering with the Anglo's freedom to act as he sees fit. (1976, p. 30)

When Gloria's team members acted as though they had the right to help her make her own decisions, she couldn't tell them to stop because that would interfere with what *they* chose to do. Gloria did the only thing *she* could choose to do and still be polite. She controlled her own participation in the meeting by turning off her hearing aids.

Valuing noninterference directly conflicts with valuing interven-  tion, a value held by most helping professionals who take for granted that a person should intervene in situations of danger or inequity and with people for whom one is responsible, such as children or elderly parents. Intervention is closely associated with the value of helping others (e.g., the rich helping the poor, the boss helping his employees, the teacher aiding his students), but giving help often carries with it the implicit right to make decisions for another person. By Gloria's values, the team did not have the right to create a plan for her; however, by the values of most other team members, they had the responsibility to do so.

Although there is growing recognition in both developmental disabilities research and practice that ethnic differences have an impact on assessment (Meyer, Peck, & Brown, 1991), lead to conflicts in goals (Lim & Browder, 1994), and affect how service providers and receivers interact (Rueda & Martinez, 1992), there is less awareness that the individual planning process itself strongly reflects a certain set of values that may not be fully shared between two people in a service relationship (Lynch & Stein, 1987). Individualized plans are focused on helping the person achieve his or her full potential and include active treatment, measurable goals, minimization of risk, and access to the same rights and quality of life as other citizens. This format is based on the values of individualism, achievement, action orientation, objectivity through measurement, attention to the future potential consequences of behavior, equality, autonomy, and emotional and material well-being.

These values are not bad and obviously do not result in poorly designed services. The assumption that they are widely and completely shared, however, obscures important variations. Some of Gloria's values were similar or identical to values implied in the planning process, whereas others were in conflict with them.

Service providers are already committed to supporting each person's preferences, choices, and goals. Developmental disabilities services have been moving toward increasingly individualized services since deinstitutionalization began. Required sequences of skills and norm-referenced assessments have given way to functional skill development and criteria-referenced assessments. Placing people into programs has been replaced with designing supports to fit people (Schalock, 1996, 1997). Adapting the planning process and the design of supports to the service receiver's values is one more step along the road of decreasing reliance on standardized services and increasing acceptance of the principle that supports must be specific to each person.

Adapting the Planning Process for Gloria

Eventually, after several years of trial and error, Gloria's team found that they could support her value of noninterference by conducting meetings as information-sharing discussions instead of decision-making discussions. Rather than beginning with Gloria's strengths and needs to plan an array of supports and services, the team process was initiated by telling Gloria what kinds of services could be provided and how those activities might affect her. Then, Gloria chose which of those supports and services she wanted.

The team supported Gloria's implicit value of four-thinking by defining four goal areas—spirituality, communication, family ties, and transportation—rather than work, home, and leisure. They supported Gloria's right to find answers for big decisions through prayer rather than through team discussion. The team supported Gloria's value of noninterference even when she bought her boyfriend whiskey and cigarettes then did not have enough money to buy groceries and when she chose not to work because, she said, she could live quite nicely on her disability check.

Some of Gloria's values were not supported. For example, Gloria has a "now orientation" rather than a "future orientation" to time and would prefer a weekly or monthly team meeting. She also values personalized relationships rather than relationships based on roles; thus, she would prefer to have only family and very close friends as team members rather than an assortment of professionals. She has higher trust in the spoken word and subjectively defined needs than in written documents and objectively measured needs. She would prefer having an oral plan rather than a written plan and receiving support services because she said she needed them instead of being subjected to objective measures.

Risks and Commitment

Gloria had strong opinions about what services she wanted and how they should be offered. As service providers, we were willing to try, and we did flexibly interpret some state regulations to fit her preferences. There were times, however, when we were willing but simply did not have the resources to meet her requests (e.g., monthly team meetings with a tape-recorded service plan). There were other instances when supporting her values would involve committing illegal acts (e.g., providing services without establishing eligibility based on objective measures of IQ and adaptive behavior).

Gloria received services based on her value of noninterference because she happened to be receiving supports from a service provider willing to take risks. However, our choice to uphold Gloria's right to noninterference had a financial impact on the agency. We could not bill the higher daily rate provided by Medicaid Home and Community Based Services; instead, we had to bill on the lower hourly rate of another entitlement program available in the state. This was necessary because Gloria chose to use our services on some days but not on others.

Supporting Gloria's right to noninterference also meant, of course, that if she decided not to use a service that state reviewers determined she needed, then we as service providers had to face the consequences. Many of Gloria's choices crossed over the line that some state reviewers drew between the "right to risk" that is allowed to a person with a disability and her "need for protection." Nevertheless, if Gloria did not ask for protection, then we could not interfere without making a mockery of our claim to be providing values-based services.

Other supports and services were adapted to Gloria's values, but none were quite as challenging as her value of noninterference. Her value was in direct conflict with most team members' conceptions of how a person should intervene to help others, especially a person with a developmental disability. The postulate of values-based services, that supports must be designed in terms of the service receiver's values, cannot be applied only when it is easy or only when there are no conflicts.

Therefore, providing support services to people with disabilities in terms of their own values is not without risks. As long as tax dollars support services, service providers will have to be accountable for the use of those dollars and the quality of their services. Some will argue that this relationship prevents change because agencies are accountable to funders and to society in general rather than to the people they serve. The same argument was made about deinstitutionalization, yet the willingness of many families and professionals to take risks and their tenacious commitment to community-based services ensured that it was ultimately successful (Sundram, 1994).

The same kind of commitment that was given to deinstitutionalization is required for the implementation of values-based services. The risks incurred are usually to the agency and not to the people receiving services. When staff are adequately trained in how to identify values and design services based on those values, the outcome for the service receiver is positive. We need to learn to trust that people with developmental disabilities do know what is best for themselves.

UNINTENTIONAL PREJUDICE

Are we as a society, as helping professionals, as family and friends of people with developmental disabilities willing to extend to them the right to live by their own values? I sometimes wonder if we even believe that all people have their own values. In so many areas of assistance we play the role of the more knowledgeable helper—the parent, the teacher, the protector, the person who advocates for their best interests—that it is only a slight shift to assume that we know better than they do what is right and proper. When we discuss values with each other, without knowing the service receiver's values, we are unintentionally prejudiced; we are evaluating behavior in terms of our own values, acting as though it is not necessary to know their values, or assuming that they have no values when they cannot communicate them clearly.

Values Considered to Be Already Known

When Gloria chose to have cheese curls and orange soda for supper, team members disagreed on whether her right to good nutrition or to make her own choices should prevail. Some team members argued that good nutrition was important and that Gloria needed to be given meat, vegetables, and a salad until she chose a nutritious diet for herself. Other team members, based on their values, reasoned that her right to make her own choices was more important, although they needed to work harder at helping her to understand the consequences of poor nutrition so that she would make better choices. However, all the professionals agreed that nutrition and choice were the two values that needed to be discussed.

When service providers and receivers are from the same background and share some or most of their values, it is easy to assume that a discussion among professionals about nutrition versus choice is a discussion from the service receiver's point of view. However, when a person's values are not yet fully known or understood, as Gloria's were not, then assuming that safety and equality are the relevant values to consider in analyzing behavior and choosing an intervention is the essence of prejudice. Team members were judging Gloria's behavior in terms of their own values rather than evaluating her behavior from her own point of view.

Values Believed to Be Unnecessary to Know

Until recently, services for people with developmental disabilities have more often used the paradigm of behavioral psychology than that of cognitive science (Guess, Turnbull, & Helmstetter, 1990). Because they are studying different aspects of behavior with different tools, behaviorists and cognitivists do not directly contradict one another (Greenwood, 1987); however, the singular use of the tools of behaviorism may lead some service providers to believe that people with developmental disabilities only respond to stimuli and may have wants, needs, and urges but not values (Denzin, 1989). Behavioral explanations offered for Gloria's supper choice were that she was imitating staff who ate cheese curls and orange soda and that she liked the taste and color of them.

According to Gerber, the right of people with disabilities to speak for themselves has been denied because the label of mental retardation "has carried with it the understanding that individuals lack the power to learn and to reason. How can one admit such a voice into meaningful discussion about anything beyond the most basic, immediate needs?" (1990, p. 4). As a consequence of limiting our explanations of behavior to causes not dependent on thought and of the definition of mental retardation as an impairment in cognitive functioning, our interventions are almost always aimed at teaching skills—teaching know-*how* rather than teaching know-*why*. In not teaching *know-why,* we begin to act as if the person does not know why he is acting as he does, does not have any understanding of his own values, and may not even be capable of having values.

Values Difficult to Communicate

When I asked Gloria why she ate cheese curls and drank orange soda for supper, she pointed toward a convenience store a few blocks down the street.

"I walk there."

Sometimes, I felt like I really did have a light bulb above my head, as the understanding of Gloria's supper choice finally clicked. The grocery store was too far from her apartment for her to walk there, which meant that she would have had to ask her community living coach for assistance. The convenience store was within walking distance.

Gloria and Donna made weekly trips to the big grocery store to purchase the week's groceries. This knowledge prompted me to ask whether Donna helped her buy enough groceries for a whole week. I was thinking that planning for a whole week might be difficult, and perhaps Gloria might prefer two or three trips per week to the grocery store; however, Gloria's reasoning followed a different track.

"I have friends."

I finally made the connection between, on the one hand, buying a week's worth of groceries, and, on the other hand, having friends and walking to the convenience store for cheese curls and orange soda. When Gloria had a week's worth of groceries, she shared with her friends. They were not exploiting her; in return, they usually shared their groceries, cigarettes, camaraderie, transportation, or whatever else they had to share. Under these circumstances a week's worth of groceries could be used up in a day or two.

Gloria's reasons for choosing orange soda and cheese curls had nothing to do with her team members' values on nutrition and choice or with behaviorists' causal explanations of imitation or pleasure. Her reasons flowed from her values: sharing—knowing who your friends are and how you interact with them; noninterference and independence— walking to a nearby store rather than asking for help with transportation; and "making do" and a present-time orientation—adapting to situations as they presented themselves rather than controlling the environment or the actions of others.

Asking people why they make certain choices or behave as they do will not necessarily help us to understand their values because people are not always aware of their own values. All humans, not just those with developmental disabilities, act relative to their values without being able to analyze the nuances of each one. Even so, some answers are possible and asking people about their values will preclude unintentional prejudice that arises from assuming that our own values are better than theirs or believing that they do not have any values. To provide supports to people with disabilities in terms of their own values— whether those values flow from ethnicity or from other social identities and experiences, whether they are explicit or implicit, and whether we agree with them or not—we need to accept that people with disabilities have their own values and the right to live according to them.

When puzzling situations with Gloria arose, I automatically considered the possibility that, because Gloria is Native American and I am not, we were facing a difference in values. As an anthropologist, when there is an ethnic difference between me and another person, I am more likely to look for value differences than personality, cognitive, or skill differences. Sometimes there were value differences between Gloria and myself and sometimes not, but at least I frequently asked myself what values gave meaning to Gloria's behavior. In doing this, I came to realize that the question of value differences must be asked every time, of every person I seek to help, not just of Native Americans whom I know have some values that are different from mine; people with developmental disabilities have their own values just as every human does. As Nathaniel Hawthorne said, "He deemed it essential, it would seem, to know the man before attempting to do him good" (1960, p. 123).

POINTS TO REMEMBER

To design values-based services for each person who is receiving services, we need to remember the following four guidelines:

1. *Discover the other person's values.* Do not assume that values are shared. For example, not everyone agrees that punctuality is proper meeting behavior.

2. *Become aware of our own implicit values.* Important values may simply seem like common sense. For example, most Americans use "three thinking" because it feels right rather than out of an awareness of its connection to the Christian Trinity.

3. *Think of the other person's values as different, not bad.* When we embrace pluralism, we cannot judge the other person's values as inadequate or incorrect and, thus, ignore them. For example, we must always support noninterference for Gloria, not just when we think it is safe to do so.

4. *Look for the values that give meaning to behavior.* All people have values that shape their behavior, regardless of whether they can fully communicate them. For example, understanding why Gloria chose to eat cheese curls and orange soda depends on knowing Gloria's values.

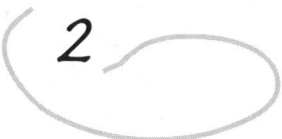

2

Values Give Meaning to Behavior

"This is neglect."

Actually, it looked like a pair of old underwear. A state inspector was waving them under my nose for emphasis as he told me we were neglecting Robert because he had so few pairs of underwear; and, he continued, the underwear Robert did have was in poor condition, as the pair in front of me certainly proved.

I wanted to ask the inspector what his underwear looked like but figured it probably was pristine white, nearly new, and in the latest fashion. The pair I had on, although clean, looked worse than the pair flapping in my face. In reality, I could care less what my underwear looks like. I can afford to buy new underwear but would rather spend money on season tickets to the symphony.

Because underwear has no universal meaning, an argument between professionals cannot answer the question of what kind of underwear is evidence of neglect. Interpreting the condition of someone's underwear, or the meaning of any object or activity, depends on beliefs and values that are constructed (Holland & Quinn, 1987). Therefore, only Bobby, as he preferred to be called, can determine, based on his own beliefs and values, when services are inadequate. This view prompted my rejoinder.

"It's his choice to wear them."

I suspect that the state inspector saw me as one of those service providers who uses the argument of choice as an excuse for poor service. It was several years before I could look back on our argument and see it through his eyes. How frustrated he must have been that something as obvious and basic *to him* as "decent" underwear wasn't being provided. At the time, the argument raged on. The inspector told me that it was my responsibility as a service provider to furnish Robert with underwear that was in a condition most people in American society would find acceptable because Robert was not aware of other options. How, he asked me, could Robert make a choice if there was nothing else available?

BELIEFS

The state inspector and I interpreted the situation differently not only because we had different values but also because we had different beliefs. Whereas values describe how the world ought to be and distinguish right from wrong, beliefs define how the world is and delimit true and false (Goodenough, 1990; Hahn, 1973). Beliefs also outline the facts of a situation for the observer (D'Andrade, 1984; Pepitone, 1994).

The state inspector believed that a person with a severe or profound disability, like Bobby, has certain limitations. In the state inspector's view, I was either reading more meaning into Bobby's behavior than was "really" there, or Bobby had been mislabeled. I, however, believe that all humans have values, although they may be constrained from acting on them, and that the meaning of an actor's behavior to the observer is not based on the actor's intent but on what the observer chooses to notice (Cohler, 1992).

Bobby's Behavior

I first formed an impression of Bobby's values about 6 weeks after I started my new job as director. Trudy, the job coach, called and asked me to come to her office because Bobby wanted to talk to me. I didn't find this surprising because Bobby knew me from the all-agency meetings we'd been having to negotiate new rules in the workshop. When I entered Trudy's office, Bobby tapped his empty coffee cup on her desk.

"Cof!"

I looked at Trudy for an explanation.

"We've had a rule that clients can't have coffee or pop except at break time."

Then she laughed in embarrassment as Bobby looked pointedly at the full cup of coffee on Trudy's desk. Bobby's meaning was clear to all three of us, so I made my pronouncement.

"Rules in the workshop apply to everyone."

As Trudy started to remove her coffee cup, correctly assuming that I meant that whatever rules applied to clients also applied to staff, Bobby left the office, went to the coffee pot, filled his cup, added 10 teaspoons of creamer, and returned to his workstation. Following this incident, several lively team discussions took place regarding whether that much creamer was good for Bobby and whether it was a situation that warranted intervention; however, it was at this point that Bobby's team and I began to see Bobby as a person who understood the concept of rules and the equal application of rules—values that are not uncommon in American culture (Stewart & Bennett, 1991).

We also began to see Bobby as able to set his own priorities. One time, when Bobby's family dropped in for an unexpected visit, he'd gestured for them to leave. They were understandably surprised because he usually enjoyed their visits and the Norwegian cookies they always brought. They thought that perhaps he was ill or was being mistreated; however, we believed that Bobby's reason for making his family leave was because he had tickets to go to a concert with a friend that night and wanted to do that rather than visit with his family.

Interpretation Based on Beliefs and Values

The state inspector and I were so enmeshed in the battle of who championed the most up-to-date philosophy of the rights of people with disabilities that neither one of us could see that it was not a question of who was right or wrong. We were simply using different values to judge the acceptability of the underwear and different beliefs to determine neglect.

I evaluated the underwear as acceptable because I saw the similarities between Bobby and me. Neither of us particularly cares about underwear, we both love concerts, and we're both thrifty—a value that is not surprising for Bobby, who had grown up on a farm with his Norwegian American family during the Great Depression. I was unwilling to accept that any particular value, such as cleanliness, is so widely shared that anyone, regardless of whether they knew Bobby personally, could make a judgment about Bobby's care. Although there are overarching general values in American society, such as equality, decency, and thrift, the specific meaning and application of them varies (D'Andrade, 1991). I not only believe that Bobby has his own specific values, regardless of the severity of his disability, but also argue that those values should determine the services provided to him. According to the principles in values-based services, forcing someone who values thrift to buy new underwear is neglecting his values.

The state inspector, however, was charged with carrying out a set of regulations about neglect based on values he accepted as obvious and widespread. He saw the underwear and made a judgment according to his own values and supported by the standards set forth by the state. For the state inspector, not providing the same quality of life that others in the community appeared to have was neglect of a person's right to equal treatment. He further believed that people in the community would judge Bobby negatively because they would attribute the condition of his clothing to his disability rather than to what the inspector classified as inadequate care.

Our interpretations of events and objects differed because we did not share the same system of meaning. Communication depends on shared meaning; however, meaning varies from group to group and even among people in the same group because meaning is constructed by choosing to notice some features (e.g., behaviors, objects, qualities, feelings, sounds) and ignoring other features as meaningless background noise (Shweder & LeVine, 1984). In addition, the selected features have beliefs, values, and other ideas associated with them (Holland & Quinn, 1987). These are called *propositions* to convey the point that the beliefs, values, and other ideas are set forth without proof. Because the state inspector and I attached different propositions to certain features, we did not share an identical system of meaning and thus miscommunicated.

MEANING IS SOCIALLY CONSTRUCTED

Meanings are arbitrarily assigned to body gestures by various groups throughout the world (Hall, 1959). Communication is possible because members of the group share the knowledge of which gesture stands for a particular message. For example, a widening of the eyes accompanied by a slight lift of the eyebrows, termed the "eyebrow flash" (Hinde, 1987, p. 94) by ethologists, has a different meaning for each of the various ethnic groups in the United States. To most Anglos, the eyebrow flash signifies incredulity or surprise, whereas many African Americans use the same gesture to communicate innocence, Latinos to express confusion, and Chinese Americans to convey anger (Samovar & Porter, 1982). These different meanings may cause Anglo teachers to mistakenly evaluate African American students as impudent or Chinese American students as docile.

More important, what makes one person angry and another surprised also varies if the individuals have different beliefs and values (Lutz & Abu-Lughod, 1990), just as Bobby's treatment and his behavior had different meanings for both the state inspector and me. Meaning is not confined to the definition of the word or phrase that serves as the linguistic label for an object, action, concept, emotion, or any feature chosen to denote. Meaning is also conveyed by propositions arbitrarily associated with those features (Beatty, 1994). Some bras and bikini tops, for example, may look exactly alike but are distinguished by values governing how each should be used. Wearing a bra in a way it is not *meant* to be worn, such as with no outer clothing as if it were a bikini top, communicates a message because of the entire meaning of the object, not just the definition of *bra* as a word.

If objects, gestures, and behaviors only had simple definitions, translation would be much easier. Instead, they come wrapped in contexts with ramifications, overtones, connotations, and implications. To know and translate only the definition and not the beliefs and values associated with the object or behavior omits the rich variety and complexity of communication. Two people can observe the same situation yet notice different features and apply different propositions; therefore, they arrive at different conclusions about the meaning of the event. If rules, values, beliefs, attributes, attitudes, customs, norms, expectations, motivations, and other propositions were universal, there would be little variation among people. Because meaning is socially constructed, however, interpretations can vary, leading to miscommunication and disagreement.

When Meaning Is Not Shared

The ways in which beliefs and values affect the interpretation of the meaning of behavior became clearer to me one time when I individually interviewed all employees at the agency I directed on the topics of neglect and abuse. All employees gave similar definitions and hypothetical examples of abuse and agreed on the definition of neglect as *not taking proper care of people*. However, when they were asked to give an actual example of a situation or circumstance they had observed that might be considered neglect, most Indian staff members cited examples of non-Indians interrupting people, withholding assistance when it was clearly needed, forcing people to comply with requests, and being in a hurry. Non-Indian staff, in contrast, cited examples of Indians not allowing independence by giving assistance when a person had not asked for help, removing the object of a disagreement rather than settling a dispute, and allowing people to do things that might be mildly harmful.

The employees did not give examples in terms of Indian and non-Indian categories of staff, and, when I commented on this difference at a staff meeting, some people disagreed with the observation. They were afraid that commenting on cultural differences would be interpreted as stereotyping (Goodenough, 1994), and people often consider their own views as obvious and right rather than shaped by culture (LeVine, 1984). However, different features were noticed by Indian and non-Indian staff because, although they defined neglect the same way and talked about the importance of respect and autonomy, what those values meant to each group varied.

Even the words used by the employees to talk about the differences presuppose certain beliefs and values. "Allowing" a person to do something that is potentially harmful implies that one person has the power and the right to control whether another person does or does not perform a specific act. Non-Indians would use the word "allow" to describe some situations, but Lakota staff would *never* use this word for those situations. Most Lakota believe that humans are able to control their own actions, regardless of what others want them to do, and they value the right of each individual to make her own choices (Ross, 1989). In Lakota culture, both people involved in an interaction have personal autonomy and are supposed to be observant of the other's needs; however, neither person can or should control the other (Powers, 1988).

In contrast, the values of autonomy and control are interpreted by most non-Indians to mean that people are compelled to make their own choices and should take initiative in seeking what they want but are legitimately controlled by others in some situations (DeVita & Armstrong, 1993). For example, parents and work supervisors have the right

and the responsibility to control their children and employees by allowing or not allowing certain types of behavior. These values make sense
when combined with the belief that humans are affected by external
events and can be controlled by others, for example, through peer group
pressure or by being punished and rewarded by others.

The features that people notice in a situation and the meaning they
infer depends on their own beliefs and values (D'Andrade & Strauss,
1992). Therefore, miscommunication occurs when people with different cultural backgrounds assume they share the same values when they
use the same words (e.g., one should not neglect people with disabilities and should take proper care of them) but construct different propositions for what those words mean (e.g., the action that was described
by a Lakota employee as a non-Indian forcing a person to comply with
a request—"Don't touch that sharp knife"—was seen by a non-Lakota
employee as preventing a person from harming himself).

Meaning and Social Norms

I remember quite well my irritation one day when I heard the insistent
knocking on my office door, which I usually left open as I didn't mind in-
terruptions but had closed that day because I had a deadline to meet.
Maybe if I didn't answer the knock, the person would go away; however,
that hope vanished when whoever it was knocked again. After the louder
and longer third knock, I knew it was Bobby and rose to let him in.

In the records from the institution where Bobby had lived after his
parents died, he was described as defiant and aggressive. I wanted to reject that characterization of him, thinking that we just didn't understand
him yet, but it was difficult; his behavior often was what I would classify as overly insistent. It was especially difficult to interpret his behavior in some other way on this day; when Bobby did come into my office, he simply watched me work—something he had done on many
other occasions.

When Gloria wanted to visit me in my office, she would stand quietly in the reception area in such a way that if I looked up I could see
her through the open doorway. After a few minutes, if I didn't notice
her, she would leave. I always felt bad if I didn't notice her because
usually no paperwork was as important to me as talking to Gloria. I
often just didn't "hear" her request because my way of gaining attention depends on sound, such as a knock on the door, the ring of a telephone, or a verbal greeting.

I might have concluded that Gloria is shy if I had applied my own standards to her behavior. I assumed, however, that her behavior meant something different. Her behavior was governed by rules of conduct, that is, *norms* she had learned as a member of a social group with values that were different from mine. Norms provide a pattern for action, a step-by-step set of directions on how to act to carry out the values embedded in the culture of the community (D'Andrade, 1984). Gloria showed respect by recognizing my right to decide whether to be interrupted, a behavior that makes sense in terms of Lakota beliefs and values. Norms are also the rules against which everyday variation is understood. Thus, other Lakota who share these social norms with Gloria quite easily and correctly label her behavior as respectful rather than as shy.

With Bobby, I assumed that I already understood and shared the norms governing his behavior; therefore, I labeled his behavior as pushy when he continued to knock after I didn't answer his first summons. However, when I began to interpret Bobby's behavior in terms of his Norwegian American background, his actions took on a different meaning. Norwegian American social norms for polite interaction are based on valuing self-reliance and a lack of greed; these values are shown by offering, seeking, or denying a service three or more times. In response to the first two or three requests, the person from whom assistance is sought must deny her own ability to help to show that she recognizes the other person's self-reliance. The recipient must turn down assistance or hospitality at least two or three times so as not to appear too greedy (MacGregor, 1990). Although I now recognize this behavior and understand its meaning, it still feels pushy to me when someone "won't take no for an answer" and insists on asking for or offering the same thing several more times. Yet, I probably appear controlling to Bobby when I respond too quickly to his initial requests for service or greedy when I take a cookie the first time he offers me one.

SCHEMAS

Although social scientists distinguish among definitions, norms, beliefs, and values, humans interact in terms of whole sets of meaning without needing to identify the particular norms and values that guide how to act or the underlying definitions and beliefs that specify what features of the environment to notice (D'Andrade, 1984). For ease of reference, these sets are called *schemas* (D'Andrade, 1991, 1992), which is a particularly apt choice because *scheme* has two definitions: "a scheme" is an outline or sketch, and "to scheme" means to plan a program of action. Schemas guide both what to notice and how to act by providing an *outline* (i.e., definitions that arbitrarily delimit the features that are important to notice and beliefs that shape what is accepted as truth or fact) and a *plan of action* (i.e., values that construct what a person ought to do and norms that regulate how to do it).

All the schemas available to be learned and shared by members of a particular society make up that society's culture (Geertz, 1973, 1983; Goodenough, 1994). Individuals and groups within one society learn different combinations and parts of the available schemas, thus accounting for why people within that society think and act alike in some ways yet differ in others (Dougherty, 1985). People with very different cultural backgrounds may still have some similarities because they share some schemas or parts of schemas even when many of their schemas are constructed differently.

A Football Analogy

For example, a football fan can describe a game to another fan by detailing the various plays without having to explain the permissible moves of each player or define what a "player" is because they share a schema of football. The *behavior* of the participants (the plays on the field) is interpreted with reference to the *norms* (the rules of the game) that guide the actions of the players involved and use words with *definitions* that are shared (e.g., the size and shape of the field and the ball, the attributes of a good player, the qualities of a good coach). The rules make sense because they are based on *values* (e.g., competition, achievement, well-defined roles and responsibilities) and are supported by *beliefs* (e.g., humans are naturally competitive, people try harder when properly motivated, clearly defined rules decrease misunderstanding).

The actions of the players to a person who has no schema of football, however, are a meaningless jumble. Describing the rules may help him begin to separate significant features from background noise; for example, physical contact among players on the field is important to notice, but jostling among players on the bench is not. Even when he learns to identify who is a player and what a player is supposed to do, football may still not "make sense" (e.g., if he values cooperative intellectual pursuits and believes intense physical activity will cause illness), although small parts of the schema might seem familiar (e.g., if he, like most football fans, defines fairness as an equal application of the rules).

What to Notice and How to Act

The most difficult part of understanding how schemas affect behavior is the proposition that humans do not notice all the features of the environment available to be noticed. Schemas guide them toward noticing some actions, qualities, sounds, and so forth and dismissing other features as background noise. It is not that the features do not exist (Watson, 1991); they simply are not noticed and have no impact on the actions of the person using that particular schema (Denzin, 1989).

For example, if a person does not have a schema for "chopsticks," then she sees only two slender pieces of wood lying on the table if she notices them at all. If there is nothing on the table that she identifies as a utensil in her schema, she might discover that one of the pieces of wood can be used to stab a bite of food, but she will not use it in the way that someone who does know a specific schema about chopsticks would use it.

In developmental disabilities, the idea that the concept of mental retardation is socially constructed (Biklen & Duchan, 1994; Greenspan & Granfield, 1992; Manion & Bersani, 1987; Serpell, 1988)—that is, that it is a schema rather than a biological "fact" that exists independently of any definition—draws on this characteristic of schemas. Mental retardation only exists when certain behaviors and physical characteristics have been identified as being due to something called mental retardation. If no behaviors or characteristics were selected as features to notice, there would be no mental retardation. The features would simply exist as background noise and have no meaning.

Some specific schemas (e.g., "how women should act," "how people with mental retardation should be treated," "what behavior is appropriate in the workplace") affect what to notice and how to act; they provide the broad themes around which a person's own actions are organized and the actions of others are judged (Strauss & Quinn, 1994). There are also schemas available in American culture for "how people think" (D'Andrade, 1987) and for "emotions people feel" (Rosaldo, 1984). Seeing others through these schemas then guides analyses of and responses to situations and other people. If, for example, a schema about stigma has been learned and includes a proposition that certain physical characteristics identify a person as less valued, it is more probable that those characteristics will be noticed. Even an attempt to change stigma (e.g., by the "two-pronged strategy" [Wolfensberger & Thomas, 1983, p. 24] of the principle of normalization) is guided toward changing the physical characteristic and the definition of the characteristic as devaluing rather than ignoring the characteristic as irrelevant background noise. If there were no schema of stigmatizing physical characteristics, they would carry no meaning and would not be noticed just as chopsticks, without a chopstick schema, are only two slender pieces of wood.

Learning Schemas

Some schemas, especially those encoding explicit values, are learned by linguistically guided interaction (Cole, 1985; Schwartz, White, & Lutz, 1992) and depend on explicit learning. Children are specifically taught some definitions ("See his trunk? That's an elephant") and norms ("Don't cry. Big boys don't cry"). Other definitions are learned through correction ("This is a blue crayon, not a green one. Show me the green one"). Rhetorical questions are often used to remind the child of propositions learned earlier ("Is that how big boys act?"). Adages and proverbs are also used to teach schemas (Lakoff & Johnson, 1980; Strauss, 1990) by providing prepackaged, easily remembered explanations of complex propositions (e.g., "The early bird gets the worm" is about competition, initiative, industriousness, and possibly even punctuality and thinking ahead).

Other schemas, especially those encoding implicit values, are learned through observation and daily social interaction in much the same way as rules of grammar (Borofsky, 1994): by recognizing the general regularity in form shared across several actual experiences (Heath, 1986). This type of learning, called *implicit learning* (Reber, Walkenfeld, & Hernstadt, 1991) or *procedural memory* (Whitman, 1990a), does not depend on language. However, it occurs more readily in situations where those being observed are using very similar schemas (Shweder, 1984).

Two people never learn exactly the same set of schemas or all the specific parts of schemas in general use because they interact with and observe different people (Goodenough, 1994), learn inconsistent versions of the same schema from different people (Horowitz, 1991), make mistakes in learning, have different experiences, and remember different parts of their experiences (Quinn & Holland, 1987). They are, however, more likely to share similar schemas if they interact regularly (Goodenough, 1994). Schemas are also created by individuals as they encounter situations that do not fit the schemas they know; for example, a family adjusting to the birth of a child with a developmental disability might construct a schema about why it happened and how they should cope (i.e., there is a "family-constructed 'meaning' of their circumstances" [Bernheimer, Gallimore, & Weisner, 1990, p. 221]).

All the schemas a person learns comprise his *world view*. Schemas provide broad themes around which a person's actions are organized, the "master motives" (D'Andrade & Strauss, 1992) for that person. People use schemas inconsistently (Horowitz, 1991; Paine, 1989), although they may become more consistent if they are challenged by others and must argue their position (Shweder, 1984). However, schemas can also be flexibly applied and have internal inconsistencies (Shweder, 1984), and a person can know and use several mutually incompatible schemas (D'Andrade, 1987). Humans are not machines or computers. They can be quixotic, mistaken, illogical, whimsical, and irrational; however, they usually stick reasonably well to the definitions, beliefs, norms, and values of the schemas in their world views.

Schemas and Miscommunication

Children in the United States learn what color term to apply to objects as well as beliefs about colors, such as which ones are primary and what color will result when two others are mixed. They might also learn what colors ought to be worn to a wedding or a funeral; what colors babies ought to wear; and what certain colors symbolize, such as danger, envy, or cowardice. In short, there is a general American schema about color that includes definitions, beliefs, norms, and values. In the same way they learn about colors, American children also learn a schema of mental retardation: what it is, how to identify who has it, how to act toward that person, what to expect from that person, whether it is a good thing to have, how to avoid the label, and many other beliefs and values.

Communication and interaction are possible when people are using the same schema (e.g., of colors, mental retardation, or some other set of meanings), regardless of whether they live in the same society or have exactly the same culture. However, people do not expect to be able to communicate when meanings are not shared at all. It is the middle ground, when shared meaning is incomplete, that is most difficult and leads to *miscommunication* because it is mistakenly assumed that the complete schema is shared when only parts of it are.

Shared Focal Point but Different Boundaries for Definitions   A misunderstanding might occur if a husband wears a shirt that his wife classifies as orange when he believed that he was wearing a red shirt as she suggested. This occurs because people can share the focal point of the color red (i.e., what is "really red") but may differ in where they place the boundary between what is red and what is orange. Colors are not natural units that exist to be discovered and named but are constructed by segmenting the spectrum at certain arbitrary points and creating boundaries between one color and the next.

The focal points of some definitions may be widely shared among many cultures because, even though meaning is arbitrarily constructed, it must conform to human biology and the natural world (Hill & Mannheim, 1992). For example, there are more cones in the human eye to perceive wavelengths at the focal point American English labels as "really red" than for any other range of wavelengths. Human biology, therefore, probably accounts for why the focal point of the color red is named in every language (Berlin & Kay, 1969; Burgess, Kempton, & MacLaury, 1985), although the boundary between what is labeled as red and what is called by another color label differs. The natural world also sets guidelines for the organization of a schema of color, without determining exactly how colors will be identified or whether they will even be selected to carry meaning. For example, no language groups together, as one color, wavelengths that are widely separated in the spectrum—calling red and blue by one color term and orange and green by another—although adjacent colors, such as those the English language labels as being red, orange, and yellow, might be identified as two colors in another language with a boundary in the middle of the orange range.

Even when the focal point of a definition is entirely arbitrary, rather than partially based on the natural world or on human biology, it can still be more widely shared than the boundary between what is labeled with one term rather than another. For example, there are no natural or biological reasons to distinguish cups, mugs, glasses, and steins. Most speakers of American English readily identify items that are clearly in each category because they fit the ideal prototype, yet can still differ in how they classify a particular item that is halfway between two categories (e.g., between being a mug or a stein). So, too, even if people agree on what features arbitrarily define mental retardation, they can still differ in where they place the boundary between "mentally retarded" and "not mentally retarded" (Gelb, 1997), leading to disagreement and miscommunication.

Shared Definitions but Different Propositions   Miscommunication can also occur when definitions are shared but the associated beliefs and values differ. For example, most American women understand the sentence, "I didn't wear the red dress because I didn't want him to think I was loose," because they know not just the definition of red but the propositions associated with it, such as the connotations of red as hot, sexy, and dangerous. A red dress in another schema might have a very different interpretation—in Chinese culture, for example, it means luck and is the preferred color for a wedding dress. Part of a schema of color, the definition of red, is shared, but other parts of the schema—the propositions associated with red—are not shared.

When people who have been labeled as having mental retardation talk about the stereotypes that the general public has about them, they are grappling with this type of miscommunication. Even when people agree that a person is appropriately classified as having mental retardation (i.e., they have the features that by definition constitute mental retardation), they can still disagree on what that means. Statements such as "Just because I'm disabled doesn't mean I can't live on my own" or "Retarded isn't stupid, Mom" (Kaufman, 1999) challenge the propositions contained in the generally accepted schema, not the definition of mental retardation.

Shared General Schemas but Different Specific Schemas   Miscommunication can also occur when people share general definitions and propositions but do not share more specific parts of that schema. For example, definitions of basic color terms such as red and green are shared widely in American culture. The complete color schema, however, also defines more specific colors, such as fuchsia, puce, mauve, and magenta, yet only artists and dress designers may learn this part of the schema.

Professionals in the field of developmental disabilities learn more specific parts of a schema about mental retardation than the general population. For example, if a layperson uses the term *developmental disability,* he probably uses it interchangeably with the term *mental retardation,* possibly leading to misunderstanding with a professional who distinguishes mental retardation from other developmental disabilities. The layperson is not wrong but is simply using a general schema rather than the more specific schema also available in American culture.

SCHEMAS AND VALUES-BASED SERVICES

People with developmental disabilities do not differ from people without developmental disabilities in implicit learning abilities, although they do differ in explicit learning abilities (Reber et al., 1991; Wyatt & Conners, 1998). Therefore, people with developmental disabilities are no different from other people in learning what to notice and how to act simply by observing the schemas in use around them. However, people with developmental disabilities have difficulty applying schemas (Soodak, 1990) and sometimes have language deficits that affect their ability to manipulate the ideas contained in schemas (Whitman, 1990b). They might also learn fewer schemas or learn general rather than specific parts of some schemas or vice versa because they are placed in environments where their interactions with and observation of others are curtailed. They nonetheless learn to apply many of the same definitions, beliefs, norms, and values as others around them.

To understand a particular person, his behavior must be interpreted from the point of view of the schemas he is using. If the service provider and receiver are from the same background, they probably share some or most of their schemas; therefore, the service provider is able to more accurately understand the meaning of the person's behavior and possibly even predict it. Other meanings might be more personal; therefore, the service provider must also learn the unique, idiosyncratic parts of the person's world view. Because meaning is not universal but constructed, it should never be assumed that the service provider and receiver share all their schemas or all the specific parts of each schema and thus agree on the meaning of every action or choice.

Identifying Bobby's Schemas

Bobby taught us to look for the schemas that provided the broad themes, the master motives, to understand his actions. According to his social history, Bobby had for the past several years pulled all his clothes out of his dresser every night and piled them on the closet floor. His team tried having Glen, Bobby's community living coach, help him put them away each morning, but that only made Bobby laugh. Moving the dresser into the closet didn't help. Going out for ice cream if the clothes stayed in the drawers for 3 days in a row helped once in a while because Bobby really loved ice cream and trips, but, still, he persisted.

One day, as Glen and I helped another person move his possessions into the bedroom next to Bobby's, Bobby watched intently as each box and piece of furniture passed his door. When a new dresser went by, Bobby's face took on such a look of longing that Glen and I simultaneously realized the reason for the clothing on the closet floor. Glen tested this hypothesis by asking Bobby if he wanted a different dresser.

Bobby's nod was vigorous enough to convince us that he'd been telling us for a long time that he wanted a different dresser. To be fair to the team, the dresser Bobby had was in excellent condition. From everyone's, except Bobby's, point of view, there was absolutely nothing wrong with it.

Glen took Bobby shopping at both new and used furniture stores. Bobby chose a used dresser, helped move the furniture in his bedroom around until the dresser was located in a place he wanted, then put his own clothes in it. He did occasionally take all the clothes out and throw them on the closet floor; but, eventually, he also put them away again. Essentially, the behavior that had concerned the team disappeared on its own.

The puzzling part was that the dresser Bobby chose and the dresser that had originally been provided for him were nearly identical. We knew that there was some subtle difference important to Bobby but unrecognized by us; however, we could not discover his reasons by asking him. It was necessary to look beyond this single instance of behavior in search of the schemas that gave meaning to many of his actions. This is difficult because humans do tend to interpret behavior within the immediate context in which it is displayed (Burke, 1989). For example, at a picnic one day, Glen was helping Bobby serve food onto a paper plate from a table loaded with potluck goodies. Suddenly, Bobby grabbed the plate from him and threw it in Glen's face. Glen exclaimed:

"But, Bobby, you like *chocolate pudding!"*

Because Bobby's action occurred just after Glen scooped up some chocolate pudding, Glen concluded that Bobby was rejecting the choice. At other times, Bobby had hit and spit at certain staff; thrown his lunch box through a window, thereby breaking both lunch box and window; overturned work tables at the workshop where he spent his days; eaten nonedibles, such as beads; and, in general, displayed a variety of behaviors labeled maladaptive by the professionals who had previously worked with him.

Eventually, Bobby's team came to understand that he had extremely strong values on autonomy and self-reliance. He wanted to pick out and serve his own food and hold his plate himself. He wanted to purchase his own dresser and put his clothes in it by himself. He wanted to make his own lunch, choose his work, and control which staff members assisted him. Although these two values did not explain all of Bobby's actions, identifying them helped us begin to see the pattern and cohesiveness of Bobby's world view.

Some service providers might argue that throwing food, stuffing clothing into a closet, and all of Bobby's other "maladaptive" behaviors are not acceptable under any circumstance. They might (and did in the records of services provided to him in previous years) describe Bobby as quick to anger, emotionally unstable (he was on psychotropic medications at one point), willful, dangerous to himself and others, unable to conduct himself in socially appropriate ways, in need of constant supervision, and violent. However, Bobby had no other way to communicate his determination to make his own choices and take care of himself. He persisted in applying his values despite years of failed communication.

Schemas and Behavior Objectives

"At 12:15 when lunch is announced, Bobby will put away his work and come to the lunchroom."

When I first read this description of a behavior objective for Bobby, I was confused. Were we trying to teach Bobby how to follow orders, when to put his work away, or how to tolerate being interrupted? I asked the staff members who were on Bobby's team at that time why they determined that Bobby needed to learn this. They all agreed that the reason they had chosen this behavior objective was that Bobby often violently refused to stop what he was doing when it was time for lunch and that this type of behavior limited him from some jobs he might otherwise be able to hold.

"Why does Bobby refuse?"

This question, unlike the first one, elicited a spirited discussion. Responses varied from "because he's stubborn" (which he was on some occasions), to "he's showing perseverative behavior" (which he did with some other types of behavior), to "because he's not hungry" (he was physically small and did not eat large meals), to "because he didn't choose the time" (we were learning!). We finally decided that the question was unanswerable because we did not know what constituted good work behavior in Bobby's world view.

After much more discussion, his team finally decided that Bobby's rural, farm labor background was the key to his behavior. As a child, he had learned a schema of work, including what it is, how to value it, and when to do it. Farm work has its own rhythm. Breaks are taken relative to the needs of the job at hand, not relative to a clock. One makes hay while the sun shines; ignores minor inconveniences, such as being hungry or tired; and pushes to get the work completed. Also, much of the work is a one-person job. There are no immediate bosses, and work does not have to be closely coordinated with the work of others such as it does on an assembly line.

The sheltered workshop, however, is not a farm, so why did Bobby act as though completing a task was more important than eating lunch at a specified time and as though his actions were independent of others with no need to coordinate a shared lunch break? Bobby's schema of work contained certain basic values that were not easy to change, perhaps because of his disability, his age, or his personality or maybe because he also valued stability and tradition. Whatever the reason, Bobby apparently did not want to change. Consequently, the team turned to finding work that made sense to Bobby in terms of his schema: a task where independence, perseverance, and task orientation, rather than clock orientation, would be important.

I do not know whether Bobby ever did farm tasks when he lived at home. He still, however, had lived in an environment where the people around him had work values associated with rural living. That Bobby would learn these values and apply them in his life at the workshop really is not that surprising; after all, humans do adhere to their values, even in the face of incredible pressure to change. His behavior makes sense if we look at it through his schemas and give it the meaning he and other rural people give it.

Schemas and Communication

Understanding other people's schemas in order to interpret their actions and choices requires the use of some form of communication. People are usually able to communicate something about their reasons, even though they probably do not separate definitions, beliefs, values, and norms; may not know their exact reasons; cannot express their implicit values (Borofsky, 1994); and often give different reasons before and after events and to various people (Quinn & Holland, 1987). These reasons can still be misunderstood by a person who shares general but not specific schemas, has different specific boundaries for particular definitions, or has different propositions associated with those features.

Therefore, even in the best of situations, communicating about values is difficult. When working with a person who is limited in his ability to communicate, we may be tempted to give up trying to talk about the person's reasons and search instead for the observable causes of behavior, a process that does not require communication. This can lead to inadvertently interpreting behavior in terms of our own schemas, even when trying to infer the other person's beliefs and values. When communication does not seem possible (although some communication is always possible, we just are not always listening), we should employ our knowledge about the characteristics of schemas. That is, schemas construct meaning by identifying some features as significant and ignoring others as background noise; schemas organize sets of meaning by constructing propositions and associating them with particular features; schemas provide broad themes and master motives across many behaviors; and schemas are generally, though not identically, shared with others of similar backgrounds.

Because most service providers are from middle-class backgrounds in which finding the correct or best way of doing something is valued, based on the belief that there is always one right or best answer to any problem (Bader & Nyce, 1993), it is difficult for them to stop substituting their interpretations for those of others. However, the essence of multiculturalism and of values-based services is that there are multiple truths in any situation and opposing interpretations of events, all of which are true in the sense that each is true for at least some of the participants (Goodenough, 1987). Truth, therefore, is not something "out there" to be discovered but resides in the minds of the participants (Harding, 1994), whether they are state inspectors who see neglect in the condition of a pair of underwear or Depression-era Norwegian American farmers who see thrift.

POINTS TO REMEMBER

To understand another person in terms of the schemas he is using, we need to follow these four rules:

1. *Identify the schema that gives meaning to the other person's actions.* Choices are not simply accidental but make sense in terms of definitions, beliefs, norms, and values that are part of the schema being used. For example, based on his rural schema of work, Bobby chose when to break for lunch.

2. *Remember that schemas guide both what we see (the outline constructed by definitions and beliefs) and how we act (the plan of ac-*

tion built on values and norms). How we see others' actions and how they see their own actions differ when we are not using the same schemas. For example, I saw Bobby's behavior as pushy, and he saw it as polite.

3. *Assume that the other person is using a different schema before attributing behavior to a skill deficit or personality defect.* Why people act in certain ways may be the result of reasons based on a schema we do not share or have not yet identified. For example, much of Bobby's "violent" behavior disappeared when services were provided in terms of his value of self-reliance.

4. *Recognize that miscommunication is most likely when schemas are similar yet not identical.* People may share the focal point of definitions, especially when they are based on human biology and the natural world, but still differ in specific boundaries and associated propositions. For example, Indian and non-Indian staff agreed on what acts are abusive but unknowingly differed on what constitutes neglect.

Values Correlate with Ethnic and Class Identities

"I don't want to go shopping by myself. I might goof up."

This perfectly groomed, slightly overweight, young woman stood by the door, grasping the door frame in her insistence on not doing her own shopping. Margaret's world was filled with exacting rules and overwhelming expectations that she could never hope to meet. When I first met her, she was unwilling to make a simple choice about what to wear or what to eat without asking at least several staff members what was correct. She often said things such as, "I'm disabled you know. I can't do that," or "I need special help because I'm retarded." She's the only person I've ever known who has called herself retarded.

Margaret had lived with her parents for many years in several middle-class suburbs as her father was promoted and transferred; then after her father's death, she had lived at a residential mental health facility with the dual diagnosis of mental retardation and bipolar disorder. She also experienced psychotic episodes due to unresolved grief. Now that she was stabilized on a combination of psychotropic medications,

Margaret was receiving services in the small, rural town where I worked because there were no openings at the agency that provided services in her community.

Margaret, set adrift in a small town without the moorings of family and familiar surroundings, reacted by demanding constant staff attention by using stomachaches, headaches and, if all else failed, attacks of "falling down" to gain attention. Margaret's team saw these feigned illnesses as a result of her low self-esteem, of being in unfamiliar surroundings, and of being without her father who had protected her—overprotected her according to some team members—by providing her with a highly structured, well-regulated, safe environment with few demands or challenges.

Within a few months, verbal reinforcement for making good choices seemed to increase Margaret's self-esteem. Her "falling down" episodes disappeared, and her behavior was exemplary. She dressed neatly and in appropriate color combinations without seeking staff recommendations. She kept her room clean, packed her own lunch, and was ready on time for work without asking whether it was time to do those activities. She independently chose leisure activities and began making friends.

Because of her improvement, the team decided Margaret was ready to learn the skills necessary for her to achieve one of her goals—living independently in her own apartment. Thus, Margaret began to learn how to do her laundry, handle her money, use the microwave to cook hot meals, and perform several other tasks she had never been allowed to do at home. Almost immediately, her behavior deteriorated on two fronts: Her dependency-seeking illnesses returned, but in the more serious form of self-injury, and her choices were all the bad and wrong choices she could find or invent.

Because they were familiar with the "self-fulfilling prophecy" aspect of labeling theory (Rosenthal & Jacobson, 1968), by which a label "may cause those who are labeled to believe that they do indeed possess such characteristics" (Sue & Sue, 1990, p. 13), her team reasoned that Margaret's behavior might be the result of living up to her father's expectations of her as being unable to do things for herself and in need of protection, a schema of people with disabilities not uncommon in the United States (Ferguson, Ferguson, & Taylor, 1992). They also recognized that Margaret's insistence on making "correct" choices was connected to her background; finding the one right or best answer is valued in middle-class culture (Gardiner, 1994). During the initial intervention, complimenting Margaret on making a good choice reinforced her value of finding the "correct" answer as well as filled her need to meet others' expectations; Margaret knew quite well what choices were considered to be good by the people who worked with her.

Margaret's team revised their original plan of reinforcing her for making good choices and turned, instead, to the far more difficult challenge of reinforcing autonomous behavior. To do this, they complimented her for making any choice, even when that choice was, by the values of most of the people working with her, a bad choice or a choice they would not have made for her. They reasoned that teaching Margaret to exercise her autonomy would enable her to live by her own values rather than according to others' expectations of her. Margaret's team was aware of the irony that their expectations of Margaret, based on their own schema of "autonomous adult American woman," affected her just as her father's expectations had and, thus, might be just as much of a stereotype.

AN INDIVIDUALIST PERSON SCHEMA

"All societies are confronted by the same small set of existential questions," including "the problem of the relationship of the individual to the group" (Shweder & Bourne, 1984, pp. 189–190). To characterize, describe, and perceptually apprehend other selves, individuals use culturally constructed schemas that define a person's relationship to society (Gergen & Davis, 1985). There are two main types of person schemas (White, 1992): 1) collectivist person schemas, which focus on society as primary with each person defined by his interactions with others, and 2) individualist person schemas, which view the person as primary with society built of voluntary associations of individuals.

An individualist person schema abstracts the image of a person as composed of a collection of traits (Shweder, 1980). Some of these traits are unchanging attributes and account for a particular person's personality (Holland, 1985). Other traits are the beliefs, values, and attitudes she has chosen, based on personal experiences or what she has learned from others, that account for her behavior (e.g., polite or sassy, lazy or hardworking) and choices (e.g., clothing, job, spouse). Researchers have also noted how people using this schema intentionally manage the impression made by traits, such as skin color, that are not open to personal selection (Domínguez, 1986). In addition to personal traits, the person has individual rights, tempered by responsibilities to others in the groups he chooses to join (Marsella, DeVos, & Hsu, 1985). A belief central to this conception of the person is that humans have autonomy and select their own unique combination of traits and group memberships (Shweder & Miller, 1985).

Using an Individualist Person Schema

In the United States, an individualist person schema provides the framework for how most people deal with the complex world of strangers (Goodenough, 1987; Levy, 1994). Because each person is defined to be made up of a collection of traits, some of those traits, especially the more visible ones such as skin color or clothing choices (Fouquier, 1981), can be selected as the identifying features of a category of people (Brislin, Cushner, Cherrie, & Yong, 1986) with other behaviors or characteristics then attributed to the category. There are, in other words, schemas that outline how to recognize kinds of people (Greenhouse, 1985) and associated propositions about how to act toward them and what other characteristics and behaviors to expect.

These schemas oversimplify the available information by de-emphasizing variation within categories and accentuating distinctions among them to create an easily useable template for interacting with strangers (Garbarino & Kostelny, 1992). They might define, for example, who is a working stiff and who is a bigwig, who is elderly and who is generation X, who is Chicano and who is a gringo, or who is a city slicker and who is a country bumpkin. Because the identifications are not always correct (e.g., "That man in the white shirt and tie is a stand-up comedian, not a middle-class accountant"), the associated propositions are not shared (e.g., "He's not a country bumpkin but a hardworking American farmer") and the attributed features do not apply to everyone in the category (e.g., "She may be 80, but she just ran the 10K"); these schemas are stereotypes in the negative sense of the term. That is, they provide "assumptions about an individual's behavior" that sometimes result "in inaccurate, inappropriate, or harmful generalizations" (Hanson, 1998, p. 15).

Predictions for the behavior or the beliefs and values of members of a social category can be based on ignorance and hatred and thus bear little relationship to those people's actual behavior or beliefs and values (vanDijk, 1984). They can also be based on personal knowledge through positive involvement with members of the category (Singer & Salovey, 1991) and on increasingly sensitive insights, achieved through research and education, about the schemas that give meaning to their behavior.

This later information is the type needed when the service provider and receiver are from different ethnic groups or social classes, although many professionals are still concerned that the information is oversimplified and not applicable to everyone in the category (Sue & Sue, 1990).

Resistance to Generalizations

Americans resist connecting cultural variations to specific social categories, even when generalizations are based on research. They will quickly point out, for example, that not all middle-class people value correctness and not all Lakota show respect by not interrupting. This resistance is partly based on a conscious effort to decrease stereotyping and prejudice (Stewart & Bennett, 1991). It is also a reaction to the challenge to their conception of a person as freely choosing his own unique collection of traits and group memberships. According to Althen, Americans

> resent generalizations . . . and may be offended by the notion that they hold certain ideas and behave in certain ways simply because they were born and raised in the United States, and not because they had consciously thought about those ideas and behaviors and chosen the ones they preferred. (1988, p. xv)

Type of Category   Various types of social categories are dissimilar in their potential for correlating with cultural and behavioral differences among the people whom they classify. Generalizations about the behavior of people categorized by age, gender, class, role, locality (e.g., Western, Southern, rural, urban), or religion can only be accurate to the extent that the people thus categorized have had similar experiences, adapted to similar environments, or learned similar explicit ideologies and might, therefore, share some schemas (Ross, 1975). In contrast, descriptions of beliefs and values of people categorized by ethnicity can be particularly accurate if the people classified as similar actually interact with each other or did in the recent past (Alba, 1990). The category labels a group with a shared culture rather than just a type of person.

Level of Generalization   Statements about all working-class people or all Italian Americans in the United States are at one level of generalization and thus one level of accuracy for any particular person categorized. A description of Italian Americans in a working-class neighborhood in south Philadelphia is also a generalization. However, it is a generalization about people who interact with each other rather than just people who share certain similar experiences. Even highly specific descriptions of beliefs and values of interacting groups can appear to be inaccurate because they are sometimes stated as hard and fast rules rather than as contingencies (Borofsky, 1994) related to variable conditions and constraints (Hill-Burnett, 1987).

Confusing Race, Language, and Culture   Generalizations associated with "ethnic/racial" labels typically used in the United States (i.e., African American, Asian, Hispanic, Native American, White) are particularly problematic. These categories are used in census forms, affirmative action questionnaires, and research protocols in various fields, but they rarely correlate with specific information about cultural differences. Although they may have political significance (Nagel, 1996), they do not label interacting groups with shared systems of meaning. These terms label people who are culturally distinct only in a very general way because members of these categories share some of the same schemas. For example, there are some similarities in the schemas used by Hispanics because schemas are embedded in language. There are some similarities in the schemas used by African Americans because of the shared experiences of slavery, West African derivation, and contemporary prejudice and discrimination. However, when African Americans or Hispanics do not share all their specific beliefs and values with others similarly categorized, the problem is that "African American" or "Hispanic" does not label an interacting group. The only similarity it is reasonable to expect to find among the members of such broadly defined categories, other than the feature that defined them as a member of the category in the first place, is that because they are categorized similarly they share the experience of being treated similarly by others.

Michael (1995) and Szwed (1975) argued that attributing any cultural differences to race is a racist argument. Culture is learned from interacting with members of the group sharing that culture. Because culture is learned, any cultural trait may be learned by anyone. Therefore, just because a person has certain physical features does not mean that the person has learned or must learn the cultural traits usually associated with people with those features. However, trying to separate race from culture falters because to look similar there must have been a group that interacted long enough to procreate over enough generations to pass on similar physical features. Even though culture is learned and not predetermined in one's genes, the parents who contributed their genes are also, except in the case of adoption, the parents who passed on their system of meanings through interaction with the child. Thus, the correlation between race and culture persists after an interacting group has dissolved.

Individual Variation   Finally, cultural descriptions are generalizations about schemas shared by members of a group, but interaction, whether between a service provider and a service receiver or between two strangers on the street, is between individuals. Individuals have different experiences and learn only part of the system of meanings shared by other members of their group. Nonetheless, they are more similar to others in their social group than they are to others from a different group. The culture they learn is generally shared within their group and continues to be more or less shared by being passed on through parent–child interactions (Alba, 1990), by being kept on track through the normative framework of continuing interaction within the group (Borofsky, 1994), and by being publicly affirmed through shared symbolic performances (Turner, 1967; Varenne, 1986).

ETHNIC GROUPS, CLASSES, AND SELF-IDENTITY

When using an individualist person schema, a person must choose an identity (Spindler & Spindler, 1982). Therefore, it is possible for a person to choose an identity that does not match the ethnicity or class assigned to him by others or to ignore that identity entirely (DeMott, 1990; Smith, 1980). For example, a particular person might identify herself as Native American but not be identified as such by others or vice versa, depending on what definition is applied. The legal definition uses the feature of "blood quantum," a metaphor for combinations of Native American and non-Native American parentage, leading to the situation in which a person can have a high blood quantum but "look very white" or vice versa (Feraca, 1990), with neither blood quantum nor looks predictive of whether the person was reared among people who shared a specific set of Native American beliefs and values (e.g., Lakota, Navajo). Two other definitions are also used: residing on a reservation and speaking the native language (Daniels, 1970) or being recognized as Indian by other Indians (Brave Bird & Erdoes, 1993), with some congruence but far from perfect correspondence among the four categories generated and with only one definition labeling people who also interact as a group.

Assessing Ethnic and Class Background

For service providers, determining a service receiver's ethnic group and class enables them to provide services that support the person's beliefs and values. Therefore, an identification that focuses on interaction with others in the labeled group is the most useful, followed by categories that reflect social differences meaningful to that person, such as religion or location. Objective definitions, such as genetic parentage for ethnic/racial categories (Smith, 1980) or family income or occupation for class categories (Goldschmidt, 1974; Wohlfarth & Van Den Brink, 1998), are necessary for certain types of research but are not useful for establishing the meaning social categories have for the people using them (Grella, 1990). In other words, the question is not whether a particular person is working class in terms of the observer's objective definition but whether the person thinks of himself as "blue collar" or as a "working man," however he defines those terms. In addition, it depends on whether the person interacts with others she perceives as similar to herself. That is, the schemas people use to make choices about themselves and their interactions with others are based on local terms with local meanings (Nagel, 1994). In the same vein, outsiders may use a general category such as African American, Hispanic, or Native American, but the people thus categorized have more finely tuned labels for differences among themselves (Domínguez, 1986).

Self-identity might be based on what Alba (1990) called *symbolic ethnicity,* whereby the person chooses to identify himself as a member of a particular ethnic category based on one grandparent or great grandparent's place of birth although he has never interacted with a group of people of that ethnicity. Or the reverse can occur. For example, the person may have been reared in an ethnic group but chooses to ignore it (Smith, 1980) or actively disavows that membership because he is struggling with a stigmatized identity (Sue & Sue, 1990). Class differences are especially denied because "classes are social categories that cannot be understood in terms of individual motives and desires" (Ortner, 1991, p. 171); that is, they challenge the belief that individuals freely choose their own traits and group memberships. In all these cases, self-identity is emotionally important to the person but problematic as a source of information for a service provider.

Assessment of Ethnic Background   Figure 3.1 identifies the importance of one or more ethnic groups in a person's background and the probability that values characteristic of that group are part of the person's current world view. If an individual's family has been part of an interacting group for many generations and the individual has been part of the same interacting group and has stayed in contact with others who share her ethnic background, that individual is likely to share the beliefs and values associated with that particular ethnic group. However, the correlation is not completely positive; a person with a relatively low score might have stronger emotional ties to or actively seek more involvement with a particular group because of her self-identification, and a person with a higher score might reject that identity. Therefore, the second part of the assessment tool explores the person's self-identity.

Assessment of Class   Figure 3.2 identifies the relative importance of working-class (and below) and middle-class (and above) affiliations for the person being assessed because social mobility, either up or down, may alter a person's class identity during his lifetime but not change all of his beliefs and values. For example, a person reared in a working-class home might have graduated from college and work in a white collar job yet still act in ways more closely associated with the values he learned as a child. People may also aspire to live a certain way but be denied the opportunity to do so because of poverty and discrimination (Sue & Sue, 1990). Thus, their current behavior and choices may not be a reflection of their values but of strategies chosen by necessity, a situation that is explored further in Chapter 8.

Learning Relevant Schemas   If assessments indicate that a specific ethnic group or class is significant for a particular person, then he and his family can be asked about that background. Some information on beliefs and values can be gathered this way. However, people are often not specifically aware of their implicit values because the values are so obvious that they are common sense and rarely described when others inquire.

Reading about a person's specific type of background and having in-services on beliefs and values characteristic of that group also increase familiarity with that culture. Presentations given by people from this background speaking about their culture and lectures by social scientists who have studied this culture are equally important as they provide different kinds of insights, and, of course, in many cases this might be the same person. In-services on the general topic of cultural sensitivity are also helpful because Americans in general, particularly middle-class white professionals (Gaines, 1982), tend to see behavioral varia-

Assessment of Ethnic Background

Part One: Score one point for each "yes" response on the following questions. The higher the score for the individual assessed (especially scores above 17), the greater the probability that significant parts of his or her world view are similar to the world view of others who share his or her ethnic background, regardless of whether he or she claims this identity in Part Two.

Language

	Yes	No
1. Was a language other than English spoken in your home when you grew up?		✓
2. If yes, did you learn it before you learned English?		
3. If yes, can you still speak this language fluently?		
4. If yes, can you still understand this language, even if you cannot speak it?		
5. Did either of your parents speak a language other than English when they grew up?		
6. If yes, did they both speak this language?		
7. Did any of your grandparents speak a language other than English when they grew up?	✓	

Location

1. Did you grow up in a place(s) where most of your neighbors were of the same ethnic background as one or both of your parents?	✓	
2. Did one or both of your parents grow up in places where most of their neighbors were the same ethnic background as they were?	✓	
3. Was one or more of your grandparents born on a reservation or in a country other than the United States?		—
4. Was one or both of your parents born on a reservation or in a country other than the United States?		
5. Were you born on a reservation or in a country other than the United States?		
6. Do you still live in a place where most of your neighbors are of the same ethnic background as you?		
7. Did your parents come from the same ethnic background (or closely related backgrounds, for example, Norwegian and Swedish)?		

Religion

1. Did you attend church/synagogue/mosque (or other religious service) regularly as a child?		

(continued)

Your Values, My Values, Pengra, ©2000 Paul H. Brookes Publishing Co.

Figure 3.1.   Assessment of ethnic background.

Figure 3.1. *(continued)*

Religion *(continued)*   **Yes**   **No**

2. If yes, was this the same religion that one or both of your parents professed?

3. If yes, was this the same religion that one or more of your grandparents professed?

4. Did at least three of your grandparents profess the same religion?

5. Did your parents profess the same (or closely related) religion?

6. Did you attend a religious school for any portion of your childhood?

7. Do you still attend the same kind of (or very similar) church/synagogue/mosque (or other religious service) regularly?

Relatives

1. Do you have two or more siblings?

2. Do you still see one or more of them or talk to at least one of them at least once per month?

3. Do you see or talk to any of your cousins on a regular basis?

4. Do you live within 100 miles of at least 10 relatives (even if you do not see them regularly)?

5. Do you go to at least one family gathering per year (e.g., weddings, funerals, holidays, reunions, christenings, bar mitzvahs)?

6. Do you go to three or more family gatherings per year?

7. While your parents were still living or if they are still living, were you or are you on good terms with one or both of them?

Customs

1. Do you regularly eat food similar to the food you ate when you were growing up?

2. Do you fix special recipes or eat particular foods from your ethnic or religious background for special occasions?

3. Are the decorations/artwork in your current residence similar to the ones that were in the residence(s) where you grew up?

4. Are the furnishings in your residence or the arrangement of your furnishings and belongings similar to how your childhood home was furnished or arranged?

(continued)

Figure 3.1. (*continued*)

Customs (*continued*)   **Yes**   **No**

5. Do you own any piece of clothing that you consider characteristic of your ethnic or religious background (even if you do not wear it)?   _____ _____

6. If yes, do you wear it on some occasions?   _____ _____

7. Do you regularly listen to a television or radio station or read a newspaper or magazine specifically marketed to people of your ethnic or religious background?   _____ _____

Add up the "yes" responses to calculate the **TOTAL SCORE.** _____

Part Two: The following questions are designed to focus on the person's self-identity, which may or may not correspond with the importance of his or her ethnic identity as assessed in Part One. A specific self-identity noted in Question 10 is important to know to provide services that support the person's values.

1. If you answered "yes" to any questions in the Language section, what language(s) were/are they? _____

_____

2. If you listed one or more languages in the preceding question, which language, if any, do you consider to be the most important one in your background? _____

_____

3. What were/are the ethnic background(s) of the places mentioned in the Location section? _____

_____

4. If you listed one or more ethnic backgrounds in the preceding question, which one, if any, do you consider to be the most important one in your background? _____

_____

5. If you answered "yes" to any question in the Religion section, what religion(s) were/are they?_____

_____

6. If you listed one or more religions in the preceding question, which religion, if any, do you consider to be the most important one in your background? _____

_____

Figure 3.1.   (*continued*)

Part Two (*continued*):

7. If you answered "yes" to any of the questions in the Customs section, with what ethnic group or religion are those customs associated? _____

_____

8. If you listed one or more ethnic groups or religions in the preceding question, to which one, if any, are you closest? _____

_____

9. If you are closer to one side of your family, one parent, or one grandparent, what is his/her/their ethnic background, language, and religion? _____

_____

10. Summarize all the ethnic groups, languages, and religions mentioned in Questions 2, 4, 6, 8, and 9. Is one or more of these particularly important to you? _____

_____

_____

_____

_____

tions as personality differences rather than as normative class or ethnic social patterns (Holland, 1985).

Staff Diversity   It is essential to have staff from diverse backgrounds, especially from all ethnic groups and social classes served by the agency, and at all levels from direct support to board members. This does not mean that services should only be provided to people by others who share their backgrounds based on the false assumption that this will ensure that they have shared values (Pedersen, 1988). Instead, it means that all discussions and decisions, whether at the team level, at staff meetings, or at board meetings, are made by people with diverse and possibly conflicting views. In addition, an atmosphere of trust that allows all voices to be heard (Friedman, 1979) is created by including value differences as part of every discussion, whether the discussion is about moving office furniture or rewriting the policy manual, and not just when there is a conflict.

Assessment of Class Background

Score one point for each "yes" response to the questions in Parts One and Two. Total the scores for each part and compare them. If the Part One score is higher than the Part Two score, the person being assessed probably comes from a working-class background. The greater the difference between the two scores, the greater the probability that significant parts of his or her world view are similar to others with a working-class background. If the Part Two score is higher than the Part One score, the person being assessed probably comes from a middle-class background. The greater the difference between the two scores, the greater the probability that significant parts of his or her world view are similar to others with a middle-class background.

For the occupational terms that are in italics, substitute "blue collar" and "white collar" if used in your area or insert locally significant terms. Whether the person applies those or similar terms to him- or herself, as he or she defines them, is the goal of the assessment. It is not the goal to determine whether the person is working class or middle class by externally defined income ranges or occupations. For activities that are listed in italics and enclosed in parentheses, substitute locally significant equivalents (e.g., mah jong rather than bridge, slow pitch rather than horseshoes).

Conduct the assessment with the person who is receiving services, if possible, as well as with a member of his or her immediate family. The family member should answer the questions from his or her point of view, not as he or she thinks the questions would be answered by the person who is receiving services.

Part One   Yes   No

1. Did you grow up in a place(s) where most of your neighbors held (*manual* or *technical*) jobs?   ____   ____

2. Did one or both of your parents grow up in a rural area or in places where most of their neighbors held (*manual* or *technical*) jobs?   ____   ____

3. Did your father, stepfather, or other man present during your childhood hold a (*manual* or *technical*) job, if he worked outside the home? (If he was unemployed, mark "yes.")   ____   ____

4. Did your mother, stepmother, or other woman present during your childhood hold a (*manual* or *technical*) job, if she worked outside the home? (If she was unemployed, mark "yes" if you marked "yes" for Question 3.)   ____   ____

5. Do you currently live in a place where most of your neighbors hold (*manual* or *technical*) jobs?   ____   ____

6. Did one of your parents have a high school education or less (i.e., *no college or specialized vocational training*)?   ____   ____

(continued)

Your Values, My Values, Pengra, ©2000 Paul H. Brookes Publishing Co.

Figure 3.2.   Assessment of class background.

Figure 3.2. *(continued)*

Part One *(continued)*   Yes   No

7. Did both of your parents have high school educations
   or less (i.e., *no college or specialized vocational
   training*)?   _____   _____

8. Do you have a high school education or less (i.e., *no
   training beyond high school*)?   _____   _____

9. Was your family income at or lower than the average income in the community in which you lived?   _____   _____

10. When your parents socialized outside their home, did
    they do so mostly with other family members?   _____   _____

11. When you go out now, do you socialize most often with
    other family members?   _____   _____

12. Did your parents go (*bowling* or *play horseshoes*)?   _____   _____

13. Did your parents play (*pinochle* or *cribbage*)?   _____   _____

14. Did your father belong to a (*lodge, fraternal,* or *veterans
    organization*)?   _____   _____

15. Was your evening meal called supper?   _____   _____

Add the number of "yes" responses to calculate the **TOTAL
SCORE** for Part One.   _____

Part Two

1. Did you grow up in a place(s) where most of your
   neighbors held (*managerial* or *professional*) jobs?   _____   _____

2. Did one or both of your parents grow up in places
   where most of their neighbors held (*managerial* or *professional*) jobs?   _____   _____

3. Did your father, stepfather, or other man present during
   your childhood hold a (*managerial* or *professional*) job,
   if he worked outside the home? (If he was unemployed,
   mark "no.")   _____   _____

4. Did your mother, stepmother, or other woman present
   during your childhood hold a (*managerial* or *professional*) job, if she worked outside the home? (If she was
   unemployed, mark "yes" if you marked "yes" for Question 3.)   _____   _____

5. Do you currently live in a place where most of your
   neighbors hold (*managerial* or *professional*) jobs?   _____   _____

6. Did one of your parents attend or graduate from college
   or the equivalent?   _____   _____

(continued)

Figure 3.2.   (*continued*)

Part Two (*continued*)	Yes	No
7. Did both of your parents attend or graduate from college or the equivilent?	_____	_____
8. Did you attend or graduate from college or the equivalent?	_____	_____
9. Was your family income at or higher than the average income in the community where you lived?	_____	_____
10. When your parents socialized outside their home, did they do so mostly with friends rather than relatives?	_____	_____
11. When you go out now, do you socialize most often with friends rather than relatives?	_____	_____
12. Did your parents play (*golf* or *tennis*)?	_____	_____
13. Did your parents play (*bridge* or *whist*)?	_____	_____
14. Did your father belong to a (*business* or *civic association*)?	_____	_____
15. Was your evening meal called dinner?	_____	_____

Add the number of "yes" responses to calculate the **TOTAL SCORE** for Part Two.   _____

Assistance from a Cultural Specialist   A new specialization in the fields of health care (Nichter, 1991; Weidman, 1979) and educational evaluation (Fetterman, 1987) has emerged. A cultural specialist is a person who is available, much like a behavior specialist, to consult with a team to facilitate qualitative rather than quantitative data gathering and analysis (Angrosino, 1976; see also Chapters 4 and 5) to assist the team in planning and implementing culturally relevant supports and services for a particular person. The task of the cultural specialist is "clinically applied anthropology" (Chrisman & Johnson, 1990), which involves focusing on the beliefs and values of a person and his or her family rather than on the imparting of general information about an ethnic group or social class background (Chambers, 1985). The cultural specialist actively participates in interpretation and compromise, serving as mediator and broker (Esber, 1979) during team discussions to translate schemas so that misunderstanding is not mistaken for disagreement.

Supporting Gloria's Self-Identity

"I'm not Indian anymore."

When Gloria said this to me, I was standing with a bill in my hand for a pink sweatsuit she had charged to the agency, ready to talk to her about who pays for what; however, now I was faced with a far more important issue. Actually, I was shocked, as Gloria had seemed to be very secure in her Indian identity. Thus, I asked her what made her Indian. She quickly told me two things:

"Wearing dresses. No haircuts."

She was quite right that she now only occasionally wore the dresses she had worn every day at home on the reservation, opting instead for the pink sweatsuit, and that she had asked to get a haircut. We assumed that Gloria had chosen both changes, although she may have stopped wearing dresses and had her hair cut because she wanted to be like the others in her new group. I did not realize that these changes would make her feel less Indian or that, maybe, she had succumbed to subtle pressures we, the staff, were unknowingly exerting.

We had tried to communicate a message of acceptance. For example, we added Native American art as part of the decorations in the group home; tuned radios to the local Indian station; subscribed to the Indian newspaper, *Lakota Times*; showed videotapes that had positive images of Native Americans; added Indian tacos to the menu; and provided transportation to the reservation so Gloria could visit family and participate in powwows and ceremonies. These things were helpful; but clearly, there were other features that meant more to Gloria. Over the next several weeks, we continued to talk about what it meant to be Indian, and she added two more behaviors to her list: "talking Indian" and going to church. Eventually, her team found a bilingual friend for her with whom she had pie, coffee, and Lakota conversation once a week (O'Connor, 1993). We also assisted her in attending several different churches, a choice not unusual for Lakota who accept that there are many paths to spirituality, not just a single, right one (Powers, 1987).

Gloria and I and several other people attended a Native Americans with Disabilities conference in Albuquerque, New Mexico, where Gloria met some people active in the People First organization. As a result, she founded a local People First group and participated in a self-advocacy training sponsored by the state advocacy office. Gloria eventually stopped attending People First meetings; she discovered that her motivation had been to learn to stand up to racism and prejudice about being Indian, not to be an advocate because she had been labeled as having a disability. According to Strenta and Kleck, "individuals with stigmatizing characteristics often take it for granted that their treatment by others is causally linked to these attributes" (1984, p. 279). In the town where Gloria received services, both her Indian identity and her disability were stigmatizing. Gloria, however, identified herself in the same way other Indians did, as Lakota, not as a person with a disability; therefore, she saw her mistreatment as a consequence of her Indian identity. In Lakota culture, having a disability is not stigmatizing (Ross, 1989); therefore, helping Gloria see her treatment as being due to her disability would have challenged her schema of what it means to have a disability. To provide values-based services to Gloria, it is necessary to support her self-identity and her analysis of the reasons for her mistreatment.

Gloria and I continued to talk about being Indian. I explained the concepts of values and value differences. She explained to me what it was like to be hurt and disrespected just because you are Indian. Once she asked me to write a letter to complain about a state employee who had treated her disrespectfully. Together, we wrote a letter to the employee's supervisor and received a typical "he was only doing his job" response that Gloria knew was further proof of how little others understood her value of respect. Another time, we visited a museum that prominently featured Lakota artifacts. Gloria contributed to their fundraising campaign because she believed they were helping people respect Lakota history and culture.

Identifying Bobby's Ethnicity

Unlike Gloria, whose ethnic background was clearly identified by herself and others, Bobby's Norwegian ethnicity and farm background were simply not recognized in his records as potential factors in his or his family's behavior. The knowledge that Bobby's family brought him Norwegian cookies and wanted him to attend a Lutheran Church was vaguely recognized as having something to do with his Norwegian heritage; however, his family showing up without calling ahead to make arrangements was not recognized as part of a common Norwegian visiting pattern.

Norwegian Americans often drop by to visit their neighbors without planning a particular task or activity but just to "be there" for each other and to support each other by their presence (Aamodt, 1981).

Bobby's family's habit of dropping by, however, had occasionally been discussed at staff meetings with a note of irritation by some and shoulder shrugging by others. Although we explicitly agreed that it was Bobby's family's right to visit anytime, for some staff members it was a little like being subjected to a surprise inspection. Efforts to convince his family that a special activity could be arranged if we knew when they were coming did not solve "the problem." At the time, we did not know that having a special activity would interfere with the family's behavior of "being there" for Bobby. The staff members who were unconcerned and not surprised by the unannounced visits were Scandinavian American.

We did not suspect that an assessment of Norwegian American beliefs and values would be an appropriate part of developing services for Bobby because neither he nor his family actively identified themselves as Norwegian American. Their values were not that unfamiliar to us, and their behavior was not abnormal, illegal, or harmful—just mildly irritating to some people. Yet, Bobby's Norwegian American heritage was apparent from his love of coffee with a lot of cream to his values on making independent choices, taking care of himself, and being thrifty. Even coming to visit me in my office was his way of "being there" for me, a pattern that I did not recognize and misinterpreted before I began reading about Norwegian American values. Ethnicity does not have to be recognized by the individual to have an impact on him (Cerroni-Long, 1993) if he was reared, as Bobby was, in a group that shared those values.

One time, Bobby chose to attend the district Special Olympics. We were surprised because Bobby generally hated physical exertion, never watched sports on television, disliked group activities, and rarely chose to participate in sports or games. However, Bobby's behavior at the event quickly made sense of his choice; while there, he joyfully greeted and visited with many people, particularly his friends from the institution where he had previously lived. Bobby attended the Special Olympics not because it was what he wanted to do but because we had not offered him the supports he needed to do what he wanted to do, which was to support his friends by "being there" for them.

To say that someone has a particular ethnic or class background, regardless of whether she identifies with it, does not mean that all services and supports must be offered only in terms of the values characteristic of those social groups, nor does it mean that the person must be taught to behave by those values. If, for example, Bobby liked black coffee, it would be absurd to encourage him to add cream just because other Norwegian Americans drink coffee that way. Identifying the person's background, however, does make it possible to offer an array of choices, including ones based on values characteristic of that ethnicity or class, and to enable the person to live by those values if he so chooses.

Identifying a cultural background also does not mean that all problems will be related to it (Trotter, 1991). Bobby also regularly flooded the bathroom, flushed his socks down the toilet, threw his shoes out the window, and lay on his back while waving his feet in the air; however, none of these behaviors appear to be associated with being Norwegian American. The team, however, did eventually realize that they were part of a single problem (see Chapter 6).

Learning from Margaret's Search for Identity

Margaret and I were returning from her hometown where I had attended a meeting and she had visited her mother in the nursing home. Afterward, we went to the cemetery to put flowers on her father's grave. Together we read the triple headstone that had Margaret's and her mother's names already chiseled next to her father's with spaces left to add their years of death. All the way home, Margaret described her father's funeral and asked questions about her mother's approaching death, a discussion that I hoped would help her prepare for that event. Her next comment, however, led us in a completely different direction, as conversations with Margaret had a way of doing.

"When I die, I'll go to heaven like my father. Then I'll be able to think like everybody else."

Margaret's discussions with me on the ride home and with her friends in People First during the following months revolved around two issues—her disability and wanting to belong somewhere. Being treated as a member of the social category "people with mental retardation" often impedes people from living by their own values, an issue discussed in Chapters 7 and 8, and eventually solved by Margaret in her own way (see Chapter 5). However, Margaret was also grappling with rootlessness and not belonging to a community, a concern she shared with other geographically and socially mobile middle-class Americans (Spindler, Spindler, Trueba, & Williams, 1991).

Community for the working class in the United States is the urban ethnic neighborhood or small rural town settled by one ethnic group,

characterized by a strong web of extended kinship and "more tradi-
tional patterns of resource sharing and social interaction" (Foley, 1989,
p. 154). These communities are physical places where class and ethnicity intersect, where neighbors work at the same factories or neighboring
farms, attend the same churches and schools, and identify themselves
as members of the same group.

For middle-class Americans, community is no longer a place but a
concept. "Moving" into the middle class in the United States literally
requires moving out of one's former neighborhood and away from the
intimacy of kin and friends (Ortner, 1991), shedding or denying all
traces of ethnicity or working-class roots to become part of the "culturally invisible mainstream" (Rosaldo, 1989, p. 209), and finding identity
through talk (Chock, 1987; Foley, 1989) and role performance (Dussart, 1993). "The *workplace* tends to become the neighborhood as well
as the family" (Spindler, Spindler, Trueba, & Williams, 1991, p. 111
[emphasis in original]); individuals create groups based on shared interests, belonging because, as Margaret said, they are "like everybody
else." Conformity becomes the glue that holds middle-class people together, however weakly, because common interests define who is a
member (DeMott, 1990) rather than a shared heritage where ties bind
tightly because of the overlapping connections of family, neighborhood, religion, and work.

Margaret's search for identity and her anxiety about doing things
exactly right may have been more intense because she did not yet have
work or motherhood to define her place in middle-class society. Instead, she was defined by her role as a mentally retarded person, a stigmatized identity conferred on her by others. Margaret's questions, however, were not that different from those asked by other middle-class
Americans: Who am I and where do I belong? Initially, it seemed that
Margaret was concerned with these questions because she had been labeled as having a disability. This analysis, however, is just another form
of *diagnostic overshadowing,* a term originally coined to "represent the
tendency for a diagnosis of mental retardation to overshadow a coexist-
ing psychopathological disorder" (Spengler, Strohmer, & Prout, 1990,
p. 205) but used here to include the tendency to see behavior as related
to a person's disability rather than to her class, ethnicity, or other social
identity.

An individualist person schema combined with the rejection of the
importance of class in the United States made it difficult for us to see
Margaret as a normal, middle-class American woman searching for her

own identity. There is a strong denial in the United States that classes really exist (DeMott, 1990) or that people from various classes differ in their values (Ortner, 1991). It is barely acceptable to refer to someone as middle class or working class and pejorative to call someone impoverished; therefore, class membership is generally ignored. Instead, behavioral differences among people from different classes are attributed to personality variations (Stewart & Bennett, 1991) or personal choice (Lear, 1984) for fear that relating them to class might seem to be a stereotype.

GENERALIZATIONS ARE NOT STEREOTYPES

Using generalizations about beliefs and values of various ethnic groups and social classes to interpret behavior decreases the misunderstandings and hurt feelings that develop when people have different backgrounds. To deny or be unaware of differences allows people to use their own schemas to evaluate others; this is actually a form of stereotyping, as these judgments are often inaccurate and harmful. If the cultural contexts of behaviors are unknown, Bobby's family's unannounced visits might be mistakenly evaluated as mistrustful, Gloria's behavior of sharing all her groceries as impulsive, and Margaret's quest for conformity as dependency. However, knowing generalizations about cultural differences allows these events to be understood rather than judged as abnormal, unusual, or wrong.

Generalizations about beliefs and values are also not stereotypes because they are about differences in meaning, not predictions of behavior. Knowing that someone is Norwegian American or middle class does not mean being able to predict that he will choose not to buy new underwear too often or that she will be overly concerned with knowing the correct way to dress. Descriptions of behavior rather than of culture are particularly apt to stereotype members of various ethnic groups and classes because they are incorrectly used to predict specific behavior rather than only to anticipate possibilities. Cultural descriptions enable people to understand a particular behavior if it does occur.

When I was helping Gloria find a house to move into on her own, she told me that her dream home would have a white picket fence in front and a cat inside. When I asked her whether having running water and indoor plumbing mattered to her, she said that having those would be nice but she could get along without them, an answer that didn't surprise me because I was aware of her values on fortitude and "making do." Because I also was aware of another generalization, that Lakota culture includes a strong value on family, I asked Gloria if she needed room for visiting family and friends. She laughed—the thought of having a home without room for family to visit was absurd. It hadn't even occurred to her to list that as part of her dream because she assumed it was obvious. Gloria probably would have said she was satisfied regardless of what house we helped her move into because she so desperately wanted her own home. But I know she was ultimately happy, not because of the running water, indoor plumbing, or even the cat and the white picket fence, although those were important, but because her home was large enough for guests.

POINTS TO REMEMBER

To support a person's identity, we need to employ the following four strategies:

1. *Study research-based generalizations about cultural differences characteristic of the ethnic group and class membership of each person.* Generalizations are not stereotypes, although they still must be used carefully when applied to individuals identified as members of categories that are not interacting groups. For example, when working with Bobby, generalizations about rural people in the United States were less useful than generalizations about Norwegian American Lutheran farmers in the Midwest.

2. *Interpret how a person forms his own identity by understanding the beliefs and values characteristic of his ethnicity or class.* All people develop an identity, although in a society employing an individualist person schema, it is particularly difficult because the individual must find his own identity. For example, Margaret's search was similar to other middle-class Americans' quests for community, except she had the additional task of coping with a stigmatized identity.

3. *Support each person's self-identity by helping her deal with prejudice, whether due to ethnicity, class, or disability.* Supports for advocacy activities must be offered in terms of the person's analysis of her own situation. For example, Gloria connected others' unkind acts to their racism and not to her disability; therefore, she was assisted in pursuing some activities that strengthened her Indian

identity as well as advocacy activities that sought respect because of that identity.

4. *Assist each person's management of his own ethnic or class identity by providing culturally appropriate activities and choices to him.* Generalizations about activities that are characteristic of ethnic groups and classes can help the service provider offer an array of activities that include those activities as choices, whereas generalizations about beliefs and values help the service provider interpret and evaluate those choices if they are made. For example, supports for Bobby ought to include the chance to visit another community to "be there" for his friends, an expensive option that, when evaluated in terms of Bobby's values, is worth it.

Part II

DESIGNING
VALUES-BASED SERVICES

Part II applies the three themes developed in Part I by demonstrating a technique for discovering variations in schemas about particular kinds of behaviors and how to provide values-based support services that build on those variations. Chapter 4 uses an extended example of an assessment tool developed to understand an image schema—in this case, values about when an act is theft—and intervention programs designed for one person based on that tool. This example is useful because the process of developing an assessment tool for discovering values is the same when working with any person whose social identity differs from the service provider's, regardless of the specific schema in question.

Chapter 5 provides a second example of an assessment tool, one developed to understand a proposition schema—in this case, values about the best way to make decisions. As with all values, decision-making values cannot be analyzed out of context but must be related to schemas that the person has in common with others who share his social identity.

Chapter 6 investigates how unrecognized, partial, or disordered schemas can contribute to problem behavior. Embracing the main postulate of values-based services does not mean that all behavior must be accepted as equally good. However, interventions to change problem behavior, as with all values-based services, must be from the service receiver's point of view, based on how she, not the service provider, defines the problem.

Intervention Using Schema Analysis

"Gloria stole some pretty barrettes and hair ribbons!"

The news traveled quickly throughout the agency. An outsider might have been puzzled or even shocked by our excited reaction. This was a happy event. Gloria was making progress.

For the first time since Gloria moved here from her reservation community, she had taken something other than canned goods, towels, blankets, soap, and sanitary napkins. Taking something pretty, something not related to survival, was a change in her behavior and, we thought, a breakthrough.

When Gloria first moved to the group home, there had been a flurry of incident reports about her stealing things. Her room looked like a shelter prepared for World War III, containing all the supplies necessary for survival. After stuffing every nook and cranny, she started packing trunks and duffel bags to put in the storeroom.

Perhaps Gloria was simply adapting to her background of extreme poverty, having come from the poorest county in the United States (U.S.

Census Bureau, quoted in *Rapid City Journal,* 1994), and to the recent loss of her main caregiver by stockpiling against future poverty, planning for when she would be living on her own again without her present level of resources. Or, maybe, her actions were guided by the Lakota value of sharing, but in the community where she lived now these actions were interpreted as theft. It was also possible that she just liked to accumulate things and didn't know that taking them was stealing.

We didn't completely understand why Gloria was taking things, although we suspected cultural differences and an adaptive response to poverty. However, other Lakota with low incomes lived in this community and didn't steal; therefore, we reasoned that there might also be some misunderstanding or new skill she needed to learn. Because we didn't want to limit her independence, we had to teach Gloria what was and was not considered stealing in this town where she now lived; however, we wanted to do so in terms of her values. Therefore, the team needed to determine Gloria's beliefs and values about taking things as well as the schema of theft in the local community to find the points of conflict and agreement.

When I asked Brenda, Gloria's case manager, how she defined stealing, she said that it was "taking something that doesn't belong to you." That was basically my definition, too, but I was having difficulty applying it. For instance, I pick up aluminum cans even though they don't belong to me because I value recycling. If I see a quarter on the sidewalk I pick it up; however, if I were to find a wad of $100 bills, I probably would advertise in the local paper for the rightful owner. At what point should a person decide not to pocket the money but to advertise for an owner? $1? $10? $100? Would the amount of money I found determine whether I advertised, or would I be more likely to keep a large amount if no one saw me pick it up or if I was out of work at the time? I could easily understand if Gloria was having difficulty knowing what was acceptable behavior and what was stealing.

SCHEMA-BASED INTERVENTION WITH GLORIA

Figure 4.1 is an assessment tool written to uncover variations in theft schemas used by staff and people in the local community. It was designed to make respondents think about their stated values about theft as well as their actual behavior. Before reading the discussion of the schema and how we helped Gloria once we understood her values about theft, take the assessment yourself.

Assessing Your Schema of Theft

The middle column describes various situations. Read each situation, and then, in the column on the left, mark whether you have ever done this or would do this if you were in the described situation or a very similar situation. Mark "yes" if you have done or would do this and "no" if you have not done it and would never consider doing it, regardless of whether you think the scenario actually constitutes theft.

At least 1 week later, take the assessment again on an unmarked copy of the assessment form or with the answers in the left column covered. Read through the situations a second time, and in the column on the right, mark whether you think this is theft. Again, mark "yes" if you think this is theft and "no" if you think it is not theft, regardless of whether you have actually done or would do any of the actions described.

Have you done or would you ever do this?			Is it theft?	
YES	NO		YES	NO
✓		1. Before leaving a restaurant, you take the 30 packets of sugar, salt, and pepper that remain on the table.		
	✓	2. A week after a community pot-luck at your local community center, there is still one casserole pan that has not been claimed, so you take it home.	✓	
	✓	3. You sell a nearly new frost-free refrigerator but neglect to tell the buyer that the frost-free feature no longer works.		✓
✓		4. You pick up a quarter you see on the sidewalk.		
	✓	5. A well-dressed man getting into an expensive car drops his gloves. You wait until he drives off and then take them.	✓	
	✓	6. You are out of money and very hungry, so you take a half-price item from the damaged goods basket.	✓	
✓		7. You buy one drink during happy hour, then eat a meal's worth of free snacks during the next 3 hours.		✓
	✓	8. You pick up a $10 bill you saw fall out of the pocket of an elderly lady walking in front of you.		

(continued)

Your Values, My Values, Pengra, ©2000 Paul H. Brookes Publishing Co.

Figure 4.1.   Assessing your schema of theft.

Figure 4.1. (*continued*)

Have you done or would you ever do this?   Is it theft?

YES   NO   YES   NO

_____ _____   9. You take an old highchair from   _____ _____
                the curbside garbage because you
                recognize it as a valuable antique.

_____ _____   10. You take an old highchair from   _____ _____
                the front yard of a very run-down
                house with other junk in the yard
                because you know it is a valuable
                antique.

_____ _____   11. You take an old highchair from   _____ _____
                the front porch of a house that
                appears to be unoccupied because
                you know the chair is a valuable
                antique.

_____ _____   12. You go through the garbage   _____ _____
                behind the local photo-developing
                store to collect empty film canisters
                for a craft project.

_____ _____   13. Before leaving a restaurant, you   _____ _____
                take one packet each of sugar, salt,
                and pepper to keep in your car for
                emergencies.

_____ _____   14. You pocket your tips at your   _____ _____
                restaurant job without reporting
                them to the IRS.

_____ _____   15. You are refunded the full price   _____ _____
                for an item you bought on sale, but
                you do not tell the cashier.

_____ _____   16. You buy five or six drinks during   _____ _____
                happy hour and then eat a meal's
                worth of free snacks during the next
                3 hours.

_____ _____   17. You are very cold and have no   _____ _____
                money, so you take a sweater you
                find on the bench at the bus stop.

_____ _____   18. Your car breaks down while you   _____ _____
                are in a strange city, so you take the
                telephone book from a phone booth
                to use the maps.

_____ _____   19. The customer preceding you at a   _____ _____
                restaurant table left a sweater behind
                that will exactly match the pants you
                just bought, so you take it.

(*continued*)

Figure 4.1. (*continued*)

Have you done or would you ever do this?   Is it theft?

YES   NO   YES   NO

_____ _____   20. You tell the mail order company   _____ _____
              that an item arrived damaged even
              though it did not so that you can get
              a free replacement.

_____ _____   21. While doing laundry at the   _____ _____
              laundromat, you see a nice t-shirt in
              the lost and found. It is still there a
              week later, so you take it.

_____ _____   22. You take a personal telephone   _____ _____
              call at work that lasts about 1
              minute.

_____ _____   23. You advertise in the local news-   _____ _____
              paper, but no one claims the dia-
              mond ring you found in a public
              restroom; therefore, you keep it.

_____ _____   24. A very nice coat in your size is   _____ _____
              left for a week on the coat rack at
              your place of employment, so you
              take it.

_____ _____   25. The clerk gives you a quarter   _____ _____
              too much in change, and you keep
              it.

_____ _____   26. You are on a fishing trip and find   _____ _____
              an expensive rod, reel, and tackle
              box abandoned in some reeds, so
              you take them instead of turning
              them into the lost and found.

_____ _____   27. Your child brings a nice toy   _____ _____
              home from playgroup, but because
              you do not know whose it is, you
              keep it.

_____ _____   28. The clerk gives you $20 too   _____ _____
              much in change, and you keep it.

_____ _____   29. You are out of money in a   _____ _____
              strange town and get very sick, so
              you take a bottle of aspirin from the
              store without paying for it.

_____ _____   30. You are at a local store when the   _____ _____
              munchies hit; you do not have
              enough money with you to buy a
              snack, so you take a bag of cookies
              without paying for them.

(*continued*)

Figure 4.1.   (*continued*)

Have you done or would you ever do this?			Is it theft?	
YES	NO		YES	NO
_____	_____	31. You take a personal telephone call at work that lasts about 20 minutes.	_____	_____
_____	_____	32. You forgot to bring money and it is a long walk home, so you just take the milk you came to buy.	_____	_____
_____	_____	33. You are on a picnic and find a half-full bag of charcoal, so you use it.	_____	_____
_____	_____	34. Your friend at the checkout lets you redeem coupons for items you have not purchased.	_____	_____
_____	_____	35. You helped distribute commodities at the Senior Citizens' Center, so you take the three extra boxes of food home with you at the end of the day.	_____	_____
_____	_____	36. You trade meal receipts with your friend because his is higher than yours and you get reimbursed for your expenses.	_____	_____

Variations in a Schema of Theft

There were six strands of meaning in the schema of theft used in the local community: ownership, location, value of the item, quantity of the item, theft by deception, and personal need for the item. These strands of meaning were established by five volunteers who sorted approximately 75 situations into what they considered to be similar events. The volunteers based these similar events on each set of situations sharing a single reason, or strand of meaning, for why they might be considered theft. Then, differences in sorting were discussed and items were rewritten or eliminated until there was agreement on the sorting of 36 items that varied with respect to these strands. There may have been alternative interpretations in other communities, or other volunteers might have divided these differently because there were no right or wrong answers. There was just increased understanding of some of the significant features of a schema of theft as well as insight into when and how people choose to use it.

Two trends emerged in discussions with Gloria's team and with participants in workshops on assessing values. The most consistent pattern in the variation of answers was a tendency for younger people to see fewer situations as theft and older people to rate more behaviors as theft. The second trend was for working-class people (generally direct support staff in the audiences I addressed) to say that taking something associated with need was not theft more often than middle-class (generally the professional and supervisory staff) respondents did. Both of these patterns were overlaid with differences in whether the respondent also valued recycling or thrifty behavior and a difference in how Indian and non-Indian staff defined sharing.

All staff members agreed that sharing was using something owned by someone else. The difference between Lakota and non-Indian ideas of sharing lay in whether the person had to ask permission or could just use the other person's possession as needed. The norm for people who were not Lakota was that a person should ask permission of the owner to borrow his things because ownership confers the right to control use of those items. The norm for Lakota staff members, however, was that a person could use, but not take, someone else's possessions when she needed to, particularly if she knew the other person well. Asking permission would be like accusing the owner of being stingy.

Figure 4.2 provides a chart to analyze responses on the assessment in terms of the six identified strands. The simple definition of theft, taking something that does not belong to you, identifies ownership as a significant feature. Yet, picking up aluminum cans, finding spare change on the sidewalk, or taking something from a lost-and-found box if the item has been there for a long time is not considered to be theft by many people because some items are classified as not really being owned by anybody. Theft, then, is not just taking something one does not own, it is taking something owned by someone else. Another strand, location of the item, allows taking things from no-man's land, such as public restrooms, roadside ditches, and restaurants because items found in these places have no readily identified owners.

Taking something of very minimal value is sometimes not classified as theft or is seen as less serious than stealing something of great value. Even U.S. laws reflect this distinction with the categories of petty theft and grand theft. A related idea is that the quantity taken also defines what is theft; taking a little of a low-value item is permissible, but taking too much of it is not. For example, a quick personal telephone call at work or taking an occasional pen or paperclip is all right.

Taking too many pens, using the telephone for too long, or taking too many extra catsup packets at the fast-food restaurant crosses that invisible "too much" line and, for some people, becomes theft.

Getting something by deception—through lying, because no one saw or because it was someone else's mistake—is not considered to be

Scoring Your Theft Schema Assessment

Score one point in the left columns of the scoring charts for each situation you said you would not do or had never done (for which you checked "no" in the left column of Figure 1). Total the number of points for each section to calculate your left-column scores.

Score one point in the right columns of the scoring charts for each situation you said was theft (marked "yes" in the right column of Figure 4.1). Total the points in the right column for each section to calculate your right-column scores.

A right-column score of zero indicates that that factor may not be in your schema of theft. A score of six indicates that that factor is a very important factor in your definition. Your weighting of all six factors describes your schema of theft.

Personal adherence to your own values about theft is described by how closely your left-column scores ("No, I've never done this") match your right-column scores ("Yes, this is theft"). Responding to the right column too soon after responding to the left column, or not covering your left column answers while filling out the right column, may result in self-generated validity (i.e., softening your definition of theft to make more of your behavior conform to your stated values).

A.	Ownership		B.	Value	
5.	⎯⎯	⎯⎯	4.	⎯⎯	⎯⎯
8.	⎯⎯	⎯⎯	12.	⎯⎯	⎯⎯
18.	⎯⎯	⎯⎯	25.	⎯⎯	⎯⎯
23.	⎯⎯	⎯⎯	26.	⎯⎯	⎯⎯
27.	⎯⎯	⎯⎯	28.	⎯⎯	⎯⎯
35.	⎯⎯	⎯⎯	33.	⎯⎯	⎯⎯
Totals:	⎯⎯	⎯⎯	Totals:	⎯⎯	⎯⎯

(continued)

Your Values, My Values, Pengra, ©2000 Paul H. Brookes Publishing Co.

Figure 4.2.   Scoring your theft schema assessment.

Figure 4.2.   (*continued*)

C.	Deception		D.	Location	
3.	____	____	2.	____	____
14.	____	____	9.	____	____
15.	____	____	10.	____	____
20.	____	____	11.	____	____
34.	____	____	21.	____	____
36.	____	____	24.	____	____
Totals:	____	____	**Totals:**	____	____

E.	Personal Need		F.	Unwritten Boundaries	
6.	____	____	1.	____	____
17.	____	____	7.	____	____
19.	____	____	13.	____	____
29.	____	____	16.	____	____
30.	____	____	22.	____	____
32.	____	____	31.	____	____
Totals:	____	____	**Totals:**	____	____

theft by some people. Some respondents clarified this by saying that if taking the item did not hurt an individual then it was all right. Hurting a corporation, the government, or a business is not considered by some to be hurting anyone. For them, this kind of action—"getting away with it" or "beating the system"—was not theft but, rather, an acceptable show of prowess.

Personal need is the final strand for defining when taking a particular item is not theft. A value increasingly common in the United States is the personal right to a decent quality of life; thus, individuals are entitled to health and a certain minimum standard of living (Muyskens, 1992). Some people carry this idea one step further, arguing that if a person does not have these necessities, then it is acceptable for that person to take what he needs.

The First Intervention: Learning Self-Regulation

Using the schema assessment tool helped team members to state more clearly their values about theft and begin to unravel the strands of meaning in Gloria's behavior of taking things. The local schema varied with age and class on the "no apparent owner" and "I need it" factors. Therefore, because Gloria was young and earned less than minimum wage, she might evaluate taking certain things as permissible, whereas the older professionals working with her would rate the same action as theft. When the assessment tool was used with Gloria, it appeared that she shared these two strands of the schema with other young, working-class people in the community. However, Gloria's definition of whether she needed an item was very different from that of others in the community, possibly because of her experience with extreme poverty.

The hypothesis that taking things was related to Gloria's fear of being without resources rather than to a lack of knowledge about acceptable behavior was supported because each time the team would begin to talk about her getting her own apartment, she took more survival items. When Gloria's fear subsided and she began to take things not related to simple survival, the team designed an intervention to help her decide what things she needed.

Thus, the first intervention with Gloria focused on her analysis of her needs and ways to meet them. Rather than saying, "Don't take that towel. It doesn't belong to you," her community living coach would say, "You already have six towels. Do you think you need more?" Then, the instructor would connect the idea of her ability to work and earn money to the idea that this ability would be with her no matter where she lived. "You don't have to take those towels. You know how to work and earn money. You can buy more towels when you need them." Sometimes Gloria said she needed the towels and sometimes she said she did not. The purpose of the intervention was not to get Gloria to agree with her coach's definition of how many towels were necessary but to help her think about her needs and ways in which she could meet them.

If I had believed that Gloria would never again live in poverty, that she would have a good income for the rest of her life, then I might have accepted that it would be permissible to teach her that needing an item is not a reason for taking it. However, changing her values would have decreased her ability to adapt to the poverty she would face if her Medicaid was decreased or eliminated or if a policy exclusion between Medicaid and Indian Health Service eligibility put her back on the street on her own. In my cynical view, these situations might, in fact, occur.

Therefore, we did not challenge the idea that people take things when they need them or sell them to make money. We worked with the concept of whether she needed the item and whether she had other ways to earn money. Instead of simply teaching her a list of rules—don't take this, or it's okay to take that—we were teaching self-regulation of behavior (Siegel et al., 1990; Wehmeyer, 1992a, 1992b; Whitman, 1990a, 1990b) by helping her to make decisions about her own level of need and what she could do about it. Some staff saw this as "allowing her to steal" until she had a job that paid well enough to make stealing unnecessary. After all, although it is easy to say that services should support the service receiver's values, it is more difficult to accept this philosophy when values conflict. In terms of Gloria's schema of theft, she was not stealing nor were her actions inappropriate.

One day Gloria came to the sheltered workshop with a half full bottle of whiskey she had found on a walk in the park to pick up aluminum cans. I listened with bated breath to the conversation between Gloria and her middle-class, non-Indian job coach.

"Sell him. Good money."

"Yes, you could sell it if you needed the money. Do you have a place to sleep?"

"Yes."

"Are you warm?"

"Yes."

"Do you get enough to eat?"

"Yes."

"Do you have a job so you can earn more money?"

"Yes."

"Do you need to sell the whiskey?"

"No. Okay. I don't sell him."

I was thrilled. Never once did Gloria's coach slip back into her own value system. She did not say, "This is dirty. Throw it away." or "You shouldn't do this." She did not challenge Gloria's knowledge of how the world works. In fact, Gloria could quite easily have sold the whiskey.

With this intervention Gloria's behavior improved, as evaluated by professional staff and probably by many in the local community. Rather than directly challenging her values, her team worked with them to help her understand her situation and make her own decisions.

The Second Intervention: Learning Code-Switching

Learning how to identify ownership was the basis of the second intervention that the team devised. Gloria and her community living coach went for walks together in the community, stopping to discuss things they saw that Gloria might potentially take. The idea was to work on Gloria's understanding of ownership. She already knew that things belonging to others should not be taken; although, in her view, they could be shared. She just had difficulty knowing when something was owned by someone else if she did not know the people involved. Her former community was filled with relatives and people she knew on a first-name basis, but this new community was filled with strangers. Her community living coach would point, for example, to a message board on the door of an apartment neighbor and say, "Think how sad the lady who lives here will be when she doesn't have paper on her message board. She won't be able to get messages from her friends." Taking a ball from an unattended front yard was addressed by saying, "Think how sad the little boy will feel when he comes home from school and can't find his ball."

I suspect this approach came close to challenging values Gloria held because of her cultural heritage. Why not use the ball if no one else was using it? Why not share some of the paper on the message board? There was plenty there. Eventually, however, Gloria learned the difference between what she had to do to live in the white man's world and what she could do when she went home.

One day when Gloria had taken all of my pens and I asked for them back, she said:

"Eee, you white woman. You greedy. I'm Indian."

Gloria's tone of voice, use of the Lakota exclamation "eee," and body language all expressed resignation over the silly ways of the white world. She gave back most of the pens but kept some to show me I really did have more than I needed and should share. Because I agreed (but only when challenged by Gloria to think carefully about my own behavior) and also recognized that she had as much right to guide my behavior by her values as I had to guide hers by mine, I accepted her compromise and learned a valuable lesson from her.

It is possible for people with developmental disabilities to learn, just as others do, that some people have different values and that it is sometimes necessary to act in terms of those values regardless of whether they agree with them. Working-class people and ethnic minorities, for example, quickly learn how to *switch* from the behaviors that are natural in the context of their own families and neighborhoods to the middle-class *code* of socially accepted behavior in more public places—such as school, work, and hospital—thus disguising their differences from teachers, bosses, and doctors (Medicine, 1987). Code-switching may take its toll on those who master it, especially if one's own group evaluates the resulting behavior negatively (Ogbu, 1987), or may allow people to operate effectively in more than one culture if they consciously manage the codes (Goodenough, 1987).

Therefore, the third intervention the team designed was based on separating Gloria's actions regarding "free food" from other types of stockpiling. Donna, a Lakota staff member, explained that on the reservation, when Gloria would attend a community event where there was food, it was expected that everyone would bring a container and take home some of the extra food. In fact, more food than necessary was prepared for the event because having leftovers to take home was part of how community dinners were conducted (Powers & Powers, 1984). Gloria's community living coach did not use the "Do you need this?" or the "You can buy your own if you want to" strategies. Instead, she helped Gloria to know when to switch codes by identifying events that followed Lakota norms—dinners at the local Lakota Chapel—or situations that followed non-Indian norms—cookies and punch at the grand opening of a local business. Helping Gloria learn to classify different food-related events extended her schema of how to survive in the non-Indian world without changing her knowledge of how to act in her home community. Perhaps this approach strengthened Gloria's opinion that whites are stingy; but then, from her point of view, they are.

The Third Intervention: Learning Appropriate Quantities

The assessment in Figure 4.1 led the team to another insight; some of Gloria's behavior of taking things, such as taking 50 packets of catsup from a fast-food restaurant, had nothing to do with theft but occurred because she had difficulty understanding quantities. This hypothesis was bolstered because Gloria also often used a whole bottle of shampoo when taking a shower, a whole can of cleanser to clean one sink, and a whole roll of toilet paper when using the bathroom. The team eventually helped Gloria learn to use appropriate quantities but not in the context of whether it was theft. Learning to use an adequate amount of shampoo generalized to taking only a few packets of catsup from the local fast-food restaurant.

The team's positive experience with Gloria can largely be attributed to the use of the schema assessment tool as an avenue for exploring values and demonstrating that different groups vary in their schemas of theft. We were forced to inspect our own prejudices about Indian versus non-Indian and working-class versus middle-class values. It also called into question our almost automatic assumption that people with disabilities simply do not know the rules of how to behave correctly. We had to look more closely at Gloria's specific actions rather than just quickly categorize them as theft and proceed with an intervention to teach her the "right" way to behave.

If we had tried to teach Gloria new ways of behaving that challenged her basic schema of theft, we might not have been as successful. We needed to build on her values and knowledge by teaching her skills, such as quantity recognition, self-regulation, and code-switching, that were reasonable in her world view—not recreate her as a middle-class white woman. She is young, poor, female, and Indian. With time, she will no longer be young. With a good job placement and a support plan, she will not be as poor. She will always be female and Lakota; although, what it means to have those identities may change and, thus, her values may also change. Values-based services are not inflexible nor do they preclude intervention. However, they must carefully relate interventions to the person's self-identity and schemas used by others sharing those identities.

CREATING AND USING A SCHEMA ASSESSMENT TOOL TO PLAN AN INTERVENTION

All service providers are faced with the dilemmas of how to decide what skills to teach, when and how to intervene to change behavior, and how to help people become accepted and valued members of their communities. Focusing on the service receiver's goals and strengths, making decisions as a team, including people important to that person on the team, and teaching behavior that is valued in the local community (Luckasson et al., 1992; Lynch & Hanson, 1992; Meyer, Peck, & Brown, 1991) are strategies employed to find the best possible solutions to these dilemmas. Creating a schema assessment tool focused on one behavior and then using it to make judgments on when to intervene and what to teach is another strategy that teams can use.

Creating a Schema Assessment Tool

The method of assessing a schema can be varied to match the complexity and importance of the behavior being addressed. A 10-minute team discussion might suffice for one situation, while another situation might require the services of a cultural specialist to design a schema assessment tool, especially if most team members have class and ethnic identities that differ from those of the service receiver. However, the team can effectively address less complicated problems by developing their own schema assessment tool.

Describing Situations   The first step in creating a schema assessment tool for a specific type of behavior is to ask people (e.g., team members, other staff, possibly even volunteers from the community) to describe variations of where, with whom, how, and when this behavior might occur (Gallimore, Goldenberg, & Weisner, 1993). Do not, at first, ask whether the behavior is right or wrong, acceptable or unacceptable, or within the norms of the community. Focus, instead, on marginal instances of the behavior that is being analyzed. The point is to find variations in interpreting unclear situations, not the shared core of what all agree is acceptable in a clear-cut situation.

Schemas guiding common behaviors might not be easy to describe because, as LeVine and Langness pointed out, "everyday thinking, because of its pervasiveness and 'familiarity,' tends to be taken for granted. It becomes, in a way, invisible" (1986, p. 204). As Figure 4.1 shows, there are many strands of meaning involved in what seems simple and obvious on the surface. This is also the case with other behaviors. Think, for example, about sharing. Most people do not share the food on their plates but do share the food on a serving platter. Of course, there are exceptions to this rule; husbands and wives may share food from the same plate, though, perhaps only at home and not at a formal dinner. To share some things, permission of the owner must be sought. A person shares the television and the refrigerator in a group home but not the bathroom. Or, perhaps you do share the bathroom but use individual toilet stalls. A person does share the same bed with another person under certain conditions but not under others and so on.

Suggesting variations for different types of behavior is often fun, and people can get quite silly coming up with situations that push the limits of their definitions and values. The discussion also sensitizes team members to how they differ from each other. I have heard some pretty spirited discussions about the who, how, when, and where of spitting, hugging, interrupting, swearing, teasing, smoking, disagreeing, and doing housework.

Sorting Situations   The second step is to sort the situations into similar sets. Write each situation on a 3- by 5-inch card, and ask several people to sort them into piles of similar situations. Determining the similarities among the situations in one pile forces people to think about the strands of meaning involved in judging when a particular type of behavior is acceptable. Cognitive scientists call this process "unpacking a schema" (Strauss, 1992) because most schemas encode up to seven strands of meaning (D'Andrade, 1987). If people sort the cards very differently, particularly if they have different ethnic or class identities, they may be using different schemas rather than variations of a single schema, and all sortings should be used to interpret responses when the tool is baselined.

Baselining Variations   To find general trends and interpretations of behavior acceptable to different groups of people, the next step requires baselining the schema assessment tool. Choose three to six situations (or any number that reflects the complexity of the topic) from each set of similar situations by selecting situations that vary with respect to the strand of meaning identified for that set. Incorporate the selected situations in random order into a single questionnaire. Then, ask a broad range of people to take the assessment twice—once to identify whether the respondent has done or would do the action described and a second time to rate each situation in terms of whether it is an instance of a particular kind of behavior. Depending on the topic, this rating can be a response to a specific question, such as "Is this prejudice?" or, "Is this harassment?" or a general question, such as "Is this wrong?" Or, the question may be "Is this independence?" or, "Is this acceptable?" if a positive behavior is being analyzed. Taking the assessment twice is necessary because there is a difference between knowing a schema and choosing to apply it.

Group the respondents by their social identities (e.g., the older respondents versus the younger, male versus female, Native American versus non-Native American), and look for similarities in their responses. Because this is not a research project, this step may be accomplished through discussion with the respondents. It is critical to look at areas in which people from the same background have not marked any of the situations in one set, which could indicate that the strand is not meaningful to them, or in which they have marked all the situations, which could indicate that the feature is particularly important to them.

Pay special attention to the types of miscommunication that are described in Chapter 2. For example, in her study of the joking behavior of Puerto Rican students and Anglo teachers, Hill-Burnett (1987) found that the focal point of a definition may be shared but not the boundary. Both students and teachers used joking in the same situations but had different definitions of when joking crossed an invisible line and became malicious baiting. This was similar to how Gloria's team members differed in whether they viewed some of Gloria's behavior as theft; they, too, varied in where they placed the boundary between taking a small but permissible amount and taking too much. Or, the definition, but not the associated propositions, may be shared; this was the case when Indian and non-Indian staff agreed on the definition of sharing but differed in whether their norms required them to ask permission of the owner.

The amount of variation between the first set of responses to a schema assessment (Have you done this or would you do this?) and the second set (Is this theft?) for a group of respondents of the same age, gender, ethnicity, or class reflects how tightly a particular schema is connected to behavior for that social identity; schemas can generate many contradictory correct resolutions to a particular problem (Shore, 1990) or can precisely define a required course of action (D'Andrade, 1991). Schemas even include propositions about how much variation is acceptable (e.g., 5 miles per hour over the posted speed limit is a well-known "rule of thumb" for permissible speeding), which allows individuals to bend schemas to their own ends or ignore some parts altogether (Paul, 1990). Because schemas are "well learned but do not dictate [an] unvarying pattern of behavior" (Strauss & Quinn, 1994, p. 287), people who share the same variant of a schema do not necessarily behave identically.

Using the Schema Assessment Tool

Use the assessment with the person receiving services by observing his behavior or asking him about the situations, a few at a time, in several different sessions. Situations may need to be reworded, or others more familiar to the person may be substituted. Also use the assessment with the person's team members and additional family members who are not on the team. Ask them to respond to the assessment based on their behavior and values, not on how they think the person receiving services should behave. Then, analyze the person's behavior in terms of schemas shared with others of the same identity (e.g., if the service receiver is young and from a working-class family, compare her with young, working-class respondents).

Judging When to Intervene   In assessing a person's schemas, there are several kinds of discoveries that can be made, each of which might entail a different kind of intervention. Finding that a person rates an action as wrong but does it anyway will lead to a different kind of discussion than finding that a person does something she thinks is right that some people on the team think is wrong because they are using different varieties of the same schema or entirely different schemas. Thus, there is misunderstanding rather than misbehavior. If, however, the person differs from others of the same social identity, then isolating the strand in the schema that differs can be used as the basis for designing an intervention.

However, just because people of the same age, class, or ethnicity define and evaluate situations in certain ways does not mean that all people with that identity must also define and evaluate situations that way. If, for example, Gloria's schema of theft had not been defined in terms of need, it would not have been appropriate, in my opinion, for the team to teach her to take things when she needed them. There still is individual variation. However, the danger of unwarranted intervention is far greater when behavior is compared with general community norms rather than with the schemas characteristic of a particular local ethnic group, class, or other identity.

A more difficult issue would have been what to do if Gloria had used the "take it if you can get away with it" approach that a few people espoused. Service providers must still use judgment in deciding whether some variations in schemas are within normal limits; some people have disordered schemas and exhibit deviant, abnormal, psychotic, or criminal behavior, an issue that is explored further in Chapter 6. Justifying a person's maladaptive behavior by comparing it with others who exhibit similar behavior is not the intent of using schema assessment. If people have learned their schemas in abnormal environments, such as in institutions or in situations of domestic violence, changing their values rather than providing services in terms of those values may be necessary.

Bobby, for example, did not share a schema of theft or ownership with other Norwegian American farmers. His behavior was similar to Kerry's, a young woman with mental retardation described by Lovett (1985). Both Kerry and Bobby would hoard things, such as magazines, including those owned by others. Bobby and Kerry defined ownership as physical possession. Both would fight to maintain control of objects already in their possession and attempt to claim objects not in someone else's immediate control. Lovett hypothesized that this occurred because Kerry had lived in an institution where "life had taught her that you owned what you could grab or hang on to . . . the idea of property that belonged to some persons and not to others was alien" (1985, p. 135). According to Lovett, Kerry's schema of ownership was not the result of inaccurate learning or an inability to learn abstract concepts, as this definition of ownership is also used by people in other institutions such as prisons and nursing homes.

The team decided that they needed to change Bobby's definition of ownership to one more in line with that held by people who have not lived in institutions. All Bobby's possessions were labeled with a "B," and his community living coach periodically went through his hoarded items with him. Items with a "B" were kept, and those without a "B" were returned to their rightful owners. At the same time, Bobby's friends and the staff members who worked with Bobby were encouraged to return things to Bobby that were labeled with his "B" of ownership. The greatest impact was when items were returned to him, especially when staff members returned things that were left in their offices. Bobby began to change his definition of ownership from physical control to the more abstract definition of "I own it whether it's in my personal possession or not."

Gloria learned some of her schema of theft while living in poverty; because she might return to poverty someday and because this part of her schema was similar to the theft schema of some people in the local community, her team decided not to pursue changing this part of her schema. Bobby learned some of his schema in an institution. For some of the same cynical reasons Gloria might someday live in poverty again, Bobby might return to living in an institution. However, Bobby's team decided to intervene because this part of his schema was only similar to the ownership schema of a few people living in prisons and nursing homes.

There are no definite answers when using schema assessment, only more specific information to consider when making difficult decisions.

Judging What to Teach   Although teaching parts of a schema may be necessary, as it was for Bobby, schema assessment more often uncovers the need to teach people when and how to apply a particular schema, as it did for Gloria (e.g., "Is this a Lakota dinner?" "Do you need this towel?"). Choosing which schema to apply to a particular situation is difficult because, according to Holland, "the world does not seem to be laid out so that only one schema or only one package of schemas nicely applies, without discord, in every case" (1992, p. 71). Therefore, ambiguous situations require people to determine through self-regulation whether it is appropriate to use a particular schema. For example, the shared skill steps for following instructions at work found by Sherman, Sheldon, Harchik, Edwards, and Quinn (1992) can be employed when it is clear that it is a time to follow instructions—that is, when it is the boss giving the instructions in the workplace and about work tasks. But, what if it is not the boss but a co-worker, what if the boss is giving instructions at a social event, or what if the instructions concern sexual rather than work behavior?

A study by Soodak (1990) found that adults with mental retardation living in a group home knew a schema about getting ready for work (shown by correctly sequencing photographs of each step of the task) but were unable to apply it in real-life situations. This led to the hypothesis that maladaptive behavior is the result of not knowing when to apply a particular schema rather than of not knowing the schema. Whitman suggested that mental retardation could be "defined as a self-regulatory disorder" (1990a, p. 349) because people with mental retardation are seemingly unable to generalize the strategy or schema learned in one situation to a novel, but essentially similar, situation or to discriminate when a situation is different, therefore requiring a different strategy. Teaching generalization and discrimination can be more focused, and therefore potentially more successful, when schema assessment has pinpointed the strand of meaning presenting difficulties for the learner.

Choosing how to apply a schema is equally difficult because few schemas are so tightly tied to behavior that they generate only one correct solution for how to act in a particular situation (Shore, 1990). Schemas most often define a range of options with broad agreement only for the ideal choice and varying degrees of disagreement among groups using the schema as less ideal solutions or more ambiguous situations are considered. For example, two respondents to an assessment tool about "following instructions at work" may agree that a particular directive by a specific person is an instance of an instruction one must follow (they mark "yes" in the right column for a co-worker with 2 years seniority telling them to count pages in each stack of paper) and that they have followed the instruction (they mark "yes" in the left column for the same situation). For a similar but less clear situation, their responses may differ (they both mark "yes" in the right column for a co-worker with 1 year seniority telling them to count the pages; but one respondent admits in the left column he estimated the height of the stack of paper rather than counting the pages as instructed). For an even more unclear situation, they both refuse to comply even though technically it is an instance of "following instructions at work" (they both mark "yes" in the right column for a co-worker with 6 months seniority and both mark "no" in the right column for whether they actually complied). When finally an unwritten boundary has been crossed, they are in agreement again (they mark "no" in both columns for a co-worker with 1 day seniority).

Often, professionals in the field of developmental disabilities try very hard to help people act as close as possible to the focal point of what people in the community claim is appropriate behavior (i.e., their right column responses on a schema assessment tool). However, comparing the two sets of responses on a schema assessment shows that few people live at the focal point. As Racino and Walker pointed out, individuals with developmental disabilities are "held to stricter standards than others in our society," and they shouldn't be (1993, p. 74). They should have the right to estimate the stack of paper just like the other employees do, even though ideally the 6-month employee's instructions should be followed.

In fact, a person's persistently pursuing an ideal type of behavior may be evaluated as rigid or emotionally disturbed (e.g., following the instructions of a co-worker with 1 day seniority). For this reason, Margaret's team was concerned about her when she was afraid to choose a less than perfect option. She would return a paperclip with a flourish, as if to say, "See, I am following the rules perfectly." But, then, she believed she was unlovable unless she was doing things exactly right. Assisting people to be perfect by their or others' standards and values is not the goal. Although team members may make similar judgments on clear-cut examples of neglect, theft, following instructions, sharing, and many other behaviors, they may disagree when evaluating situations that are more ambiguous. Therefore, the behavior of the person receiving services should be compared with the behavior of others who share her identity because helping people with disabilities perform within the socially accepted range of actual behaviors of others is the goal. Discussing the gap between knowing a schema and choosing when and how to apply it makes the team more respectful and less judgmental of the behavior of the person to whom they are providing services. It frees them, in a way, to get to the business of what is really important in the person's life.

LIMITATIONS OF SCHEMA ASSESSMENT TOOLS

One of the weaknesses of assessing how people's behavior is related to their values by asking them whether they have actually done or would do certain things is that they might underreport certain aspects of their behavior so that their behavior conforms more closely to their stated values (Feldman & Lynch, 1988). That is, self-generated validity might occur when people are "at risk in discovering something unpleasant about themselves" (Rokeach, 1979, p. 8). Thus, if people do not already tell some form of the truth to themselves, they probably will not on this type of assessment.

The standard approaches to validity used in quantitative research are not applicable to the use of qualitative tools (Maxwell, 1992) such as schema assessments. Validity in a qualitative study does not depend on a comparison between the object studied and the account of it made by the tools used to study it, as it would in a quantitative study. Instead, it depends on the recognition or rejection of the account by the people about whom the account is written (Geertz, 1973), that is, on interpretive validity. In addition, qualitative accounts do not claim to be the one correct account but only one of many possible valid accounts. Because teams were not using schema assessment for research but, rather, to design interventions, validity was usually established by the collective "Ah, ha!" that occurred when the process of looking at variations and unclear situations, rather than at widely shared community norms, provided the insight team members needed to make sense of and interpret what was going on in a particular person's life.

However, there is no guarantee that any particular schema assessment will unpack the contrasting interpretations that reveal when there is miscommunication rather than misbehavior. For example, there was no contrast between Indians and non-Indians in their responses to the assessment given in Figure 4.1. However, it is impossible to know, without further investigation, whether this was because they shared the complete schema because the assessment tool did not include situations that would elicit the differences that did exist, or because Lakota respondents switched codes when they took the assessment.

Another limitation of the approach is that it depends on the existence of a relationship between schemas and behavior. However, groups vary in how tightly their schemas are connected to behavior because they differ in how self-reflective they are (LeVine, 1984). The schema uncovered by assessment might, therefore, be a "model for talking" rather than a "model for doing," leading to the situation where people do not do "what would seem to be entailed by the cultural beliefs they enunciate" (Quinn & Holland, 1987, p. 5).

A final limitation of the procedure is that it is time consuming and results can be fairly complicated to analyze. However, we found that although the assessment of a person's behavior took longer, teaching was easier and the results lasted longer and generalized better when we used this method than when we did not. Even if it did not have these effects to recommend it as a method, I would still advocate taking the extra time to conduct a schema analysis; for me, teaching new behaviors in terms of a person's own values is the foundation for building personalized, respectful services.

POINTS TO REMEMBER

To design schema-based interventions, we need to follow these four steps:

1. *Create and determine baseline data for a schema assessment tool by asking people with different identities to rate a series of unclear situations.* The strands of meaning defining a particular behavior are evaluated differently by various groups. For example, almost all Americans agree that taking a little bit of something is permissible but disagree about the point at which taking too much becomes stealing.

2. *Compare the service receiver with others who share his identity to pinpoint when specific parts of the schema are not being applied in the same way.* Design an intervention to teach the person to regulate his own behavior or to recognize situations that require switch-

ing codes by building on the schema the person already recognizes and partially employs. For example, Gloria's interpretation that people take things when they need them was not challenged, but she was taught to use a series of questions to determine her needs and alternative ways to meet those needs.

3. *Use judgment in determining when a person needs to change parts of her schema.* Changing a person's beliefs and values is sometimes necessary, as people have learned some of their schemas in abnormal environments. For example, Bobby's definition of ownership and his behavior of hoarding objects, including items owned by others, was similar to the behavior of other people who have lived in institutions for extended periods of time. His team chose to intervene to teach him a new schema of ownership, but another team might have made a different judgment in the same circumstances.

4. *Evaluate the service receiver's behavior relative to the whole range of behaviors chosen by others, not just to the ideals they state.* People with developmental disabilities should not be expected to be perfect by others' standards but should have the right to choose from the full range of behaviors exhibited by others. For example, Margaret had difficulty in choosing how to handle ambiguous situations because she believed she had to be perfect to be accepted by others.

Schema Analysis of Decision Making

"Cake and ice cream will be just fine, sweetie."

Anna's community living coach, Dean, was crestfallen at Anna's pronouncement. There were so many exciting possibilities for celebrating this landmark birthday. Anna was going to be 65 and all she wanted was cake and ice cream?

"Who do you want to invite?"

I could hear the hope in Dean's voice. He probably was thinking that maybe this party could be spiced up with some special guests. With a wave of her hand, Anna indicated all the people sharing the group home with her.

Dean wanted to make this birthday different. Anna wanted to make it the same. Anna knew what going out to dinner meant. She thoroughly enjoyed going out to dinner. She knew what it was to have special guests and a big party. On other occasions, she had participated in these more exciting alternatives; but for her birthday, tradition guided her decision.

Many of Anna's decisions were based on tradition, custom, or routines that she had personally established. She went to lunch at the Senior Citizens' Center on Mondays, visited her best friend for ice cream on Tuesday afternoons, and changed her bed linen and did her laundry on Wednesdays. She had a customary task or outing for each day of the week. She quickly trained new staff to adhere to her schedule by questioning them until they could list each day's assigned event to her satisfaction. She also liked to wear certain outfits: her pink sweater with a white blouse, black pants, and a string of pearls; her green sweater with a yellow blouse, brown pants, and a silver chain necklace; as well as several other favorite combinations. She liked having the same items for breakfast every day except Sunday, when she preferred a different menu.

In the past, people with developmental disabilities have been described as rigid in their thought processes and as "virtually helpless" people "who needed to be externally controlled" (Stamatelos & Mott, 1985, p. 102). According to Jenkinson, "autonomy in decision-making is withheld from people with an intellectual disability on the grounds of lack of competence or poor judgment or failure to meet some ideal model of decision-making" (1993, p. 361).

Did Anna lack judgment and need external control to make decisions because she followed what appeared to be rote routines? She was described in her case history as having very patterned and repetitive behavior; however, she could also be described as valuing predictability and regularity in her life and as making decisions based on traditions and customs, a pattern not unusual in the small, rural, predominantly German/Dutch community where she had lived until she moved to an institution at age 25.

There is nothing wrong with choosing a course of action by following a tradition, although most Americans rarely think of that as making a decision. Merriam-Webster defines *decision* as "a determination arrived at after consideration" (1993, p. 299). However, the "consideration" does not have to be of information or consequences. It might also be a consideration of traditions and customs or some other factor.

A SCHEMA OF DECISION MAKING

Many Americans have a mental image of the correct way to make decisions; they picture decision making as a process of listing options, discussing advantages and disadvantages that each option might bring in the future, and then choosing the best option in terms of their preferences for the expected results and evaluation of the risks involved (Stewart & Bennett, 1991). Learning how to make decisions this way is even described as achieving maturity (Mann, Harmoni, & Power, 1989). Yet, this is not the only way to make a decision nor do Americans make all their decisions this way.

Some of the many and varied methods for making decisions are exposed by the reasons people give for their choices (e.g., "My wife wants me to do it this way," "It just feels right," "I prayed and the answer came to me," "My neighbor did that and it worked for him)." People often use one kind of decision making for one situation, another kind for another situation (Chambers, 1985), and, most likely, two or three interconnected decision-making methods to handle a single situation (Bloch, 1994; Lieberman, 1994). Lewis (1990) found that different decision-making strategies are used in making decisions about values; these strategies include authority, logic, sense experience, emotion, intuition, and scientific strategies. According to Rosaldo, people even decide to wait and see, making no decision at all, or to just "improvise, learn by doing, and make things up as . . . [they] go along" (1989, p. 61).

As with other values, decision-making values may not be apparent or explicit to the person using them; people simply use their common sense and do what seems natural and right. However, a lack of congruence in decision-making values between service provider and receiver can lead to program failure because of the mistaken assumption by service providers that their implicit values are embraced by the people using their services (Downing & Cobb, 1990). In addition, being required to make a decision in a way that is judged to be wrong decreases motivation (Wlodkowski & Ginsberg, 1995). Therefore, values about how to make decisions should be assessed for both service providers and receivers by investigating their schemas of decision making.

Assessing a Schema of Decision Making

Figure 5.1 is slightly different from the assessment tool in Chapter 4 because decision making depends on a proposition schema rather than an image schema (Quinn & Holland, 1987). The schema of decision making unpacks the way in which a decision is made rather than determining when something is an act of decision making. The schema for theft, however, focuses on when an action is theft rather than on how to steal.

In addition, the assessment of a schema of theft is based on the assumption that everyone agrees that theft is wrong but that their ideas

Assessment of a Schema of Decision Making

Directions: The following situations describe how you might decide to do an activity. Take the assessment twice. The first time you take the assessment, if you agree that the situation describes a *good* way to make a decision, regardless of whether you have ever made a decision that way, check the first column on the left. If you think it is a *bad* way to make a decision, regardless of whether you have ever acted that way, mark the middle column. If you do not think that that particular method of making a decision is either good or bad, mark the *neutral* response in the third column.

At least 1 week later, on a clean copy of the assessment tool or with the left column responses covered, take the assessment a second time. If you have made a decision for the specified reason or in the way described for the same or a similar situation you have experienced, regardless of whether you think it is a good way to have acted, mark the *yes* response in the first column on the right. If you have never made a decision in the manner described, then mark the *no* response.

Is this a good or bad way to make a decision?				Have you made a decision this way?	
Good	**Bad**	**Neutral**		**Yes**	**No**
___	___	___	1. I might choose to learn a new game or watch a new television show just because I have never played that game or watched that show.	___	___
___	___	___	2. I would choose not to volunteer at a public event (e.g., church service, ball game, show, concert) because I might do something embarrassing.	___	___
___	___	___	3. If I found someone's lost dog, I would return it if there was a reward.	___	___
___	___	___	4. I decide what to wear to an event (e.g., party, church, work, beach) by choosing to wear what others will be wearing.	___	___
___	___	___	5. I would choose not to quit my job even if it is not that great because it might get better.	___	___
___	___	___	6. I would agree to go on a special diet if my doctor told me that I needed to.	___	___
___	___	___	7. I choose where to go on vacation by getting several options and comparing prices.	___	___

(continued)

Your Values, My Values, Pengra, ©2000 Paul H. Brookes Publishing Co.

Figure 5.1.   Assessment of a schema of decision making.

Figure 5.1. (*continued*)

Is this a good or bad way to make a decision?				Have you made a decision this way?	
Good	**Bad**	**Neutral**		**Yes**	**No**
___	___	___	8. At a new restaurant, I still order what is most similar to what I usually get.	___	___
___	___	___	9. I jog or walk three times per week because I ought to try to be as healthy as possible.	___	___
___	___	___	10. I might quit my job just because it felt like the right time to change jobs.	___	___
___	___	___	11. Sometimes I try new ways of doing things at work just to see if there is a better way to do things.	___	___
___	___	___	12. I do not walk at night on unlit streets because it is dangerous.	___	___
___	___	___	13. I might choose to do volunteer community service if there was a prize for the person who does the most work.	___	___
___	___	___	14. I might decide to have my hair cut or styled similar to a picture I saw in a magazine if I liked how that person looked.	___	___
___	___	___	15. I decide when to go to bed by how much work I have to do or by when I fall asleep in my chair.	___	___
___	___	___	16. If the police told me to turn down my music, I would, even if I did not think it was bothering anyone.	___	___
___	___	___	17. I would never leave my current job, even if I did not like it, if the information at the Job Service Center showed that there were few other jobs available.	___	___
___	___	___	18. I choose to attend events (e.g., a game, concert, play) in which my friend's son participates because we have always attended each other's family events.	___	___
___	___	___	19. If I found someone's gloves left behind at a party (park, movie theater), I would return them even if they fit me because I am honest.	___	___

(*continued*)

Figure 5.1.   (*continued*)

Is this a good or bad way to make a decision?				Have you made a decision this way?	
Good	**Bad**	**Neutral**		**Yes**	**No**
___	___	___	20. I choose to wear things that make me comfortable, regardless of whether they are the "right" thing to wear.	___	___
___	___	___	21. At a new restaurant, I would choose something I have never had before just to try it.	___	___
___	___	___	22. If I found someone's billfold, I would mail it back anonymously because I do not like meeting strangers and would not care about a reward.	___	___
___	___	___	23. I practice really hard on my baseball (or other sport) skills because I like to win.	___	___
___	___	___	24. At a new restaurant, I choose what to eat by ordering what my friends are having.	___	___
___	___	___	25. I wear whatever is clean when it is time to get dressed.	___	___
___	___	___	26. If my boss told me to do something, I would do it regardless of whether I wanted to because he is the boss.	___	___
___	___	___	27. I choose what groceries to buy by reading the information on the label about fat, salt, and nutritional content.	___	___
___	___	___	28. I go to bed at the same time every night (e.g., right after the news or after a certain television show).	___	___
___	___	___	29. I would never quit a job, even if it is very hard, because I am not a quitter.	___	___
___	___	___	30. I might leave a party (church service, bus, or other place) because the situation was making me feel uncomfortable.	___	___
___	___	___	31. I like to vacation in places I have never been before or go to new kinds of events just to try them.	___	___
___	___	___	32. I would not quit my job even if I did not like it because the next one might be worse.	___	___

(*continued*)

Figure 5.1. (*continued*)

Is this a good or
bad way to make
a decision?

Have you made a
decision this
way?

Good   Bad   Neutral   **Yes   No**

_____ _____ _____ 33. If my boss told me to do something I   _____ _____
did not want to do, I would do it anyway
because I want to get a good evaluation.

_____ _____ _____ 34. I might try a new diet if I read that a   _____ _____
lot of other people or television stars had
tried the diet and lost weight on it.

_____ _____ _____ 35. I choose what to eat at a restaurant by   _____ _____
ordering whatever the special is for that
day.

_____ _____ _____ 36. I usually wear what my friend (spouse,   _____ _____
parent) tells me to wear.

_____ _____ _____ 37. When looking for a new place to live,   _____ _____
I consider how close it is to stores, school,
and work and the cost of rent, not by
whether I like how it looks.

_____ _____ _____ 38. I choose what to wear to a social   _____ _____
occasion by wearing what is usually worn
to that type of occasion.

_____ _____ _____ 39. I might take a new training program or   _____ _____
go back to school because people ought
to pursue as much education as possible.

_____ _____ _____ 40. I go to bed when I feel tired instead of   _____ _____
at a particular time.

_____ _____ _____ 41. I might take a class or training pro-   _____ _____
gram just to learn something new.

_____ _____ _____ 42. I do not eat food that might give me   _____ _____
gas, even if I really like that food.

_____ _____ _____ 43. I would go back to school or take a   _____ _____
training program only if it led to getting a
better job or higher pay.

_____ _____ _____ 44. I do not particularly like to bowl (golf,   _____ _____
go to concerts), but I would if all my
friends were going.

_____ _____ _____ 45. If some of my friends are going to a   _____ _____
dance (game, concert, movie), I will go
with them if I have the time and money.

(*continued*)

Figure 5.1.   (*continued*)

Is this a good or bad way to make a decision?				Have you made a decision this way?	
Good	**Bad**	**Neutral**		**Yes**	**No**
_____	_____	_____	46. At a new restaurant, I would order what the waiter told me was good.	_____	_____
_____	_____	_____	47. Before buying a new washing machine (car, recliner, television), I check a consumer magazine and decide what brand to buy based on their report.	_____	_____
_____	_____	_____	48. I always go to the same place for vacation or do the same things at Thanksgiving and other holidays because it is what my family has always done.	_____	_____
_____	_____	_____	49. I sometimes choose to do things just because it is the polite thing to do.	_____	_____
_____	_____	_____	50. I only eat food that tastes good to me, regardless of whether the food is healthy.	_____	_____

vary as to what they consider to be theft. For decision making, however, people differ in how they evaluate a particular way of making a decision; some people rate one method as acceptable, while others rate it as evidence of poor judgment. Therefore, the assessment tool requires respondents to evaluate whether the actions described in a situation are good or bad or neither good nor bad (neutral).

As with any assessment, there are no right and wrong answers. Figure 5.1 is not designed to discover a perfect or universal way to make decisions. It is designed to show that people vary in their values regarding how to make decisions. It can be used in the same ways as the assessment tool in Chapter 4: to sensitize service providers to implicit values that might not be shared by all team members, to evaluate a particular person's behavior by comparing it with the behavior of others sharing his background and values, to identify particular areas where teaching may be needed, and to establish how widely behavior varies from stated values to reduce unreasonable expectations of perfection.

Figure 5.2 profiles a respondent in terms of 10 possible factors that she might consider when making a decision: innovation, risk avoidance, reward seeking, conformity, situational adaptation, author-

Decision-Making Tally Sheet

Directions: For each *good* response marked the first time the assessment was taken, check the appropriately numbered blank in the first column; for each *bad* response, check the second column. For each *yes* response marked the second time the assessment was taken, check the appropriately numbered blank in the third column. Total the number of checks, and use those scores to complete the profile at the end of the tally sheet.

Innovation

	Good	Bad	Yes
1.			
11.			
21.			
31.			
41.			
Total:			

Risk Avoidance

	Good	Bad	Yes
2.			
12.			
22.			
32.			
42.			
Total:			

Reward Seeking

	Good	Bad	Yes
3.			
13.			
23.			
33.			
43.			
Total:			

Conformity

	Good	Bad	Yes
4.			
14.			
24.			
34.			
44.			
Total:			

(*continued*)

Your Values, My Values, Pengra, ©2000 Paul H. Brookes Publishing Co.

Figure 5.2. Decision-making tally sheet.

Figure 5.2. (*continued*)

Situational Adaptation

	Good	Bad	Yes
5.			
15.			
25.			
35.			
45.			
Total:			

Authority

	Good	Bad	Yes
6.			
16.			
26.			
36.			
46.			
Total:			

Information

	Good	Bad	Yes
7.			
17.			
27.			
37.			
47.			
Total:			

Tradition

	Good	Bad	Yes
8.			
18.			
28.			
38.			
48.			
Total:			

Principles

	Good	Bad	Yes
9.			
19.			
29.			
39.			
49.			
Total:			

Feelings

	Good	Bad	Yes
10.			
20.			
30.			
40.			
50.			
Total:			

(*continued*)

Figure 5.2.   (*continued*)

Profile for Tally Sheet

Directions: In Box 1, "Good ways to make decisions," fill in the three or four factors for which you had the highest scores in column one of the tally sheet. In Box 2, "Bad ways to make decisions," fill in the three or four factors for which you had the highest total score in column two of the tally sheet. In Box 3, "Ways I have made decisions," fill in the three or four factors for which you had the highest scores in column three of the tally sheet. In Box 4, "Ways I have not made decisions," fill in all factors for which you had a zero in column three of the tally sheet. Comparing Boxes 1 and 2 to Boxes 3 and 4, respectively, shows how closely you adhere to your values.

Box 1 Good ways to make decisions:	**Box 3** Ways I have made decisions:
Box 2 Bad ways to make decisions:	**Box 4** Ways I have not made decisions:

ity, information, tradition, principles, and feelings. These factors were derived by asking people of various age, gender, class, and ethnic identities to sort 75 situations into groups. They generated 13 groups and gave each a label reflecting how the situations were similar. Twenty additional volunteers were asked to apply 1 of these 13 terms to each of the 75 situations. If at least 14 people (70%) agreed on the label, the item was kept. The situations less consistently labeled were eliminated, as were three labels that were used by six or fewer people on all items.

Table 5.1 briefly characterizes each factor that was identified by the volunteers, based on their discussion after they sorted and labeled the test items. There may be other factors that were not uncovered by

Table 5.1.   Descriptions of decision-making values

Making a decision because one values innovation means choosing a course of action because it has never been tried, because no one else has tried it, or simply because it is different from what the person is currently doing. People valuing this type of decision making may be negatively judged as thrill seekers, as risk takers, or as lacking stability. They might also be positively judged as being visionary and creative.

Making a decision because one values risk avoidance means choosing not to follow a course of action because it might involve a risk, real or imagined, such as the risk of failing, the risk of danger, or the risk of the unknown. In contrast, it means choosing alternatives that are easy, familiar, and have predictable outcomes. People valuing this type of decision making may be negatively judged as timid or overly cautious. They might also be positively judged as careful, prudent, and dependable.

Making a decision because one values seeking rewards means choosing a course of action because of the possibility of a reward or good result, even if the choice involves some risk. People valuing this type of decision making may be negatively judged as competitive or materialistic. They might also be positively judged as determined and highly motivated.

Making a decision because one values conformity means choosing a course of action because one wants to be like others, to fit in with the group. People valuing this type of decision making may be negatively judged as being prey to peer group pressure and imitating others. They might also be positively judged as a good follower, adaptable, and a team player.

Making a decision because one values situational adaptability means choosing a course of action because concrete, situational factors are more important to the person than abstract goals or principles. The person tries to adapt to the situation rather than trying to change the situation to fit her own needs. People valuing this type of decision making may be negatively judged as indecisive and disorganized. They might also be positively judged as flexible and creatively spontaneous.

Making a decision because one values authority means choosing a course of action because obeying authorities such as police, doctors, and teachers is the right thing to do. People valuing this type of decision making may be negatively judged as dependent, docile, and lacking in initiative. They might also be positively judged as respectful and dependable.

Making a decision because one values information means choosing a course of action because one has sought appropriate information, weighed the pros and cons, and made an informed choice. Value is placed on knowledge, science, and rational ideas rather than on feelings and emotions. People valuing this type of decision making may be negatively judged as cold, task oriented rather than people oriented, and lacking in spontaneity. They might also be positively

(continued)

Table 5.1. *(continued)*

judged as rational, logical, practical, and task oriented rather than people oriented.

Making a decision because one values tradition means choosing a course of action because one values doing things the way they have always been done and because one values roots, stability, and the comfort of the familiar. People valuing this type of decision making may be negatively judged as conservative, unimaginative, or afraid of change. They might also be positively judged as stable, dependable, and conservative.

Making a decision because one values principles means choosing a course of action because it is the correct action based on external standards and rules that are applied regardless of the situation. People valuing this type of decision making may be negatively judged as inflexible, dogmatic, and biased. They might also be positively judged as moral, principled, and staunch.

Making a decision because one values feelings means choosing a course of action because it seems like the right thing to do, because the result feels good, or because the person trusts his intuition. People valuing this type of decision making may be negatively judged as flighty, irrational, overly emotional, and people oriented rather than task oriented. They might also be positively judged as sensitive, insightful, and people oriented rather than task oriented.

this method as well as other valid sortings of the test items; the limitations discussed in Chapter 4 apply to any qualitative assessment tool, including this one.

SUPPORTING AND TEACHING DECISION-MAKING VALUES

Rather than defending rights of people with disabilities to choose how to make a decision, most authors discussing this issue are primarily concerned with the results of the decisions, especially when they differ from the choices the professional might have made (Dinerstein, 1994). For example, therapists Ruth and Blotzer reported that they and other therapists found themselves "supporting life choices of patients/clients that favor comfort over 'independence,' personal space over full-time repetitive work, and nontraditional options for the intrinsic value of the quest" (1995, p. 8).

A notable exception is the work by Schloss, Alper, and Jayne (1993), who developed a three-prong assessment tool to determine how much independence in decision making ought to be allowed. They developed three continuums concerning the degree of risk, the source of input (from just others, to others plus the individual, to just the individual), and the degree to which caregivers' input is binding on the individual. They did not consider the degree to which the person's decisions and decision-making values should be binding on caregivers, probably because in American society people who make their own decisions do not usually have caregivers.

To support and teach decision-making values, regardless of the content of the decisions reached using those factors, the person's current values must be ascertained. Service providers can then select their approaches and comments to reflect values important to that person. In addition, designing programs and activities in terms of values creates opportunities for people to make values-based decisions rather than choices simply based on personal gratification.

Supporting Decision-Making Values

Values can be supported by how a service provider responds to a request for assistance in making a decision. For example, if assessment has shown that the person values using personal principles to make a decision, then assistance might take one form: "I know you believe in fairness. Do you think this is the fairest thing you can do?" If the person values tradition, the response could be phrased differently: "How does your family usually do this?" If he or she values getting advice from an authority, another approach might be more appropriate: "There are several different things you might do. Let's talk about which one might be right for you."

Introducing new skills in terms of a person's decision-making values is another way to provide support. For instance, if a person values making decisions based on personal principles and is being assisted in learning to brush her teeth, the instructor can begin the teaching session with a comment related to those principles: "Being able to brush your teeth will increase your privacy, and you value your privacy," or "Brushing your teeth will make you look nice, and you've told me you want to look nice." If the person values authority and conformity, the instructor might say, "Your mom really wants you to learn to brush your teeth because other people know how to brush their teeth." This approach shifts the locus of control from the instructor, who is teaching this because the team thinks that the person needs to learn it, to the learner, who is choosing to learn it because he wants to live by his own values.

Decision-Making Values versus Risk-Free Choices

Often, service providers try to shift some control to the learner by offering choices, particularly risk-free choices that require selection based on personal wants, feelings, and desires, rather than choices requiring a decision based on consideration of personal values. A person may be given the choice of eating applesauce or eating peaches for dinner but usually not the right to decide to eat both or neither and certainly not the alternative of eating seven bowls of applesauce and eight bowls of peaches. There is no difference between choosing applesauce or peaches except for how the fruits taste to the person making the choice.

Providing a range of equally weighted choices has the appearance of increasing a person's quality of life; for example, eating preferred foods is more pleasing than eating disliked foods, wearing preferred clothing feels better than wearing disliked clothing, and organizing daily tasks in preferred sequences is more pleasant than following someone else's routine. Experiencing only pleasing and pleasant consequences may lead to a more satisfying life; however, it does not help the person learn to make decisions or to understand her own values.

Choosing from a range of safe alternatives of food, clothing, and daily schedules should not be confused with learning to make a decision. The service receiver experiences no real consequences when he does not have the right to eat so much that he gains weight; to wear old, gray underwear; or to refuse to work and watch television instead. For this reason, Schloss et al. argued that "providing limited choices . . . may preclude decision-making skills" (1993, p. 216).

Even choices with the potential for some kind of consequence are too often presented in terms of how the choice might make the person feel rather than in terms of making a decision based on the person's values. If a person values making decisions based on feelings and this is a value similar to others of his background, then helping the person make a decision in terms of his feelings is an appropriate way to support his values. However, using this approach with everyone, even people who do not value feelings-based decision making, assumes that people cannot or will not defer pleasure to attain a valued outcome or make a less pleasant choice because it is more greatly valued.

Teaching Decision-Making Values

Decision-making values, similar to all values, are learned and change over one's lifetime depending on exposure to new ideas and experiences. Therefore, service providers can and should assist people in reflecting on their own decision-making values. For example, if the fire marshal has decreed that the furniture in the group home living room must be rearranged to provide better access to the fire alarm pull box, then simply rearranging it foregoes an opportunity for people to learn. A residents' meeting can be held to discuss the requirement and decide how to rearrange the furniture. One choice is based on making the fewest changes possible because stability and tradition are valued. Another way might make access to the pull box easier as well as make exiting the house during a fire easier, a plan that focuses on risk avoidance. Or, perhaps, as long as rearranging is necessary, then maybe an arrangement allowing everyone to see the television better should be considered, a plan that focuses on situational adaptation. If the three arrangements were offered as alternatives without the attached explanations, then when residents are asked to vote on the alternative they like best, they are being taught that the basis of choice is personal preference. However, if they are encouraged to determine the best plan in terms of the values guiding the alternate arrangements, they are learning to make values-based decisions.

It is not always easy to see all alternatives as equally rational or logical, especially if a particular course of action is based on a factor that directly conflicts with the service provider's values. Often the other person's values do not make sense because they are considered independently of the cultural contexts in which they occur, making it difficult to understand how they lead to good decisions. However, understanding other values may also help the service provider accept and support the content of the other person's decisions.

SITUATIONAL DECISION MAKING

"Lilah, she has to go to the funeral."

Donna stood at my door respectfully, her voice quiet but determined. When Gloria had heard on the Indian radio station the day before that a distant relative of hers had died, she was in tears. However, the time of the funeral conflicted with her plans to attend an art show where she was going to exhibit and sell her beadwork.

I knew that another staff member had already talked to Gloria, and Gloria had decided to go to the art show and not the funeral. The other staff member is not Native American, whereas Donna is. I wondered whether Donna might be trying to impose her values on Gloria, knowing that Gloria was taking on some non-Indian ways in this nearly all white community where she now lived. But Donna persisted.

"She's downstairs crying. She wants to go to the funeral now."

What? She had changed her mind? But we had a plan. Even if she left now, she'd be at least an hour late for the funeral. Donna saw my hesitation and tried again to help me understand.

"I know she made that decision yesterday. This is the decision she made today. I don't know how to explain it to you."

Now Orientation and Future Orientation

Donna was right. We often cannot explain our values. Generally, the ones that are the most difficult to explain are the ones that are the most important, the ones so right they are simply obvious (Taussig, 1992). I take it for granted that once I have struggled through making a decision and a plan based on that decision, I then follow the plan. Donna knew that the funeral would just be getting underway when they arrived (it was) and that Gloria needed to be there to physically be part of the community of sufferers.

I did not understand why this need had not informed Gloria's choice yesterday. Donna was not just saying that a person has the right to change her mind. She implied that the right decision might be different on different days, which is a difficult concept for me to grasp. It is decision making based on situational adaptation in a now-oriented world view rather than decision making based on risk-avoiding or reward-seeking factors in a future-oriented world view.

I am very future oriented. To make a decision, I generally look at the future consequences of my present actions, including both the risks and the rewards, and evaluate the consequences in terms of my values. I may identify several potential courses of action, but the one I select as the right choice will still be the right choice when I reconsider it in the future, unless additional information has become available. My decision is based on what I perceive to be a sequence of actions, irrespective of when they start or in what contexts they occur.

A now-oriented person, like Gloria, views events as shaped by the context in which they occur. Events and actions can only be understood by looking at how they are interrelated with what else is happening. The now-oriented person makes a decision based on the situation as it is, including all the things leading up to it because the past is part of the present. If time has passed, it is a different situation. Another decision may be required because the relationship among things may now be different. Time, rather than being visualized as a straight line, may be viewed as cyclic when certain patterns and relationships recur (Shweder & Bourne, 1984).

It is a trap to think the now-oriented person cannot foresee the consequences of his actions or does not understand causality because he does, just in a way different from the future-oriented person. Causality, for the now-oriented person, is determined by considering what led up to the current situation, not by forecasting what might happen in the future because of current actions (Grobsmith, 1981). Therefore, diversifying options to be ready for whatever happens, rather than making a single plan and adhering to it no matter how the immediate situation changes, is the strategy employed by now-oriented people (Halperin, 1990).

Conflicting Values

In American society, in general, working-class people and people living in poverty tend to value situational adaptation and decisions based on feelings more than the future-oriented factors of risk avoidance and reward seeking. It has been argued that this orientation exists when people believe that the future is controlled by others. People living in poverty have a "low degree of control over life circumstances"; therefore, they might think that "God and luck weave mysterious and unpredictable connections" (Balshem, 1991, p. 165). At one time, this world view was described as being an orientation toward excitement and immediate gratification combined with an inability to manage time (Green, 1982; White, 1970). This world view was also seen as evidence of fatalism and lack of ambition for the working class (Pill & Stott, 1987). These pejorative interpretations have since been rejected (Duran, 1988), but the observation remains that a now-oriented world view, combined with a value on situational decisions and a belief in luck or God's will, is typical of American people living in poverty and the working class (Weisz, Rothbaum, & Blackburn, 1984), as well as other groups such as Latinos (Murillo, 1978; Rueda & Martinez, 1992), people living in rural communities (Halperin, 1990; Spindler, Spindler, Trueba, & Williams, 1991), and African Americans (Gwaltney, 1980).

The American middle-class, future-oriented world view has been criticized as allowing improbable, negative, and unknowable events to impede practical plans (Gwaltney, 1980) and as teaching people to avoid failure rather than to strive for excellence (Stewart & Bennett, 1991). An unwillingness to accept luck as an explanation and an inability to allow events to dictate actions rather than actions to dictate events leads to a fault-finding, victim-blaming world view (McCaul, Veltum, Boyechko, & Crawford, 1990). There are no accidents, only irresponsible people and, thus, lawsuits to determine fault. A future-oriented world view, combined with a value on risk-avoiding decision making and a belief in individual choice, can be condemned for putting pressure on a person to take responsibility for all the consequences of her behavior, even the unknowable and unanticipated consequences (Stewart & Bennett, 1991). Or, this world view can be lauded for leading to rational, logical decision making; individual initiative; and the successful achievement of goals.

Thus, now-oriented people making situational decisions are sometimes judged as impulsive for not considering the future consequences of their behavior and irresponsible for not averting possible problems. In contrast, future-oriented people are sometimes criticized as impervious to other people and relationships, making decisions out of context, and being goal driven and inflexible. Yet, seeing the world through one orientation or the other is merely a result of choosing some features to be significant and ignoring others as background noise.

Both now-oriented and future-oriented perspectives have positive and negative points, depending on the beliefs and values of the people evaluating them. Determining which view leads to the best decisions is an exercise in futility and ethnocentrism. Helping people to determine their own views and assisting them in learning to make better decisions in terms of those views is the approach needed to provide values-based services.

THE IMPORTANCE OF CONTEXT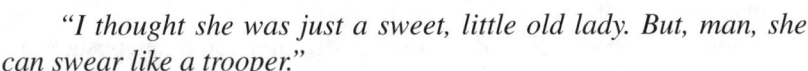

"I thought she was just a sweet, little old lady. But, man, she can swear like a trooper."

Dean made this observation when he was a new community living coach and was being trained by Anna to do things the way she liked them done. The "old hands" on the staff began to share their stories with him of their introduction to Anna's insistence on doing things a certain way; however, Dean still couldn't integrate the two seemingly contrasting sides of Anna he had experienced thus far.

"But she always seems so willing to help and is so nice to everyone. Where did she learn to swear like that?"

We didn't know where she'd learned to swear. We only knew the kinds of situations that made her swear. She liked perfection and order; when someone violated that order, she let him know that it angered her. She also respected authority and sometimes seemed almost docile as she cheerfully complied with requests, as long as those requests fit her sense of order.

Just as we had found shared characteristics between Gloria and her home community and Bobby and his, we realized that Anna might have values associated with German/Dutch ethnicity and with being reared in a small, rural town. The contrast between the sweet, docile Anna and the raging, stubborn Anna that Dean found puzzling occurred when those around her made demands that were, by Anna's definitions and values, unreasonable. However, Anna's sense of order and respect for authority might not be so remarkable or so often challenged if she still lived in a community where others shared not only these values but also the content of her traditions.

Context

By seeing people through an individualist person schema, it appears that people choose any combination of values. Yet, the discussion of Gloria's situational decision making had to be couched in terms of a now-oriented world view and other schemas, such as causality, time, and preparation strategies, because values are part of a "web of meaning" (Foster, 1994). A particular value harmonizes with other values, symbols, and customs (Barrett, 1984) and has either no meaning or a different meaning apart from that cultural context. This coherence of values has been attributed to the individual's rejection of cognitive dissonance (Neisser, 1968), in combination with his interaction with others that share a similar set of schemas (Poole, 1994).

However, people do not live in bounded and homogeneous groups or embrace a culture that is without discrepancies and internal contradictions (Wilson, 1997), especially in multicultural societies. Although culture may not be a seamless whole, as it once was envisioned (Thornton, 1992), it is also not merely a collection of traits thrown together through accidents of history (LeVine, 1984). Even in multicultural societies, people create communities where there is a "common sense of the everyday" (Taussig, 1992, p. 8) and where behavior is "collectively meaningful" because of the constant interplay between self and context (Shore, 1991).

Feelings of belonging and connectedness are created not only through sharing a set of values with other people but also through the interconnectedness of those values (Wlodkowski & Ginsberg, 1995). It is as dismaying and disorienting to try to apply a value out of the context of other values that support it as it is to interact with people who have different values altogether (Black, 1973). Requiring Gloria to use the future-oriented factor of risk avoidance in the context of her other present-oriented schemas would be frustrating for her, just as Anna's life is sometimes frustrating because she values tradition and authority but lives among people who value innovation and personal choice. Allen and Allen suggested that "it is those interactions [between self and others] that should be the focus of change, not the self or the world" (1994, p. 233).

Values Out of Context

Delbert, a Lakota man with a developmental disability in his early twenties, was referred to our services by the Department of Social Services because he was homeless; he was often seen hanging out on street corners and inhaling spray paint to get high. He was falling through the cracks—not really belonging anywhere. Delbert subsisted on his disability check, which he usually spent by the second or third week of the month; he would then resort to panhandling and stealing until his next check was issued. He was a very likeable person with a wry sense of humor and a willingness to help others. He was also artistic and often made spare change by making and selling small art objects from materials that he found. Just as often, however, he gave his work away to friends or strangers. He seemed to float through life, even when he wasn't high.

Delbert moved into the group home, but he refused to come to the workshop and chose not to market his artwork. He told us, in no uncertain terms, that he didn't need paid work. He had his artwork to do. He could live on his disability check. Telling Delbert "You can't live on your disability check" was pointless; he had already been doing just that for several years. Helping him become a professional artist and only sell his work, not give it away, would challenge his values about spirituality, artistry, friendship, and situational decision making. Insisting that paid work is good and helps to build self-esteem would clearly be imposing values on him and, thus, would ultimately result in failure.

Delbert did, however, want to get clean and straight and have more materials to use for his art projects. Therefore, the team concentrated on supporting him in attending a substance abuse support group and in finding different colors and textures of materials. Gradually, he became more interested in doing paid work similar to the type that his new friends were doing. He joined a contract work crew and began doing yard work. He seemed to be getting his life together, making his own choices, finding new friends, experimenting with new forms of art, and meeting other artists in the community. Having learned with Gloria the importance of personal autonomy, we didn't make demands on Delbert to conform, to meet non-Indian values of competition, or to work for the sake of work and getting ahead.

We were surprised, but happy for him, when he announced that he was moving to a nearby city to work at a high-paying job he'd heard about through friends. We helped him apply for support services in the new location and found a substance abuse support group for him to join. We really believed that we'd helped him to achieve his goals.

Our self-congratulatory stance was shattered, however, when 3 months later Delbert was back on the street, homeless, jobless, and getting high. I think the changes we had seen in him were part of a developing network of caring others who understood and supported his values. When he moved, he didn't take his work goals with him like he did his clothing. His goals were context dependent. Without his support network, he made different choices and decisions in an environment with different pressures and temptations. Perhaps, with time, he would have developed a new support network, but things came apart more quickly than new relationships could be constructed.

If we could have pinpointed one specific cultural conflict, as we had with Gloria's participation in events with free food, we might have been able to help him learn to switch codes in certain situations. Yet, switching to a totally new world view with different types of decision-making strategies creates dissonance for most people and can compromise mental health (Sue & Sue, 1990). We should have worked harder to find an environment in which his values were understood and perhaps even shared.

Finding the Right Context

"You goofed up?"

The amazement in Margaret's voice was unmistakable as she looked from Brenda to me. I had just popped into Brenda's office to tell her we had made a mistake on yet another government form. Brenda's response had been "Oh well. We'll know better next time." Margaret was passing by and had heard the exchange.

Brenda was quicker than I at taking advantage of the opportunity to teach. She answered first.

"Sure. The trick is to do the best you can, then learn from your mistakes."

I remembered Margaret's favorite phrase when she had moved here: "I might goof up," she always said. Thus, Brenda's first answer to Margaret was to reassure her that mistakes could be handled. Margaret, however, was going in a different direction as her next inquiry showed by its emphasis on the first word.

"You *goofed up?*"

Again, Brenda understood the significance of the moment and answered the more important question.

"Sure. I goofed. Lilah goofed. Everyone goofs up sometimes. I think maybe even your dad goofed up sometimes."

That conversation marked the beginning of another change in Margaret's behavior. She went on a binge of buying new clothes, eating fattening snacks, and staying up all night to watch television. She even had one sexual liaison, an area formerly strictly prohibited by her father. Instead of seeing Margaret's shifts in affect as bipolar disorder, which was her previous diagnosis, her current psychiatrist diagnosed her behavior as being the result of borderline personality disorder. This is a disorder characterized by quick shifting between two self-schemas: one schema of the "all good" self and the other of an "all bad" self (Horowitz, 1991).

Her team's response was to affirm her right to make decisions and to emphasize setting priorities. For example, when she came home from the laundromat with soaking wet clothes and announced she spent all her money in the candy machine, Dean, her community living coach, said, "I see you wanted candy more than dry clothes. That's your choice. Now you need to figure out what you're going to do with these wet clothes."

This approach was based on the team's positive evaluation of independence and autonomy. Similar to many professionals in the field of developmental disabilities, they were advocating for the person's right to make his or her own choices and decisions (Fullwood, 1990;

Wehmeyer, 1992a, 1995). Margaret's team members, similar to most Americans, valued making their own decisions; therefore, they wanted to assist Margaret in making her own decisions, too. They had learned that people value different ways of making decisions and had also accepted quite readily that people set different priorities for themselves. They worked hard and creatively to support rather than challenge the values of the people they were serving, even when they did not agree with the results.

With Margaret, the team struggled initially with her not wanting to make her own decisions, then with the equally difficult challenge of supporting her in making any choice, even an apparently immature or risky one. They clearly saw Margaret's ability and willingness to make decisions as connected to whether she would ever be able to live independently.

Margaret, however, had ideas of her own about how she wanted to live her life. After 6 months of her spending and eating spree, she left the large church she had been attending and joined a church with a small congregation and explicit behavior guidelines for its members. She quickly became friends with many fellow church members and joined in activities and services two or three times per week. Her life stabilized, and she moved into her own apartment; most important, however, she was really happy. She loved choosing what to wear and when to eat. The bigger decisions in her life, such as how to behave with a boyfriend and live in moderation, were guided by principles voiced at church and by her new friends.

The church and minister were not just a replacement of her father's control. In the past, Margaret had not been allowed to choose what she wanted for lunch, what to wear, or when to go to bed. She now made her own choices within the context of the clearly articulated values and principles of the church, and the people with whom Margaret socialized embraced those same values (Pargament & Park, 1995).

This solution will not work for everyone, although religious communities have been found to be helpful to some people (Hornstein, 1997; McNair & Smith, 1998). It did, however, give Margaret confidence that she could be like others because the rules were the same for her as they were for the other members of the community. She liked being able to conform to the rules along with everyone else. She was not a failure or an incompetent. She told me that other people goofed, too; then they turned to God for forgiveness and the strength to accept things they could not change, such as a father's death.

We learned again that supporting a person's values is not a matter of addressing one value at a time but requires seeing the person as whole, with a set of integrated values. This philosophy was tested when Margaret decided to take a job that paid less than the one we had found for her. The job she chose was working at a store operated by a member of her church. She answered the phone and took messages. She loved being able to use her skills of politeness on the telephone and her ability to read and write. She also liked the sociability of her workplace and being able to be like others by wearing nice clothes like they did. Margaret saw quite clearly that her job was important, not because of the size of the paycheck or even because of the tasks she was assigned, but because of the people with whom it connected her.

Building on Strengths

It is important to recognize the way people are already making decisions. Gloria, Margaret, Anna, and Delbert may all be lumped together as "people with developmental disabilities," but their choices in what factors to consider when making decisions and in how they view the world are a reflection of their values and their cultural backgrounds, not of their disabilities. Gloria and Delbert are very similar to other Lakota. Anna is very similar to other rural and small-town Americans of northern European extraction. Margaret's choices are within the range considered normal by middle-class urban Americans. Their personalities, specific experiences with mental illness or abuse, and histories of institutional living or poverty have also contributed to their beliefs and values. Thus, each individual is ultimately a unique person even if she is also similar to other people of the same class or ethnic group. Accentuating the uniqueness of each person and focusing on the label of disability, however, cannot be allowed to overshadow how each person has values similar to others (Mest, 1988). It also cannot outweigh the task of finding the context where those values are supported (Siegel et al., 1990).

POINTS TO REMEMBER

To understand and support each person's decision-making values, we need to adopt the following four practices:

1. *Recognize how a person is already making decisions.* There are other ways to make decisions in addition to the ideal model of de-

cision making usually envisioned. Anna, for example, made decisions by accepting direction from an authority and by following personally established routines and traditions.

2. *Assist each person to use his decision-making values when selecting among alternatives or choosing activities.* Whether teaching a new skill or leading a discussion about rearranging living room furniture, the instructor can characterize each option by the values it incorporates.

3. *Relate decision-making values to the context created by the person's other values and experiences.* Gloria's value on situational adaptation could easily be mislabeled as indecisiveness or impulsiveness unless it is viewed within the context of a now-oriented world view.

4. *Find the social context most conducive to bringing out the strengths of each person's decision-making values.* Margaret's use of conformity and authority to make decisions might be evaluated as weaknesses or as succumbing to peer group pressure if she was in a social context of peers who were drug addicts and criminals. However, her need to belong and the value she places on conformity led to a happier result in the context of the religious community she joined.

Problem Behavior
and Schema Analysis

When I first met Ted, he seemed lost in a world of his own. He was
blind in one eye, partially sighted in the other, and also deaf, reacting
only to very loud sounds or vibrations. He spent hours holding his
fingers in front of his eye and gazing at a light. He flicked his fingers
and sometimes poked his own eye, probably to make colors and
shapes appear. When he wasn't staring at the light, he was wandering
around the room, pushing people out of the way or grabbing them by
their necks and pulling at their earrings or hair. Because Ted's team
hypothesized that his wandering and stereotypy might be due to bore-
dom (Guess & Carr, 1991), they gave him different fragrances to explore, objects with a variety of textures to feel, and even a kaleidoscope through which to look. He enjoyed each new item for a while
but quickly lost interest.

Brenda, Ted's case manager, was the one who first realized that
Ted's grabbing people by their necks wasn't aggression. He was exploring things in his environment in the only way he could, by pulling

them closer to his eye or by testing them with yanks and pokes. This insight led Brenda to suggest that Ted needed glasses.

There was no record in his current files that he had ever worn glasses. He was from a middle-class, urban, Norwegian/German family but had been institutionalized shortly after birth some 40 years ago, which was a common practice at that time for babies born with Rubella syndrome. Institutional practices during those years didn't particularly stress getting glasses for someone with as little vision as Ted appeared to have. Even if glasses had been tried and rejected at some point, he was in a new environment now; it certainly couldn't hurt to try them again.

Ted smashed his first several pairs of glasses, but gradually, as staff gave him interesting things to look at and directed his attention further afield, he wore them for longer periods of time and began to enjoy watching the activity in the room and looking out the window. This success led Ted's team to look for other ways to involve him; over the next few years his life became more interesting. We were thus caught off guard when 3 years later, he put his glasses away and again began to wander around the room, pulling people's hair and staring at the light flicking his fingers, at first for short periods of time but gradually for increasingly longer periods.

We wondered whether what little vision he had in his one eye was failing; however, when he did wear his glasses, he seemed able to see as well as ever. It occurred to us that his return to a former, familiar pattern of behaving might be a way to comfort himself. An aggressively thorough medical exam finally revealed that Ted had gallstones and probably was experiencing pain. After gall bladder surgery, Ted started wearing his glasses again.

IDENTIFYING PROBLEM BEHAVIOR
AND DESIGNING INTERVENTIONS

Certain behaviors, selected for special attention in developmental disabilities, have variously been called problem behavior, challenging behavior, or maladaptive behavior. Carr et al. used the term "severe problem behavior" and included in its definition the behaviors of "intense forms of aggression (punching, scratching, biting, and kicking others), self-injury (head-banging, self-biting, and self-slapping), property destruction, and tantrums (prolonged screaming and crying . . .)" (1994, p. 3). Turnbull and Ruef included pica, the eating of nonedible substances or items, as problem behavior in addition to "aggression toward others, property destruction [and] self-injurious behavior" (1996, p. 280). Sometimes stereotypy, repeating an action multiple times without variation, such as flicking one's fingers, is also included (Lakin, Bruininks, Chen, Hill, & Anderson, 1993). Challenging behavior has been defined as injury or damage to self, others, or property and to "actions that . . . interfere with the acquisition of new skills, or socially isolate an individual" (Sigafoos, Reichle, & Light-Shriner, 1994, p. 147). McGrew and Bruininks defined maladaptive behavior as "behaviors which interfere with effective adjustment" (1990, p. 55).

Although the definitions vary, these are not labels for different types of behavior nor are the listed behaviors defined relative to their meaning or context (Demchak & Bossert, 1995). Sometimes, they are not even named and defined but simply called "behaviors," as if everyone knows the referent. The common factor for this class of behaviors is that they are considered unacceptable and in need of interventions to change or preclude them.

Intervention Based on Hypothesized Causes

Changes in the label for this class of behaviors have signaled changes in hypotheses for their causes and, therefore, possible interventions. Intervention is based on how a person conceptualizes the cause of the behavior. For example, Scheibe pointed out that "bizarre and deviant behavior has been looked upon . . . as the result of demons entering a person . . . [or] as due to an unfortunate history of conditioning" (1970, p. 31), with the person treated differently depending on whether the interventionist is trying to rid the person of demons or overcome his conditioning.

Changes in terminology eliminated the implication that this class of behaviors was bad, thereby suppressing most punishment interventions (Gardner & Cole, 1989). The hypothesis that some of the behaviors were caused by medical and psychological conditions led to a medical treatment model of intervention and to the recommendation to look for medical and psychological causes before proceeding to other interventions (Evans & Meyer, 1985; Gaylord-Ross, 1980). Calling it maladaptive behavior encouraged interventions aimed at the fit between the behavior and the environment in which it occurred. Behaviors were changed or eliminated by adjusting the environment or by placing the person in a different environment. Another shift in intervention resulted from the hypothesis that behavior is a form of communication (Durand, Crimmins, Caulfield, & Taylor, 1989). If the communicative function of the difficult behavior can be determined, then other, more acceptable behavior that sends the same message and is equally efficient at producing the desired results can be substituted (Carr et al., 1994; Reichle & Wacker, 1993).

The focus, however, is still on a class of behaviors categorized as similar because the observer considers them to be a problem. The function, cause, or meaning of the behavior is sought only after the target behavior has been identified. The decision to intervene may then be based on whether the behavior is dangerous, limits the person's participation in activities, interferes in having social relationships, decreases the person's quality of life, or in some way negatively affects the person's development (Crimmins, 1994; Weiss, 1990). These evaluations are from the observer's point of view. A person-centered, values-based approach, however, requires asking what the person considers to be the problem (Ferguson, 1994).

Identifying the Problem from the Person's Point of View

The problem from the person's point of view may be that she is not receiving enough attention from others, does not want to perform a certain task, wants to participate in preferred activities, or some other problem. She may be using a variety of behaviors to solve her problems as she sees them, only some of which are labeled by the observer as challenging or maladaptive. For example, when a person is not doing the next step of a task, it might be that he does not want to do the task rather than that he does not know the next step (Brown, 1991). The person's inattention or off-task behavior might be his way of communicating this. If the service provider continues to prompt, the person's response might be to bite himself. Arguing about whether he does or does not actually think to himself, "I'm going to bite myself so that I can stop this task," is irrelevant. The person's behavior is no different from the service provider's, who finally stops prompting him to do the task whether she says to herself, "I'm going to stop this task so he stops biting himself." The point is that the inattention or off-task behavior is not identified by the service provider as a problem behavior. Thus, the service provider does not seek to understand its function and instead continues to prompt until the biting begins.

Clearly, the person has a well-formed schema about what he wants, or no one would be able to figure out the message when they eventually do look for it. A person may use self-injury to escape a task, but not just any task. He uses it to escape tasks that he does not like or that are new, difficult, or unpleasant. That is, seeking escape is not arbitrary and accidental. It is not done because the sunlight hit his arm a different way today or because the person next to him is wearing a red sweater. The message can be understood because service providers share his schema of tasks or infer his schema from the pattern of his choices.

When the message is understood, the person is taught an acceptable and more effective way to express the same message. Service providers do not try to teach the person that the task really is pleasant or easy; that is, they do not try to change the person's schema of tasks or his application of it. The medium of the message is the focus of intervention, not the message itself.

When service providers and receivers do not share the same schemas, the message may never be understood or the pattern of the person's choices may never be discerned. For example, if it is indeed the red sweater that has elicited the self-injury, this may never be discovered, even if self-injury always occurs when someone wears a red sweater, because no one else has a schema that evaluates red sweaters as unpleasant. Red sweaters are so much a part of the background noise that no one would probably even think to keep track of such an irrelevant detail when data are collected about the antecedents to the person's self-injurious behavior.

Designing Interventions from the Person's Point of View

To design an intervention from the person's point of view, service providers may need to reframe how they view people's actions and question what they do or do not know about how the person views her own behavior (Rhodes, 1992) and how others who share her background view her behavior. The approach offered here, values-based services based on schema analysis, is not intended as a replacement for interventions that teach communicative alternatives based on a functional assessment of problem behavior. It is an extension of functional behavior analysis, particularly in determining which schema is guiding communication.

Functional behavior analysis is based on gathering information on the antecedents and consequences of behavior, the environments in which the behavior occurs, and its relationship to interactions with other people (Reichle & Wacker, 1993). However, there is an assumption for some analysts that the interpretation of that information is not problematic because it is assumed, to recapitulate earlier examples, that everyone knows and agrees on the difference between red and orange, between theft and nontheft, or between good and bad ways to make a decision. That is, there is the assumption that service providers and receivers share their schemas.

A values-based approach necessitates considering several possibilities when conducting a functional analysis of challenging behavior. Are schemas shared between the service receiver and provider? If so, is the schema being used by the person simply unrecognized by the service provider, or is it a partial or disordered variant of the schema? If the schema is not shared with the service provider but is characteristic of others with the same background as the service receiver, is it a partial or disordered variant of that schema? The possible combinations of answers to these questions are illustrated in Table 6.1.

The simplest, least intrusive intervention is when the schema is shared but unrecognized by the service provider. Once the schema is identified, interventions can be geared toward teaching socially accepted communicative alternatives. If the schema is shared but the service receiver is using a partial or disordered variant of it, then the person's team must decide whether to change the person's schemas.

If schemas are not shared, then the schema being used by the service receiver is more difficult to recognize and may mistakenly be evaluated as a disordered variant of a schema that is known to the service provider. Once the service provider understands the person's schemas relative to the world view of others who share her background and values, the only change necessary may be for the service provider to learn to communicate with the service receiver and interpret her behavior in terms of her schemas. It may also be necessary to design an intervention that is minimally intrusive from the service receiver's point of view. That is, a communicative alternative that is accepted by others who share her social identity can be taught to the service receiver and learned by the service provider. Finally, the most difficult situation to analyze is when the service provider and receiver do not share schemas and the schema that the service receiver is using is a partial or disordered variant of the schema used by others similar to her in social identity.

WHEN SCHEMAS ARE SHARED BUT UNRECOGNIZED

"Have you ever looked at his feet? They're gross."

This comment from Bobby's community living coach, Glen, irritated me slightly because we were trying to concentrate on why Bobby

Table 6.1.   Problematic combinations of schemas to consider when analyzing behavior that is difficult to understand

Quick reference label	Description	Responses to consider
Schemas shared but unrecognized	Service provider and receiver share a schema but the service provider does not recognize that the service receiver is using it.	*Service provider:* Reframe service receiver's behavior by recognizing the schema being used. *Service receiver:* Learn communicative alternative.
Schemas shared but incomplete or disordered	Service provider and receiver share a schema but the service receiver is using an incomplete or disordered version of it.	*Service provider:* Reframe service receiver's behavior by recognizing the schema being used and use only the parts that the service receiver recognizes. *Service receiver:* Learn additional parts of the shared schema or an ordered version of it.
Schemas not shared and unrecognized	Service provider and receiver use different schemas and the service provider does not recognize or understand the service receiver's schema.	*Service provider:* Reframe service receiver's behavior from the point of view of the service receiver's schema and learn communicative alternative. *Service receiver:* No change needed.
Schemas not shared and incomplete or disordered	Service provider and receiver use different schemas and the service provider does not recognize or understand the service receiver's schema. Service receiver is using an incomplete or disordered version of a schema that he or she does partially share with others of similar ethnicity, class, gender, or other social identity.	*Service provider:* Reframe service receiver's behavior from the point of view of the service receiver's schema and learn communicative alternative. *Service receiver:* Learn additional parts of the schema or ordered versions of it that others of similar social identity use.

flooded the bathroom. It is difficult enough to develop behavior intervention plans without getting sidetracked on irrelevancies. It sounds so easy in the instruction books. Just gather data on what happens before, during, and after the targeted behavior. Then, change the stimulus or consequence or teach an alternative way of communicating. Yes, exactly; but first you have to formulate an hypothesis.

There seemed to be no rhyme or reason to when or why Bobby flooded the bathroom. For that matter, we hadn't pinpointed any possible explanations for why he got angry and lay on his back waving his feet in the air (a behavior we sometimes called "temper tantrums"), ate beads, threw his shoes out the window, or flushed his socks down the toilet. Although I eventually learned that often an unfocused comment or a silly suggestion opens new ways of looking at old problems, it was my frustration with our lack of progress that made me respond to this diverting comment.

"No. I've never seen his feet. Why are they gross?"

Glen, whose job it was to assist Bobby with bathing and dressing, gave me more information than I wanted.

"His toenails are thick and difficult to trim, and they smell."

My quick response, to make an appointment with a podiatrist and have his toenails looked at, would allow us, I hoped, to get back to the task at hand and figure out why Bobby flooded the bathroom.

In retrospect, it might seem amazing that such a small, seemingly irrelevant remark provided the key to understanding Bobby's reasons for many of his actions, except that direct support staff often do know more about the people they are working with than other staff do. This knowledge may be intuitive and difficult to express, or they may not be encouraged or rewarded for offering subjective comments. But, direct support staff discover, by trial and error or by close and sensitive observation, what does and does not work with one person and what is unusual about that person.

Bobby's Schemas of Pain and Self-Reliance

Glen was quite right that Bobby's toenails were a problem. The podiatrist said Bobby needed surgery and follow-up treatment to rid him of the fungus that was painfully compressing the tissue beneath his toenails. No wonder he flushed his socks down the toilet and threw his shoes out the window. Eventually it hit us. When he lay on his back with his feet in the air, he was not having temper tantrums. His "tantrums" were the actions of a person in pain, elevating his hurting feet. Flooding the bathroom was Bobby's attempt to soak his feet to make the pain go away. It was months later that the final piece fell into place. Eating beads occurred when he had a headache or when his feet hurt because the beads looked like pills.

We had not even considered pain as a possible reason for his actions because Bobby used the sign for pain at appropriate times, such as when he fell or cut his finger. Possibly, he did not use the pain sign for his aching feet because he was similar to other men, such as laborers and factory workers, who put up with pain for years, even developing routines for handling pain but never complaining and certainly never going to a doctor (Zola, 1966). Chronic pain becomes the usual state of affairs. In other words, Bobby might class sudden and unusual pain, such as a cut finger, differently from chronic pain and thus use the pain sign for acute but not chronic pain.

However, he may have tried to report the pain and received no response. I learned later that the personnel at the institution where Bobby had previously lived knew about the fungus. His team had decided that surgery and the physical restraints they believed would be required for postsurgical procedures would be more difficult for Bobby than living with the fungus, which in milder cases does not cause pain. Therefore, Bobby's behavior of dealing with the pain on his own might have developed because no one appeared to do anything to help him when he told them about it. We certainly did not hear his message for a long time and continued, from his point of view, to ignore what he was feeling.

Probably all three situations—our view of Bobby as having the knowledge and skill to report pain, Bobby's experience in trying to report it and getting no response, and Bobby's rural, manly schema of chronic pain as something to be endured and taken care of independently—led to our slowness in developing an hypothesis for any of his actions or realizing that they were related. Understanding the final piece, eating beads as self-medication, resulted from reframing many of his actions as motivated by his very strong value on taking care of himself, a value commonly associated with rural culture (Groce, 1981). The team opted to help Bobby live up to this value safely by having him carry small quantities of acetaminophen rather than limiting his self-reliance by teaching him to ask a staff member for it.

When we finally identified Bobby's schemas of pain and self-reliance, they were not that different from schemas we recognized as characteristic of some Americans. For example, Glen shared these same schemas. It was also not difficult for his team to accept them as the basis for designing other supports because doing so decreased problem behavior and, more important, resulted in an improved quality of life for Bobby. For example, postsurgical procedures were conducted without physical restraints because Bobby determined when they would occur and who would conduct them.

Anna's Schemas of Hunger and Self-Reliance

At one time, Anna took part in a program to learn better table manners, a second program to learn to clean her room, and a third to take appropriate amounts of food when eating in public. My translation of these programs was "don't take food from other people's plates," "don't store food in your pillowcase and dresser drawers," and "don't leave the restaurant with your purse and pockets full of food." Her team was aware that all three programs revolved around the issue of food but had not really considered food as the main issue.

When Anna's team looked for another way to frame these actions, seeking to interpret them from Anna's point of view using her schemas, they generated the hypotheses that she was afraid of being hungry and that she was adapting to an environment in which she did not control her access to food. Therefore, the interventions designed needed to address Anna's definition of the problem. The tricky part was that Anna had been on a reduced-calorie diet for weight control at the institution where she had lived prior to moving to this community. Her current dietician had also recommended a reduced-calorie diet. Anna did not have Prader-Willi syndrome or any glandular condition, but she did have a problem with weight because of her small stature and low level of exercise.

Therefore, the team was faced with the problem of considering competing values. If Anna's fear of hunger was addressed by telling her that she could always eat as much as she wanted, then the resulting weight gain could compromise her health. When the issue was framed from Anna's point of view, weight gain was not her concern; therefore, the team decided it should not be an impediment to designing interventions addressing her fear of hunger. Potential weight gain could also be handled by increasing her exercise. Because she loved walking in the park, daily walks were an obvious way to increase her exercise.

Without a reduced-calorie diet, the way was cleared for staff members to encourage Anna to take second helpings from the serving platter rather than from the plates of others at her table. However, rather than saying, "You can have as much as you want," they said, "You can have seconds now if you still feel hungry, but you have places you can get food if you feel hungry later." Dean had helped Anna find a pretty canister to keep in her room where she could store nonperishable snacks. She had a box with her picture on it in the refrigerator where she could keep her perishable snacks. She went grocery shopping once per week with her own money and could buy snacks if she chose to do so.

At first, her weight did increase as she helped herself liberally to seconds and snacked often; however, she gradually stopped stuffing her pockets with food to hide in her room and, eventually, she lost weight. She even stopped snacking, although she continued to purchase and store snacks. Perhaps she was enabled to eat less at mealtimes because she knew snacks were available if she wanted them. She could eat because she was hungry and stop when she was full rather than eat to excess so as not to be hungry later when no food would be available.

If Anna had simply eaten all the food that was within her reach and eaten whenever food was available, then the intervention might have needed to focus on helping her learn to associate certain physiological feelings with "being hungry" and "being full" to pair with starting and ending a meal. We tend to assume that this is natural and does not need to be taught; however, hunger and satiation are defined and evaluated in a schema. If they were not, we could be satisfied with a very filling gruel and would not be affected by color, texture, temperature, taste, popularity, and tradition.

Anna's schema about food, feeling hungry, and having access to food was complete and not unfamiliar to any of us when we looked at the situation from her point of view. The problem for Anna was that she had to apply her schemas in an environment where others limited her access to food. Because she valued self-reliance, she found ways to adapt to that environment. Changing her environment and showing her how her environment had changed built on the strengths already in her repertoire, that is, self-reliance and planning ahead. For Anna, it really was only a slight shift from "stealing and hiding" food to "buying and storing" food. But for us, it was a much larger shift from seeing her behavior as a problem in need of intervention to recognizing and reframing it as adaptive behavior designed to solve a problem.

WHEN SCHEMAS ARE SHARED
BUT INCOMPLETE OR DISORDERED

Ted was once involved in a recreational project to plant a garden. Participants were given styrofoam cups filled with dirt to start the seeds indoors. Ted picked up the cup full of dirt and tried to drink it. People who are deaf and blind often do use their sense of taste to explore the world; therefore, this would be one way of framing Ted's behavior. However, Ted rarely used this method, probably because he had learned not to in the past when mouthing things was considered to be unacceptable behavior. The interpretation that makes the most sense is that Ted was using the cup in the way he knew cups were supposed to be used, by drinking or eating something from it. Styrofoam cups had also, in his experience, been presented full of pudding, candy, peanuts, or raisins. The problem, from Ted's point of view, was that someone used a cup in a way that cups are not supposed to be used.

One intervention might be to teach Ted that cups can be used in other ways; that is, the team could expand Ted's schema of containers to match the schema used by his service providers. However, having a fully formed schema about containers is probably not going to lead to significant improvements in Ted's life. The simplest, least intrusive change for Ted is to have service providers learn to use cups with him only in the way that he defines them—as containers for food or drink. However, sometimes it is necessary to expand or change a person's schemas to enhance his quality of life, as we learned from the following situation with Ted.

Ted's Incomplete Schema of Pain

Ted had a vocabulary of sounds he made, one of which we had established meant "I have a headache" because he also hit the top of his head when he made this sound. Giving Ted acetaminophen usually stopped both his verbalization and the hitting shortly after administration. We had learned from his response to gall bladder attacks that he did not use this sound or hit the spot that was hurting when the pain was in an area other than his head. He had learned or invented part of a schema about pain, but not a schema that encompassed every possibility.

Researchers have noted that some people with developmental disabilities appear not to react to painful stimuli, possibly because of differences in neurology or indifference to pain. They have recommended careful observation of behavior changes that might signal illness or an altered emotional state: pacing, inattentiveness, behaviors that are inter-preted as anger, increases in stereotypy and self-injurious behaviors, decreases in apparent enjoyment of food and preferred activities, or changes in sleep patterns (Biersdorff, 1991; Rubin, 1987).

Pain insensitivity or indifference may explain the behavior of some people, but it is also possible that many people who appear not to react to pain simply have not yet learned a complete schema of pain. That is, they have not learned to notice certain physiological states and how to interpret, value, and respond to them (Lutz, 1988). People learn a schema of pain and other emotions just as they learn other parts of their culture (Harkness & Super, 1985). For example, football players, carpenters, and ballerinas may ignore or even learn not to feel some things that others might consider to be painful. Childbirth is painful but can be managed by breathing a certain way. Dental work may be espe-cially painful because people have learned to expect it to be so.

Ethnic groups (Zborowski, 1960, 1969), religious groups (Wolff & Langley, 1968), and social classes (Christopherson, 1966) in the United States vary in how they construct their schemas of pain. How-ever, there may be a focal point to feelings that are labeled as painful, similar in all cultures and for all people, that is based on biological processes (Heelas, 1984). As with any schema, people vary as to how much of the available schema they learn, in whether they learn all the parts exactly as others learn them, and whether they make mistakes in applying it or do not apply it at all in circumstances where others might.

Ted may be less sensitive to pain than others, although it is impos-sible to prove or disprove this, but he did not appear to be indifferent. He simply had no way to identify for himself or to communicate to us what he was feeling because his schema of pain was incomplete in comparison to ours. Without our familiar behavioral cues for how oth-ers express pain, at first we were unable to identify pain as the problem when he was having gall bladder attacks. Because Ted had several other medical conditions that cause pain, his team decided to look for ways, other than pulling other people's hair, for Ted to communicate his needs to staff before the pain becomes severe. Although the plan has not yet been successful, Ted's team chose to expand Ted's schema of pain be-cause they believed that doing so would improve the quality of his life.

Disordered Self-Schema

John, when I first met him, was in his early thirties, was tall and strong, and had multiple episodes of what, by any definition, was very severe, maladaptive, challenging problem behavior. He was aggressive toward others, damaged property, and exploded into violent tantrums. He also had several routines that could be described as obsessive, such as flushing the toilet 30–40 times or tearing off each paper towel from a roll, crumpling it, and throwing it in the garbage. Violence alternated with periods of withdrawal. He sometimes hid under his bed in the fetal position or would rock while crying to himself in a dark corner. He licked his forearms and peeled skin off in dime-size spots. Several different psychotropic medications had been tried over the years in addition to many antibiotics for the infections that followed the self-injury.

Because John was allergic to many medications, Brenda, John's new case manager, wanted a list of all medications that he had taken during the last 19 years, his reactions to them, and his behavior during drug holidays. A 2-foot thick file of medication records and social histories from all his previous placements provided our starting point. I labeled 19 pages of paper with each year and listed the 12 months down the side. Brenda took half the pile of reports, and I took the other half. Each time one of us came across a bit of information, we noted it by the appropriate month and year.

When we finished, we spread the papers across my desk and an adjoining table to begin to reorganize the notes in terms of his reaction to each medication, especially in combination with other drugs he was receiving simultaneously. Then, the pattern jelled. The middle section of each page, representing the summer months, contained all the drug holidays that were successful, when his behavior was relatively normal. Drug holidays in the winter months showed only deterioration in behavior. This overall pattern was reported to his psychiatrist, who diagnosed seasonal affective disorder, a type of depression that occurs during the short days of winter, and prescribed light therapy and an antidepressant in the winter months.

Discovering John's battle with depression brought home to me how broad themes and patterns are just as important as events immediately before or after an episode of challenging behavior. The effects of abuse, the impact of institutional living or multiple placements with constant staff changes, affective disorders, grief, chronic pain, or just needing glasses may color a person's behavior. These experiences are "written into" a person's schema of himself and of others around him and to the kind of relationships he has with others, creating a self-schema (Horowitz, 1991). The self-schema persists even when the situation changes. For example, after Ted started wearing glasses and

John received antidepressants and light therapy, both still used aggression in some situations because unusual or abnormal self-schemas can "lead to patterned and recurrent errors of perception, interpretation and action" (Horowitz, 1991, p. 13). John often perceived others as trying to control him and sometimes they were. He also perceived relationships in this negative way when others were not mistreating him because self-schemas are preserved "even in the face of conflicting evidence" (Singer & Salovey, 1991, p. 39). That is, they are self-validating as new evidence is interpreted in terms of the current schema.

Finally realizing that John had recurrent bouts of depression and providing him with appropriate medical intervention was only part of the solution. Another part of the solution for John was to learn to identify various emotions and how to handle them in different ways rather than responding to all situations with aggression toward self, others, and property. Essentially, John needed to rewrite his self-schema to include new ways of handling familiar situations. The only image he had of others around him was that they were trying to control him and would eventually get mad at him and leave or send him away. The only image he had of himself was as a tough guy whom no one could hurt because he was going to hurt them first. His plan never worked because he tried to control his environment with obsessive routines and often ended up under his bed, withdrawn and overwhelmed by all the feelings, people, and situations he could not control.

Just as important, we needed to change our image of John, reframe our analysis of his behavior, and learn to see the world from his point of view. When people saw John's behavior as part of his depression, they interacted differently with him from when they saw his behavior as aggression. This new way of interacting with John often deescalated sequences of behavior that formerly would have progressed to the point of violence. His team learned to initiate changes in early summer so that he would have time to adjust before winter when the struggle with depression would begin again. They also began to see that John used aggression to express sadness, to control the demands of others, and to maintain his image of himself as a tough guy even when—probably especially when—he was feeling inadequate and unloved.

The real art to this analysis, however, was to separate John's disordered view due to his depression, with its associated behaviors of self-injury and compulsions, from the orderly view he had of his world and himself. Because the disordered parts of a self-schema overshadow and distort the parts that are healthy, the tendency when working with people with disordered self-schemas is to assume that the entire schema is disordered (Blotzer & Ruth, 1995). Interventions with John to eliminate his aggressive behavior, which he used to control others, should not inadvertently decrease his desire to be in charge. He liked being the center of attention. He wanted to be important and sometimes fabricated stories with himself as the hero. If people see only the disordered parts of John's self-schema, they will perceive him as violent and domineering. By focusing on the ordered parts of John's self-schema, they will be able to envision him, with the appropriate supports and additional skills, as a natural born leader.

WHEN SCHEMAS ARE NOT SHARED AND ARE UNRECOGNIZED OR DISORDERED

For several months when Gloria first arrived, every time she exploded into an episode of spitting, pulling hair, and pummeling anybody and anything with her fists, a staff member stood with her in front of a mirror, talking to Gloria's reflection in the mirror. "You have beautiful hair. You have a lovely smile. You have nice eyes. You are a good person." Finally, one day Gloria spoke to her image in the mirror.

"One nice eye."

Her first utterance to the mirror was made in a flat voice with no change in facial expression. Gloria's analysis of her eyes was brutally accurate. One eye was clouded by years of chronic infection and scarred from abuse; whereas, the other eye was bright and lively, sparkling with joy, anger, love, or determination.

The times in front of the mirror had grown to include good times, too. "You are good to have helped with the dishes without anyone's asking." "You were good to Ralph by helping him get on the van." The team's reason for designing the mirror program was to help her gain self-esteem through self-affirmation. It seemed to be working because she was hitting and spitting at other people less frequently.

Yet, we worried that when the fighting was extinguished, we would no longer have Gloria; we would have only a simulation of her, created by our well-intentioned expectations and the values implicit in what we said to her mirrored image. Therefore, we decided it was important to understand her statement. Was this a realistic view of her eyes because of mute acceptance of the abuse in her life and her powerlessness to change the results of that abuse? Or, did it flow from the

Lakota acceptance of suffering as part of life (Erdoes, 1990), even reverence for self-imposed suffering as a path to understanding? Or, was this an affirmation of the best part of herself, the glass of water half full rather than half empty? Or, yet again, maybe her reason for saying it was to correct the Pollyanna staff who didn't just ignore the "not nice" eye but pretended it wasn't there at all. "You have nice eyes," they always said, when anyone could see there was only one nice eye.

We couldn't answer any of our own questions. Some team members even argued that if the mirror work was helping her gain self-esteem and was decreasing her aggressiveness, for whatever reason, then it didn't matter what she was thinking when she made this statement.

In our search for understanding, we asked Donna why Gloria was so angry all the time, assuming that her behavior was correctly labeled as anger because at times Gloria would clench her teeth and fists, hunch her shoulders, and turn away, sometimes even leaving and walking home to be alone. Other times she would fight. However, the fights generally ended up with her crying and telling us she didn't want to be mad and that she was sorry. This was followed by a spate of kind acts to others. Donna's answer corrected the team's analysis of Gloria's behavior.

"She's not angry. She's ashamed."

With a flick of the wrist, the colored pieces in a kaleidoscope of behavior formed a whole new pattern. Donna had refocused the picture, framing Gloria with a different schema. The behavior that a non-Indian would interpret to mean anger meant something different to Gloria and Donna. We, along with many other American professionals, thought of "emotions . . . as the aspect of human experience least subject to control, least constructed or learned (hence most universal), least public, and therefore least amenable to sociocultural analysis" (Abu-Lughod & Lutz, 1990, p. 1), but emotions are not just reactions to events and body states. Emotions are interpretations of events, defined and explained through shared schemas available to members of the group (Reddy, 1997).

Gloria's Collectivist Person Schema

As Chapter 3 discusses, most white American professionals use an individualist person schema in which the person is seen as choosing his own traits and values. In addition, the individual is also seen as having personal rights, although rights are tempered with responsibilities toward other individuals (Marsella, DeVos, & Hsu, 1985). Self-control, one-to-one competition, getting ahead of the crowd, and changing situations to conform to personal needs are values included in an individualist person schema. People who work hard become successful, have self-respect, and take pride in their accomplishments (Triandis, 1989). If they do something wrong, then they are guilty as an individual for the failure. Self-esteem is built on how well the individual sees himself succeeding, compared with other people in his group.

In other cultures, most notably many Asian and Native American cultures, where a collectivist person schema is used, the individual has duties and obligations to the group with his status and identity defined by his group membership (Triandis, Bontempo, Villareal, Asai, & Lucca, 1987). Adapting to situations, sharing within the group with all members contributing as they are able, and having one's group do well are valued (Weisz, Rothbaum, & Blackburn, 1984). Not contributing to the group brings shame (Medicine, 1987). Problems are explained by events in the person's environment or as a result of the collective actions of others rather than by looking for traits in the person. Often, there is great personal autonomy in collectivist cultures because the person's obligations are so well internalized that personal autonomy leads to actions that benefit the group (Lee, 1959).

Some of the differences between an individualist person schema and a collectivist person schema lie in their contrasting emphases on feeling self-respect versus earning the respect of others, feeling guilt versus feeling shame, having personal responsibilities versus having group obligations, and having personal rights versus having civic duties. Self-esteem is a concept clearly related to an individualist person schema where transgressions against the person are met with anger, whereas transgressions by the person are a cause of blame and guilt. People using a collectivist person schema also think well or ill of themselves, but the focus is on group membership, where transgressions against a person dishonor the group and transgressions by the person result in shame and loss of others' respect.

Gloria's shame flowed from being exiled from her own group as well as from not being able to meet her obligations as a member of this new group when she was asked to do things too difficult or unfamiliar to her. Quite fortuitously, the expanded mirror program included good things she had done for others as well as her personal characteristics. Gloria's behavior changed as these comments communicated to her that staff respected her for what she did for others. Staff also changed in how they evaluated Gloria. When they saw her as a more likeable and competent person in spite of her physical aggression, they became less directive with her, a behavior interpreted by Gloria as recognition of her autonomy.

Most professionals believe that the need for self-esteem is universal, although the ways in which a person gains self-esteem may differ from group to group or even from person to person. Gloria's team had consciously tried to take her culture into account when they designed the mirror program to increase her self-esteem. The mirror, they believed, would be a way for non-Indian staff to talk to Gloria without making direct eye contact with her; they knew that direct eye contact conveys disrespect in Lakota culture. However, neither her team nor the rest of the staff ever considered that the concept of the person as having or not having a trait such as self-esteem might itself be culture bound. We were not yet experienced in working with people with Gloria's background and did not realize how many assumptions we made about the meaning of her behavior. As we came to understand how important respect, rather than self-esteem, was for her and even began to see the world through her eyes a little, we became better at providing supports that decreased acts we labeled as aggressive by helping her gain respect by being nice to others.

Gloria's Schema of Being Nice to Others

"That man. He give me two dollar."

I waited for Gloria's report to continue, although I suspected that I knew what would come next. Gloria had been labeled a prostitute because men gave her money to have sex. We didn't think she was a prostitute because she didn't view the money as having purchased sex. She saw it as people being nice to each other. The man was nice to her by giving her the money she wanted, and she was nice to him by giving him the sex he wanted even if she didn't want to have sex with him.

Gloria's team had chosen to concentrate on helping Gloria to understand that she had the right to refuse or accept sex. They chose not to complicate the issue with discussing whether money was involved or whether the man was a stranger. Just because he wanted sex didn't mean it would be mean to say no, they told her. There are other ways to be nice even if the man says that's how to be nice to him.

"He say go upstairs. Lay on me."

Yes, that's what I expected she was going to say next. Were we really doing the best thing? Was the risk too great? Were we right in letting her walk anywhere in the community without a staff member along? I agreed with her team that teaching her the skills to protect herself and make decisions would in the long run make her safer than sending a staff member with her to protect her. But, as an administrator, I was deeply concerned about the immediate safety and liability issues. What if we were wrong? What if Gloria chose to continue "prostitution"?

I really didn't think this would ultimately be what she wanted, as her interaction with these men wasn't prostitution; it had a different meaning for her. She might continue, however, if she began to see it as a way to get money rather than as a way to be nice to others. Simple survival issues were still a high priority for Gloria. Focusing on prostitution as an illegal act and something she shouldn't be doing would only cast her in the role of the offender, a victim-blaming approach. Sending a staff member with her into the community was cost prohibitive, as Gloria spent hours walking many places and talking to many people. Our choice, then, was between either limiting her freedom of movement or accepting the possibility that Gloria might contract a disease or be arrested for prostitution.

Instead of limiting her freedom of movement, the team opted to work with Gloria; they decided to teach her to use condoms, get regular health exams, learn to refuse or accept sex, know what rape was and how to report it to the police, and find other ways of being nice to men who gave her money instead of agreeing to sex. As I was getting ready to follow the current behavior intervention plan and talk to her about ways to be nice, Gloria continued.

"I say no."

Then she held up $2. Oh joy! Oh wonderful world! The plan was working even better than I had expected. I mentally thanked whatever man it was out there who hadn't taken the money back. The issues of survival and being nice were separated. It was difficult to remain calm and matter of fact when really I wanted to jump up and hug her. Because this was a critical moment of change and understanding, I needed to be as mature as she was.

"Yes. It's okay to say no and not let him lay on you. There are other ways to be nice. What are some ways to be nice?"

"Give him food. Give him blankets. Tell him thank you. Show him where to get popcorn."

Perfect! Her list had not included "Lay on him." The value of being nice to others hadn't changed. The acceptable parts of her collectivist person schema were still intact. Consenting to unwanted sex as a way to be nice was a disordered interpretation of the collectivist person schema held by other Lakota. Therefore, when Gloria redefined whose right it was to choose how to be nice and different ways to be nice, her schema conformed more closely to the collectivist schema held by other Lakota.

We had learned to see a different meaning in Gloria's behavior. It was not an illegal act of prostitution or a problem behavior to be eliminated; however, reordering Gloria's schema did eventually eliminate behavior defined by others as prostitution. When we focused on Gloria's value of civic duty, which she enacted by being nice to others, many of her other actions made more sense to us and allowed us to support this value in other areas of her life as well.

VALUES-BASED BEHAVIOR INTERVENTION

Because choosing a way to intervene is connected to the way in which a particular behavior is labeled and valued, it is critical in values-based services to begin behavior analysis by assuming that the meaning that a person gives to his own behavior is the correct meaning, regardless of whether it matches the meaning the service provider would give it. When we interpreted Ted's action of smashing his first pair of glasses as exploration, we were attempting to give his actions the meaning he gave them. If he had continued to break each pair of glasses, we might, at some point, have admitted that this was not exploration but was Ted telling us he did not want to wear glasses. However, if we had automatically labeled his action as property destruction and had not even considered interpreting it as exploration or refusal, then we would be using our definition without establishing whether Ted shared that definition.

Instead of limiting our analysis to acts of property destruction, framing Ted's behavior as exploration lead us to look for other ways Ted investigated his environment, and we found them. We also discovered that many of Bobby's actions were geared toward maintaining his self-reliance, Anna's to planning ahead, and Gloria's to being nice to others. Widening the view from a narrow focus on a particular problem behavior to the general themes and values in a person's life helped us to respond to other behaviors that were not problematic. It also provided guidelines for team discussions of vocational, residential, and social goals.

However, the approach of values-based services does not require the service provider to support every action and schema of the service receiver. It is not carte blanche for an "anything goes" attitude (Feldman, 1997). Judgments must still be made when a schema is disordered and when behavior is abnormal, unhealthy, or unacceptable relative to the beliefs and values of others who share the person's background. This does not mean that we should accept the beliefs and values of drug addicts, criminals, and psychopaths. Using sick, deviant, or antisocial behavior as the yardstick for determining acceptable behavior is not required, regardless of how many others behave that way (Slobogin, 1998). One can accept that there are diverse ways of being moral without having to accept that all the different ways of acting are equally moral. To use an analogy, a person can accept that there are diverse ways of being psychologically healthy (i.e., different personalities that are equally well adjusted), without accepting that all psychological states are equally healthy (e.g., paranoid, histrionic, or narcissistic personalities).

Nor can one just observe the behavior of people who share the person's background because a code of morality or set of schemas does not produce the same behavior in different environments. What "is" is not necessarily what "ought to be." People may behave a particular way because they have found it to be one way to survive in their current environment, but it may not be how they would behave in a different environment. Therefore, assessment tools for values-based interventions must consider what people are doing as well as what they say they ought to do. For example, because Gloria acted one way in a poverty-stricken environment does not mean that that is how she would act if she and her relatives and friends had enough money for food, clothing, housing, and transportation.

Ultimately, then, as an interventionist, I must make judgments about the acceptability of behavior. However, as a professional embracing the philosophy of values-based services, I must look for the alternative and equally healthy, moral, group-referenced ways of behaving (Boone, 1991; Chambers, 1985). As I continue my attempts to solve the mysteries behind others' actions, I never forget the lessons we learned from Bobby: Look for medical explanations first. Look at old information in new ways. Look for broad patterns and themes in the person's life because nothing is irrelevant. Consider other meanings besides the negative ones that seem to occur to us first. Always listen to the observations and interpretations of the person's family, friends, and favorite direct support staff; their insights often come from intuition born of empathy and close association. Most important, respect the person's values, and frame the problem from his point of view.

POINTS TO REMEMBER

To reframe problem behavior from a person's point of view, we need to consider the following four alternatives to seeing the person's behavior as the problem:

1. *Assume that the meaning a person gives to his behavior is acceptable even though the behavior is not.* Interventions should be designed to change the medium, not the message. For example, the goal is to help John express sadness, anger, and fear through behaviors other than aggression and to help Ted respond to pain other than by pulling people's hair. Decreasing or eliminating fear, pain, or other emotions might also be indicated but should be pursued in addition to, not in place of, finding acceptable ways for the person to communicate his needs and feelings.

2. *Analyze behavior in terms of the values that motivate it.* After some of a person's values have been established, look at problem behaviors and ask whether they are motivated by those values. For example, finally discovering that Bobby ate beads when he had a headache was the result of asking how pica might be supporting his value of self-reliance.

3. *Establish whether parts of a person's schema are disordered or missing by comparing it with the same schema used by others who share the person's identity.* Design a behavior intervention to eliminate only the part of a schema that is disordered. An intervention should not undermine the parts that are normal. For example, Gloria's value of being nice to others is shared by other Lakota but not the interpretation that being nice means acquiescing to unwanted sex.

4. *Evaluate whether the environment is hindering or enabling the person to live by her own values.* The way in which a person is acting may not be the way she wants to act. For example, stealing and hiding food was not how Anna wanted to act; it was how she had to act to cope with an environment that limited her access to food.

Part III

VALUES-BASED
SERVICES IN CONTEXT

Most Americans know one or more schema of people with developmental disabilities—including behaviors expected of them, behaviors considered appropriate to show them, and propositions about their place in society—that override categories of ethnicity, class, age, gender, and other social identities of the person with developmental disabilities. These schemas create the environment in developmental disability services because they shape how service providers perceive service receivers and define how power is exercised. Understanding how these schemas function will enable service providers to change their services in order to empower people with developmental disabilities.

Chapter 7 critiques two ways that American schemas define personhood: by distinguishing humans from animals through their communication of values and by separating individuals from each other through privacy. In these schemas, people with developmental disabilities are treated as not having as much personhood as others, giving others the power to ignore their values and invade their privacy. Therefore, humanizing and personalizing services requires supporting each person's values of privacy and self-disclosure.

Chapter 8 describes the American schema of self-control, which allows people who are judged as having internalized the proper social norms to be independent. People with developmental disabilities, in this schema, are evaluated as in need of control because they are seen as unable to adequately internalize social norms. An alternate way to analyze control, through a schema of inequality, yields a different approach to services. Independence is empowered by matching service providers and service receivers based on their values of giving and receiving help.

Finally, Chapter 9 examines the most pervasive schema of all— how Americans in general view people with developmental disabilities because of an implicit value of intelligence. This schema devalues people with developmental disabilities and ensures their powerlessness. Understanding how subtly this schema is woven into American culture might aid service providers in changing it. The results of the analysis, however, are not encouraging; but they do re-emphasize the importance of supporting people with developmental disabilities to live by their own values.

Humanizing and Personalizing Services

"My name is not Patty. It's Dean. Call me Dean. I call you Anna. You call me Dean. Okay?"

Poor Dean. I could hear the irritation in his voice. He had been on the staff for several months and was going to be very good. He generally didn't get upset, but this was really getting under his skin.

We'd talked about Anna calling all staff "Patty," with no resolution. Dean argued that Anna had the skill to use his correct name and should be prompted to use it, just as he prompted her to use other skills she had. He assumed that if she was not using his name then it was because she hadn't learned it yet. I believed Anna addressed all staff as Patty, not because she didn't know their names but because she didn't care about them as individuals. They came and went in her life with terrible regularity. I calculated that, based on the number of years she'd spent in the service system and the average staffing ratios and turnover rates, she had been in contact with more than 300 staff during her lifetime. There was only one staff member whom Anna called by name.

She had been working with Anna for 7 years and had earned Anna's recognition.

In American culture, using personal names is one way that people create a sense of self as separate and different from others in society (Peacock & Holland, 1993). Unusual spellings, first names shared across generations of the family, a nickname, or a diminutive of a person's given name can be a significant part of his identity. Bobby's discomfort when he was called Robert and Dean's frustration at being called Patty stemmed from others' apparent disregard of their chosen identities.

Service providers can be hurt by not being recognized by the people they support. They want to be accepted as unique individuals and valued for their good points. Why, then, do some service providers not recognize when they are treating people with disabilities as "Pattys"? I heard a staff member say to another staff member one day, "Are you the only one here today?" There were 12 people in the room, but only one of them was a staff member. All the rest were just "Pattys," just clients, just people receiving services and supports; it doesn't matter what label is applied when it only refers to a category of people thought of as "nobodies," individuals who are socially nonexistent and completely powerless (Ortner, 1991, p. 188).

The service environment is not only shaped by the values of service providers and receivers, but it also is affected by the values encapsulated in American schemas about people with developmental disabilities. Many professionals providing services are noteworthy for their willingness to challenge their own dogmas and embrace change; they look for better ways to provide services, and they support better lives for people whom they genuinely care about, not just care for. Sometimes, though, service providers are blinded by the implicit negative values about people with disabilities that are just as much part of their world views as they are of other Americans. At those times, services can become dehumanizing and depersonalizing.

BEING A PERSON

The floor plan of the building in which I worked made it necessary for me to pass through the workshop to get from my office to the rest of the business office. It always bothered me to interrupt, so I tried to slip through as quietly as possible. After Ted got his glasses, however, he wouldn't let me pass unnoticed. Every morning on my first trip through the room, he would always call out a high-pitched "Whoooop!" I hypothesized that perhaps he was greeting me, so I responded by saying, "Hello," and shaking hands.

One morning he didn't see me enter, so I greeted him first. He made no response. I was startled; clearly my hypothesis was incorrect. On successive days, I alternated greeting first, not greeting, and greeting in response to his verbalization. I also observed his behavior with others as they entered the room. I finally had a new hypothesis. I think Ted was saying, "Notice me. I'm here. Don't ignore me." As each new person entered, if she greeted Ted or in some way recognized his presence, he was quiet. It was when a person entered the room for the first time that day and didn't acknowledge him that Ted would call out. Furthermore, if the person didn't respond to Ted by greeting him, her next passage through the room received a more agitated "Whoooop." Once each person had recognized his existence for that day, further passages through the room were ignored.

Ted had been labeled in his service records as alingual; however, when we started listening carefully, we were eventually able to establish that distinct sounds had exact meanings: "I have a headache," "I'm hungry," "I'm cold." My favorite was "Whoooop! I'm a person. Notice me."

Greeting Ted each morning before he had to remind me became part of my daily routine. I looked forward to it, in fact, because it reinforced my belief that every person has the right to be a somebody—not just a nobody. It surprised me a little, however, that I continued to feel a twinge of disappointment when Ted never responded to my greeting. I understood Dean's irritation at being called "Patty" and Ted's insistence on being recognized. Being treated as a nobody, not being recognized as a person, and not receiving a response made me feel invisible, worthless, and disconnected from society, too.

Defining Personhood

Every society defines who (i.e., certain, though not all human individuals) and what (e.g., ghosts, animals, mythical beings) will be considered a person (Harris, 1989) in schemas that "lend the object social significance and identity" (Nicolaisen, 1995, p. 48). Although Americans often assume that their definition of a person is universal (deCraemer, 1983), "personhood is self-generated, socially determined, . . . linguistically constructed" (Storl, 1995, p. 418) and varies cross-culturally

(Spiro, 1993). There are also common general themes (Harris, 1989) that allow social scientists and philosophers to develop theories that appear to be universal, although they are based on a Western schema of personhood (Mageo, 1995). The moral and legal precepts of previous times and other places are sometimes incorporated into current thought, further complicating the issue. For example, in Roman law, only a "person" had rights; however, women, children, slaves, individuals who were insane, and animals were not considered to be "persons" because they lacked "free will" (Wise, 1996), a view that still informs parts of contemporary American law.

All societies have schemas for distinguishing a person from non-human animals (humanization) and an individual person from other members of society (personalization) that exclude some individuals (Perring, 1997), thus denying them some or all their personhood. Therefore, "by looking closer at the symbolic forms through which personhood is both perceived and expressed . . . we may dig deeper into the conceptualizations that structure . . . [the] understanding of and reactions toward disability" (Nicolaisen, 1995, p. 48).

A Person as a Human, Not an Animal   Many Americans conceive a person as being clearly distinct from other animals; humans are believed to be the only animals with values, a view that expands on the concept of a person as an individual who freely chooses her own traits and values (see Chapter 3). In discussing human evolution, Cohen, a physical anthropologist, noted that "our moralizing capability is the truly human mode of adaptation. No other species transmits so much across generations by labeling behavior as 'right' or 'wrong' " (1981, p. 205). Some philosophers, following Kant, define humans by "virtue of their capacity for rational agency, rather than their animality" (Blustein, 1991, p. 214). For example, philosophers Drews and Lipson inquired about "qualities which make us human" and found that "as human beings, we are what we value" (1978, p. 1). Albers, a nurse, claimed that "the creation and manipulation of values on behalf of individual or group interests are intrinsic features of humanness" (1979, p. 577).

To classify another individual as a person in this schema, one individual must either assume that the other has values or be convinced of it when he talks about and acts in terms of them. Thus, the boundary between humans and other animals has been defined by some American writers as the use of language because, although other animals communicate, only humans communicate their values. People who cannot use language in common ways, because of dementia, deafness, mental retardation, autism, or damage to the vocal cords, are sometimes treated as less than human (Devereux, 1991). People with mental impairments, in particular, are treated as subhuman in this schema (Walmsley, 1993) because they are believed not to have values when they are unable to communicate them or not allowed to act in terms of them. For example, when Goode discussed the goals of children with Rubella syndrome, who were deaf, blind, and labeled as having profound mental retardation, with professional staff, he was told that "such children have no ideas or goals," a statement that he found "incredible and *dehumanizing*" (1994, p. 13 [emphasis added]).

This schema operates in other areas of American life, such as when an individual is described as acting like an animal because he appears to have no values (raping, fighting too violently) or when animal terms are applied to individuals (she's a dog, he's a pig) because their appearance or behavior does not meet the standards required by the observer's values (Leach, 1964). An individual in a coma, in technical terms labeled "a persistent *vegetative* state" and in lay language sometimes described as a *"vegetable,"* further removes an individual from being a person, or even an animal, because she is neither able to communicate his or her values nor act in terms of them (Mwaria, 1990).

A Person as a Self Separate From and Part of Society   Although this American schema of a person as having, communicating, and acting in terms of values distinguishes a person from nonhuman animals, it constructs the person in such individualistic terms that two problems are created. First, the individual must maintain an integrated self in many different situations and relationships that are inherently fragmentary (Dombeck, 1991; Ewing, 1990). A person accomplishes this by constructing a self-schema, a cohesive mental image of himself drawn from personal memories, emotions, values, and beliefs (Markus & Nurius, 1986) that are kept private, providing an integrated identity but further separating the self from others (Lane & Wegner, 1994). Second, if a person maintains too much privacy and individualization, then he runs the risk of becoming alienated from society as a nonperson (Blatt, 1990) because social acceptance and personhood are established by being recognized and affirmed by others (Murphy, 1987).

Therefore, each person must disclose parts of her private self-schema to create and maintain relationships (Storl, 1995). Strangers identify each other in terms of the visual markers that classify them as members of one or more social categories, allowing them to interact in terms of the expectations associated with those categories. Then, through mutual self-disclosure, people move beyond the accessible, public categories to specific information, personal experiences, and private feelings they have shared with each other about themselves, becoming valued "not merely for being a person but for being this person" (Gowans, 1996, p. 86).

If people never move beyond the public categories, then the relationships that they have are impersonal. However, if one person learns information about the other that he did not want known, the relationship can become depersonalizing because it strips away that which makes an individual a person. What no one has the right or authority to observe or know about another defines personal privacy, a *breach* of which is called an *invasion* of privacy. The loss of personal privacy leaves a person *defenseless*. The military metaphor is no accident, as depriving a person of his privacy is an aggressive act of power of one person over another.

Gerety developed a legal definition of privacy as "an autonomy or control over the intimacies of personal identity" (1977, p. 236). Simmel defined personal privacy as the "legitimate boundaries of the personality" (1968, p. 481). Two major U.S. Supreme Court decisions concerning privacy had to use arguments of natural law rather than citing precedents from other codes of law or from constitutional rights (Simmel, 1968) because privacy is so embedded in the American world view, so much a part of the American common-sense definition of what a person is, that no one even previously considered writing it into codes of law.

Authority (i.e., legitimate power) often carries with it the right of intrusion into private matters between "the stronger and more competent person" and the "weaker and less competent one" (Moore, 1984, p. 75), for example, between doctor and patient, parent and child, or supervisor and worker (Gerety, 1977). The more people have internalized relevant norms, the less need there is for supervision. Thus, older children and more trusted workers are allowed more privacy. Conversely, intrusion into one's own private matters by someone else carries with it the implication that one is less of a person than the other is (Perring, 1997). Secretiveness on the part of oppressed populations, such as street people using street names to keep their legal names private (Wolfensberger, 1989), is a way to combat the exercise of arbitrary power (Fahey, 1995) and frees them from unwanted social control (Lane & Wegner, 1994).

Privacy also personalizes relationships, distinguishing family from friends and friends from strangers. What only a few people have the right to know or observe about each other marks the boundaries of the intimacy of family or very close friends (Fried, 1980). Less self-disclosure is permitted (e.g., what parts of the body are exposed to touch or gaze, what thoughts and feelings are shared) for interactions among co-workers or acquaintances. Therefore, there is a balance between privacy and self-disclosure. If an individual maintains too much privacy, she will have no intimate relationships and no one will recognize or affirm her personhood. If she discloses too much, she risks becoming overly dependent and exposed to control and manipulation by others (Blatt, 1990).

Having a Disability and Being a Person

Monroe succinctly expressed the self-advocacy position that others should "see that these are people, not animals" (1996, p. 123). Bogdan and Taylor found in their research on relationships between people with and without disabilities that "the nondisabled view the disabled people as full-fledged human beings" by "attributing thinking to the other . . . seeing individuality in the other . . . viewing the other as reciprocating . . . [and] defining social place for the other" (1992, p. 284). In both discussions, the key point is that whether a person is seen as having a disability is in the eye of the beholder.

Disability is not a feature of an individual that is discovered by others (e.g., a stigmatizing trait) but is a process of disablement applied by one person to another (Helander, 1995). In other words, a person with an impairment only becomes a disabled individual when he is denied participation in the culturally defined processes of humanization and personalization (Ingstad & Whyte, 1995). To help people with developmental disabilities attain greater personhood and thereby become less disabled in others' eyes, service providers should humanize and personalize services by assisting people to communicate and enact their values and to balance privacy and disclosure.

HUMANIZING SERVICES

A rather spirited discussion I had one time with Glen, a community living coach, concerned whether there are basic values that all service providers must help people achieve. He argued that service providers must teach basic body care skills before teaching community inclusion skills because privacy is a basic value in society. Teaching bathing and toileting skills, cleanliness, and dressing skills is more important, according to Glen, than teaching a person to order pizza at a restaurant or select toiletries at the drug store. He argued that having bathing and toileting skills allows one to have privacy in life's more personal functions and to be less dependent on staff. Also, people would be stared at in the community or mistreated if they were not able to dress properly or appeared unkempt or unclean.

He made a persuasive argument, one I have heard in various forms in many in-services at other facilities. His contention—that privacy in personal care is a universal basic value and, therefore, body care skills must be taught before other skills—is supported and perpetuated by the continuing impact of the medical model of body care (Pelto & Schensul, 1987) and the compelling interest of the state to see that limited funds are used to teach skills that will decrease dependence on further funding (Bannerman, Sheldon, Sherman, & Harchik, 1991). Conferring great importance to body care skills may also be based on familiarity with the Maslow triangle. Maslow (1968) suggested that physical requirements of the human body are basic and provide a natural ordering of human values and motivations, a view criticized for reflecting middle-class values (Fox, 1982; Hofstede, 1980) and lacking support cross-culturally (Wahba & Bridwell, 1976). Privacy, although differently defined by various individuals, is central to the American schema of a person as a self separate from society.

However, assuming that people with disabilities have values, finding out what those values are, and then supporting them humanizes services. When service providers assume they already know which values are most important, they are dehumanizing people with disabilities. For example, Strully and Strully said that their daughter "can live without many things in her life (e.g., learning to feed herself, learning to use the bathroom independently), but she cannot live without friendships" (1993, p. 214). Service providers must find out whether a person places priority on privacy and independence in personal care, on friendship, or on some other value. It is also important to determine, not to assume, how each person defines privacy and independence. For one woman, having the autonomy to order her own pizza may be her definition of independence because then no one will make her food choices for her, whereas requiring assistance to use the bathroom does not decrease her autonomy. Maybe her definition of privacy revolves around protecting her thoughts and opinions, but not her body, from the scrutiny of others.

Different Definitions of Privacy

That people have different concepts of privacy, prioritize the value of privacy differently relative to other values, and interpret the same interaction very differently became clear to me when Margaret, Gloria, and Bobby returned from a People First meeting in another community. They were talking about a woman at the meeting who had told the group about being forced to go to work in her pajamas because she was not dressed when the bus came to transport her from the group home where she lived to the sheltered workshop where she worked. Margaret was horrified at the indecency of this situation. Wearing pajamas was something one only did in the privacy of one's bedroom. She even became upset at her own residence, at that time a group home, when people came out of their bedrooms in pajamas and bathrobes to watch television in the shared living room. Margaret was shaken by the idea that people had seen this poor woman in her pajamas in public.

Gloria was incensed at the injustice of it. They had no right to force her to get on the bus. They had no right to force her to wear pajamas. Whether it was all right to be in public in your pajamas was less important than whether it was all right for someone to make another person's decisions. It was terrible that they were making this woman do things she didn't want to do.

Bobby's reaction was more pragmatic. Just get on with your life. Do your work. Who cares what you're wearing? All the relevant parts are covered. His definition of body privacy was minimal. Yet, it made him angry if someone talked about him. His definition of privacy appeared to be focused on the privacy of ideas rather than on the privacy of body parts or the social appropriateness of types of clothing.

Although Anna had not attended this meeting, she also had a specific definition of privacy. In fact, we had struggled to understand it because, at first, she seemed to have no sense of privacy at all. She would walk stark naked from the bathroom to her bedroom or even go into the living room when others were present. No amount of prompting changed her behavior; we eventually realized that she simply did not define her housemates as strangers. They were members of her intimate circle and, to Anna, seeing each other unclothed was permissible. She would not expose herself similarly outside the group home and, in fact, was quite particular about her appearance in public. She simply defined who was an intimate friend and, thus, who could see her naked differently from how most staff did.

Anna also occasionally refused to take a bath, a choice we did not understand because she was usually fastidious. Eventually, we realized that she would allow only certain people to bathe her. If someone offered bathing assistance and she was not on this short list, then Anna refused to bathe. One of her medications came in suppository form and inserting it usually was a major battle until we discovered that Anna would allow one particular staff member, the only staff member Anna called by name, to perform this very private and intrusive task for her. Finally, it dawned on us that her definition of privacy had two significant features: being touched and who was doing the touching. We reframed her behavior from viewing it as resistance and refusal to seeing it as the enactment of her value on privacy; thereafter, only that particular staff member assisted Anna in these private activities.

This definition of privacy made sense of another story that circulated among staff about the time somebody had reached out and smoothed Anna's hair. Anna had said to the person, "Just pat me on the head like a dog." Some considered the story to be an example of Anna's notorious sense of humor. After we finally understood Anna's very specific definition of privacy as not being touched, it became clear that she felt dehumanized. She literally meant, "I'm human. Not a dog." She may have said it in a humorous tone because using "humor" to protest mistreatment is one way that powerless people fight back (Scott, 1990). After that, the story still circulated, but it now served as a warning for new staff not to intrude on Anna's privacy.

Anna might have learned her schema of privacy in the institution where she had lived as a young adult or during her childhood from her parents and others sharing her German/Dutch ethnicity and small-town background. Or, she might have created an entirely unique schema as an adaptation to how she had been touched and who had touched her over the years. It does not matter, however, where people have learned their schemas. Once they have learned them, violating their concepts, their definitions of decent and proper behavior, is a form of dehumanization. Treating them in ways not allowed in their schemas not only violates their sense of propriety and decency but also denies them the right to choose their own values, which, according to the American schema of personhood, all humans do.

Identifying Values

Humanizing services by identifying the values that each person has and supporting the communication and enactment of them is difficult when the person is unable to communicate or the values are very different from the service provider's values. In those cases, the service provider must take extra steps to identify the appropriate values (see Part II). However, for other people, the service provider might only need to ask them what they want rather than assume that values are obvious or shared. Figure 7.1 is an example of a residential assessment with questions not unlike many residential assessments already available. However, this particular assessment also seeks to answer whether the person being assessed likes or dislikes that particular situation or believes this information is too private to disclose. Knowing that a person has three roommates, for example, does not identify whether he thinks that is good, bad, or no one else's business. The assessor needs to use extreme care in eliciting this information because disclosing "emotions and feelings" is more intimate than disclosing "facts" and makes a person feel vulnerable (Laurenceau & Barrett, 1998, p. 1239).

There is also a column in the assessment for checking whether the person wants to change the situation. Just because a person dislikes a situation does not necessarily mean he wants to change it. A person may choose to keep a job that he does not like because it pays well. However, a person may like a situation and still want to change it. For example, a person with three roommates may enjoy living with them but still want to try some other living arrangement. Finally, the person may not care one way or the other about the situation being considered.

Any assessment can easily be modified to include the assessed person's values and choices simply by adding these two additional types of information, one column for "like/dislike/too private" and a second column for "want to change/keep the same/do not care," although this should not be the only way that people's values and choices are incorporated into services. It is merely a first step in taking others' values into account rather than assuming certain values are obvious, basic, or universal.

PERSONALIZING SERVICES

"Remember when you used to say 'I might goof up'?"

That was my opening line to Margaret in a ritualized replay of an event we shared. She answered as she always does when we reconstruct this moment together.

Residential Assessment

Residential assessment by _____ Date _____

If someone helps you answer these questions, ask him or her to sign here:

_____

Signature   Title   Date

After filling in the answers and checking whether you like, dislike, or think the answer is too private to share, go back and check whether you want to change that situation, keep it the same, or do not care.

	Like	Dislike	Too private to share	Want to change	Keep the same	Do not care
1. How many people sleep in your room? _____	—	—	—	—	—	—
2. How many people live in your house? _____	—	—	—	—	—	—
3. Who chose the things in your bedroom? _____	—	—	—	—	—	—
4. Who chose the things in your living room? _____	—	—	—	—	—	—
5. Do you own your own furniture? _____	—	—	—	—	—	—
6. Do you have a key to your house? _____	—	—	—	—	—	—
7. Can you lock up your own things? _____	—	—	—	—	—	—
8. Are there places in your house that are locked so you can't get into them? _____	—	—	—	—	—	—
9. Do you have privacy in the bathroom? _____	—	—	—	—	—	—

(continued)

Your Values, My Values, Pengra, ©2000 Paul H. Brookes Publishing Co.

Figure 7.1.   Residential assessment.

Figure 7.1. (continued)

	Like	Dislike	Too private to share	Want to change	Keep the same	Do not care
10. Can you lock your bedroom door?	—	—	—	—	—	—
11. Is your home noisy?	—	—	—	—	—	—
12. Is your home quiet?	—	—	—	—	—	—
13. Can you make your place warmer or cooler yourself?	—	—	—	—	—	—
14. Do you decide when you go to bed and when you get up?	—	—	—	—	—	—
15. Do you decide what you want to eat for each meal?	—	—	—	—	—	—
16. Do you buy your own groceries?	—	—	—	—	—	—
17. Who makes your doctor appointments?	—	—	—	—	—	—
18. Who is your doctor?	—	—	—	—	—	—
19. Do you get help with your medications?	—	—	—	—	—	—
20. Do you choose what you want to wear each day?	—	—	—	—	—	—
21. Do you buy your own clothes?	—	—	—	—	—	—
22. Do you choose when you want to take a bath or shower?	—	—	—	—	—	—
23. Do you go to church?	—	—	—	—	—	—

(continued)

Figure 7.1. (*continued*)

	Like	Dislike	Too private to share	Want to change	Keep the same	Do not care
24. How often do you have friends over to visit you?	—	—	—	—	—	—
25. How often do you get invited to other places?	—	—	—	—	—	—
26. How often do you go to the movies?	—	—	—	—	—	—
27. How often do you go to concerts?	—	—	—	—	—	—
28. How often do you go to sporting events or play games?	—	—	—	—	—	—
29. Do you know your neighbors?	—	—	—	—	—	—
30. If staff live with you, do they eat with you?	—	—	—	—	—	—
31. If there are staff at your home, do they talk to you about things other than meals, baths, and programs?	—	—	—	—	—	—
32. Do you have pets?	—	—	—	—	—	—
33. Are there people living with you who scare you?	—	—	—	—	—	—
34. Is there a person in your life who loves you?	—	—	—	—	—	—
35. Is there a person you love?	—	—	—	—	—	—

"Now I say, 'I'm proud of me, too.' "

She'd only actually said it once but it had been one of those memorable events that would tie us together forever. I had been in the habit of complimenting Margaret's successes by saying to her, "I don't know how you feel, but I'm proud of you." At first she would not answer at all. Then she would respond with a flippant, "If you say so" or just "Yeah, yeah." But, one time before I could say anything, she looked me right in the eye and said, "I'm proud of me, too." Then, for some inexplicable reason we'd both laughed. It stands out in my memory as a joyous moment.

My comment and her rejoinder were part of our routine for remembering together a day that had been a turning point for Margaret in her journey to self-assurance and an interaction that had taken us one step further along the road to friendship. Sharing personal stories with each other is part of moving a relationship from a public and impersonal one to a more private and personal one (Lutfiyya, 1991; Wells, 1993) because stories are told to "maintain respect and to establish relationships" (Miller, Potts, Fung, Hoogstra, & Mintz, 1990, p. 293).

Friendship

Personalizing services requires moving beyond the impersonal, observer-defined categories of "person with a developmental disability" or "overweight, young, middle-class white woman" by finding out the self-schema and values of a particular person, but doing so in a way that does not then become depersonalizing. What kind of information is shared, when in the development of a relationship it is shared, who controls the disclosure, and whether mutual types of information are shared is part of how relationships are defined in America (Pedersen, 1982). Yet, many tasks required of service providers deal with parts of the body or types of information that are considered by some to be too private to expose. For example, Kennedy wrote about this issue using a metaphor of blankets:

> In your home, you choose when and how often you want to use your blankets . . . if you're a person with a disability, it's like the service system already has the blanket set out for you. . . .I'd like to give you some examples of how it feels under the disability blanket. First, your privacy is invaded. The service system requires that each person's goals are clearly spelled out in writing. . . . I set personal goals for myself. . . . But the goals I have are in my head and my heart, not on paper where everyone can see them. (1994, pp. 74–75)

When service providers learn private things about service receivers without responding in kind, it is a power relationship, where a more powerful person has invaded the privacy of less powerful people and potentially can then "manipulate them all the more successfully" (Taussig, 1980, p. 12). One way to guard against increasing the power differential between service providers and receivers is for them to get to know each other well enough to respect each other (Johnson et al., 1995) and become friends (Lutfiyya, 1993). Friendship, for most Americans, involves crossing from the public sphere into the private sphere (Williams & Asher, 1992) by mutual self-disclosure of life stories (Blustein, 1991).

Life Stories   Stories of personal experience, such as the moment Margaret and I shared, are woven together into a life story (Linde, 1987). The life story is neither historical nor autobiographical (Reis, 1994) but is part of a person's self-schema, a narrative about his or her experiences, including interpretations and evaluations constructed within the matrix of what is culturally meaningful (Cohler, 1992). In fact, "every adult is entitled to and indeed required to have a life story" (Linde, 1987, p. 345) because it conveys what others must know to understand the person whose story it is and so "we can be loved for who we *really* are" (Rubin, 1983, p. 68 [emphasis in original]). A life story enables a person with a disability or incapacitating illness to be seen "as a unique person with a past as well as a present, a person defined by his life instead of his illness" or disability (Rybarczyk & Bellg, 1997, p. 2).

When I started learning the stories of the people with whom I worked, then sharing parts of my life story with them, and finally creating shared stories together, I passed from having a job to having friends I cared about. I knew exactly how Sacks, a counselor, felt when he described his relationship with his client Rebecca, who had physical and developmental disabilities, as moving from initially seeing her as clumsy, then as having grace, especially when she danced. He said that as he continued to get to know her, not just as a client but as a person, "she seemed to deepen. Or perhaps she revealed, or I came to respect, her depths more and more" (Sacks, 1987, p. 182).

Control of Information

Some people might argue that service providers should have a professional relationship with the people they assist and not a personal friendship. Professionals are routinely cautioned about getting too involved with people they support because emotional attachment might decrease their effectiveness as problem solvers or make them less objective in offering advice. It might be acceptable to be a friendly professional but not a professional friend (Gaventa, 1993). The meaning of a professional relationship has become synonymous with an impersonal one. But really, all that means is that the professional does not know enough about the other person, especially her values, to see things from her point of view and to consider her opinions as valid. A parallel with the medical field is the depersonalization that develops during a medical exam, when private pieces of information shared by the patient are considered unimportant by the physician (Romanucci-Ross, Moerman, & Tancredi, 1983). The patient is powerless, and his opinions are irrelevant. He is only a thing to be worked on, not a person to be listened to.

Friendship, however, cannot be dictated, although it should be encouraged by policy and supported when it does develop (Amado, 1993). In the meantime, services can be personalized by granting control of information disclosure to the service receiver.

Telling Life Stories   Assisting people in telling or writing their life stories or telling other people's stories on their behalf if necessary is one way that service providers can personalize services. This is what happens when, for example, a teacher helps students to view a classmate with a disability in a positive light by interpreting his behavior to them (Ferguson, Meyer, Jeanchild, Juniper, & Zingo, 1992) or when a job coach prepares a place in the work environment for the supported person by telling the new co-workers about the person's interests and capabilities (Rogan, Hagner, & Murphy, 1993). It is necessary to go further, however, than to simply say, "he likes to fish"; a person's life story should be told as he might tell it—by showing his tenacity (he fished until dark), humor (he decided the fish deserved to eat more than worms), fastidiousness (he washed his hands three times after cleaning his first fish), or kindness (he threw back his second fish so it could live). It is not the fact that the individual likes fishing that is important; it is what the story about him catching his first fish tells people about him as a person.

When parents, advocates, friends, and service providers tell stories to each other about people they support and when they tell stories for people on their behalf, there should be three guiding principles. First, stories about people should only be told on their behalf, with their permission, and if they are unable to tell them for themselves. Most people can tell their own stories. In fact, probably more people are capable of doing this than service providers are willing to admit because the stories often are uncomfortable to hear (Bersani, 1996). Second, the stories that are told should not be selected by the service provider's "need to know" but should be determined in terms of the person's "need to tell," that is, in terms of her definitions of privacy and intimacy and what she would choose to tell to create friendship or service continuity. Third, when stories are told, that person's values must be explicitly and carefully incorporated. For example, telling about Anna saying, "Just pat me on the head like a dog," was demeaning until it was told from Anna's point of view, with her values shaping the moral of the story.

Daily Logs and Traveling Notebooks   Some service providers communicate by means of written messages in a daily log or notebook that travels between group home and workplace or between family and school (DeVault, Krug, & Fake, 1996). This practice should be reshaped to give control of what information is selected and to whom it is disclosed to the person whose actions are being reported. Rather than writing about the person, staff can help him rehearse what he is going to tell others about his day or, if communication assistance is needed, a tape recorder that plays a 60-second loop message can be used to record a message from his point of view. He then can control who hears the message by playing it for his teacher, job coach, parent, or friend, just as one person might tell a co-worker about the great party he went to last weekend or another might tell her husband about her rotten day at work, complete with anecdotes about what happened. Some of those anecdotes eventually become part of the person's permanent life story that explains who he is and creates him as a person in others' eyes.

Social Histories   Instead of the usual way of documenting a social history, by relating the "facts" of a person's life as seen through the eyes of professionals over the years, service providers should record the person's life story. It should be told by the person whose story it is or, for people who are not able to tell their own stories, there could be a special team member responsible for telling their stories for them. The local library is a good resource for finding people in the community who are professional or amateur storytellers and who might volunteer to assist in developing the person's life story.

Dybwad and Bersani (1996) suggested that having new staff read life stories told by advocates in People First groups is a powerful way to shape their attitudes. It is also effective to have new staff read or hear the life stories of people with whom they will be working, rather than reading social histories and research "that keeps people seeing us as statistics and objects" (Ward, 1996, p. 122); this helps to establish the tone of their relationships as personal. It also, in my experience, results in new staff more quickly recognizing the unique needs of each person and helps them shape their responses to fit that person's values.

Incident Reports   Incident reports are perhaps the most depersonalizing tool required in services to people with developmental disabilities. Not only is control of information a form of power, but, also, incident reports are one more way service providers communicate with each other about service receivers without including them in the discussion and without taking their schemas of privacy into account. Incident reporting systems should be, according to Ray (1995), consumer centered by respecting consumers' accounts of the incident, notifying parents/guardians quickly, and including the consumer in reviews of incident reports.

When it became policy at the agency where I worked for incident reports to be read to the person described in the report rather than just to the person's legal representative and the reports were read immediately rather than during the annual review, there was a change in how staff members wrote reports. Staff members no longer reported something about a person behind her back. Rather, the person involved in the report had a chance to offer her description of the incident and to respond to the staff member's account. Some staff voiced concern initially that this would make it difficult for them to tell the truth about what they observed. In actual practice, the new policy appeared to encourage more focus on what was observed and eliminated most comments that were opinions, especially negative ones. In essence, it created a balance of power between the staff member writing the report and the person about whom the report was written. Staff might be reporting private things about people, but the people involved, including those who could not respond verbally with their side of the story but who could by their behavior show whether they agreed, now also knew what the staff person thought and said. For most staff, the change turned out to be very positive. Personalizing the incident reports, changing them from a report *about* a person to a report *prepared with* the person, also shifted the focus of the reports from causes to reasons, a shift that takes the person's values into account.

Team Meetings   Team meetings are particularly depersonalizing when the discussions at the meeting involve information that is considered to be private by the person receiving services or that is only appropriate for some, but not all, of the people at the meeting to hear. Margaret, for example, believed that her privacy was invaded when all the people on her team knew about her finances. She wanted only one staff member to assist her with her money. At her team meeting, when it came time to discuss her finances, her definition of privacy required all team members to leave the meeting except the one person whom she had chosen to assist her. Their plan was written and put in her master file to meet legal requirements, but it was in a sealed envelope, labeled with the message "To be opened only with the permission of Margaret Smith."

Figure 7.2 is an example of an evaluation of privacy issues associated with a team meeting. Carefully reviewing the person's responses will assist the service provider in designing a process for that specific person that more closely follows his schema of privacy. Just because Margaret wanted her financial information to be shared with only one other person and to be stored in a sealed envelope does not mean that every person receiving services must have her financial plans handled in this manner. Doing so is just as depersonalizing as automatically sharing everyone's financial plans with the whole team.

Supporting Personhood

"Who's your grandmother?"

Hearing this question, directed to Gloria by a Lakota woman we had just met at an Indian–White reconciliation event, made me realize once again how cultural differences show up in subtle ways. Personhood in Lakota culture is group centered, not defined in individualistic terms (see Chapter 6). How Gloria was connected in the pattern of kinship relations among group members was far more significant than where she was currently living or working, information that a middleclass white American would consider important in getting to know someone (Dussart, 1993). Her mental ability was not a feature to be noted; it was background noise for the Lakota woman.

Knowing how she is connected to other group members does not affect how I see Gloria because I do not have a group-centered schema of personhood. Probably, my very careful support of her privacy is not as important to her sense of self as it is to my perception of her personhood. Learning more about Gloria's schemas increased my respect for her, just as understanding Anna's schema of privacy helped me see her

Evaluation of Privacy of Team Meetings

Privacy evaluation by: _____ Date: _____

If someone helps you answer these questions, ask him or her to sign here:

_____ _____ _____

Signature   Title   Date

Place of Meeting

1. Where was your meeting held? _____

2. Could other people who were not at the meeting see or hear what was going on? If so, did this bother you? _____

   _____

3. Do you want to hold your team meeting at a different place next time?

   _____

People at Meeting

4. Did you choose the people you wanted to invite to your meeting?

   _____

5. Were there people at your meeting you did not want there? If so, who?

   _____

6. List each person at the meeting and say whether you want that person at the next meeting and, if you do, for the whole meeting or for only a part of the meeting. _____

   _____

   _____

   _____

Topics Discussed at Meeting

7. Were there things talked about at the meeting that were too private to talk about in front of everyone? _____

   _____

8. If so, what was talked about and who should not have heard about that?

   _____

(continued)

Your Values, My Values, Pengra, ©2000 Paul H. Brookes Publishing Co.

Figure 7.2.   Evaluation of privacy of team meetings.

Figure 7.2.   (*continued*)

9.   How should this be talked about at your next team meeting?

_____

10. Were there things you wanted in your plan that never were talked about? If so, what were they?   _____

_____

Information Reviewed at Meeting

11. Did you look at all your paperwork (assessments, last year's plan, monitoring notes, etc.) with a person of your choice before your meeting?

_____

12. Were the things written about you true? If not, what things were not true?

_____

_____

13. Were the things written about you too private to tell everyone? If so, what did you want to be kept private? (You do not have to tell them again if you do not want to.)   _____

_____

_____

14. Were things you wanted people on your team to know about you left out? If yes, what things were left out?   _____

_____

_____

15. If you wanted to use a tape recorder, video, or person to help you talk at your meeting, did this get done?   _____

_____

Feelings at Meeting

16. Did you get upset at the meeting? If yes, did it bother you that other people knew you were upset?   _____

_____

_____

17. Did someone else get upset or angry at the meeting? If yes, did this bother you? _____

_____

(*continued*)

Figure 7.2. (*continued*)

18. Did you feel that you could stop the meeting and go somewhere private? If not, what do you want to do at your next team meeting if you feel upset?

_____

_____

Questions

19. Did you have questions you did not want to ask in front of all the people at the meeting? If so, did you get to ask them in private to a person of your choice during the meeting? _____

_____

20. Did you get a copy of your plan or have it read and explained to you by a person you trust? _____

_____

21. Do you want more help now or help from a different person to understand your plan now? _____

_____

Actions Needed

22. Is there anything you want blacked out of the plan before it is given to staff who work with you? If so, what is too private to tell everyone?

_____

_____

23. Is there anything you want to change about your plan? If so, we can have another meeting right away if you need to talk more about the plan.

_____

_____

24. If there are decisions you do not agree with or things that are too private that still are being shared, would you like help filing a grievance? If so, who would you like to help you? _____

_____

_____

_____

in a different light. I am still making implicit judgments based on my own schema of personhood. I respect both Gloria and Anna more because I now have more individualized knowledge of each of them.

Understanding other ways of defining and supporting personhood helps me to see how my concept of personhood actually creates disability. Even though I try to affirm more individuals as somebodies rather than nobodies and encourage other Americans to push the boundaries of their schemas, too, I do so without rejecting the idea that choice of values and control of self-disclosure is the basis of personhood. In accepting that these actions define personhood, I have also accepted that their absence is disabling.

Therefore, extraordinary care must be taken to guard against all the casual, unthinking acts that dehumanize and depersonalize people. When I ignore a person's existence by not greeting him upon entering the room where he is working, invade a person's privacy by touching her, use language that excludes some people, or disclose others' personal goals or finances to the whole team because agency policy requires it, my actions have created disability. Only by changing my actions can I hope to remove the "disability blanket."

POINTS TO REMEMBER

To support personhood for each person, we need to use the following four approaches:

1. *Revise every assessment tool to include the person's values and an option not to respond if the issue is too private.* Humanizing services means supporting each person's values, including that person's definition and prioritization of privacy as a value. For example, the staff member Anna recognized by name was the only one assigned to assist her with bathing and medications. A similar adjustment was not made for Bobby who did not prioritize body privacy, but care was taken to support his value on autonomy and privacy of his ideas.

2. *Evaluate every activity and procedure that includes the disclosure of information to ensure that it meets the person's "need to share" rather than what service providers believe that they "need to know."* Personalizing services means supporting each person's definition of a proper balance between privacy and self-disclosure. For example, Margaret wanted to disclose her financial informa-

tion to one person, not to the whole team, so that she could have private assistance.

3. *Assist people in telling their life stories and disclosing them in appropriate ways to build relationships with friends, co-workers, staff, and others.* Life stories should be told to help others understand that person's values. For example, it is not the activity of fishing that helps others respect a person who likes to fish, but what his fishing stories tell them about him as a person. Encourage others to reciprocate by sharing their life stories with that person because equal self-disclosure leads to friendship and unequal self-disclosure is depersonalizing.

4. *Affirm each person as a unique human by recognizing her as a somebody, not just a nobody to be cared for but not listened to.* Disability is in the eye of the beholder. Seeing people as unique humans with their own values requires supporting those processes that create personhood in our own value systems. For example, acknowledging Ted by greeting him or acknowledging Margaret by sharing a memory of an important moment with her helps me to see them, not their impairments.

Independence

"Not my boss. Not my boss. Not my boss."

With each repetition of his phrase of protest, John punched the nearest object with his doubled fist, then paced to the other side of my office and hit the wall with forearms, forehead, and fists, pushing off to repeat the cycle. I'd been the director for less than a week and had already heard about John. He attacked staff or lost his temper three or four times per day and had been kicked out of several previous placements because of violence.

John was a good-looking young man, although that day his hair was long and unkempt and his clothes dirty and torn. He had small, round scars in rows along his forearms from self-inflicted injuries. As he hit my desk, I was most aware, however, of the sinewy strength of his arms. His rage was so intense that I didn't know if I could or should interrupt him. Then, with a final crash and thump, John left my office.

When I arrived at the group home to determine what had initiated John's anger, Glen was furiously writing an incident report. I asked him what had happened.

"All I did was remind him to take a shower."

I was the new kid on the block and didn't really know what a hornet's nest I was hitting when I continued to question him.

"Why? He'll take a shower when he's ready to."

I am not sure which scared me more—John shouting, "Not my boss," or Glen's stinging attack of my naive view of the role and responsibilities of a caregiver. I had been hired to salvage a financially unstable agency that had failed to meet accreditation standards. To prepare for my new job, I read several books (among them, Evans & Meyer, 1985; Rusch, 1986; and Taylor, Biklen, & Knoll, 1987), all of which stressed the rights of people with developmental disabilities, including the right to make their own decisions. Because this philosophy matched my own, I blindly forged ahead, not yet realizing Glen's predicament, caught as he was between wanting to help John realize his dreams and being charged with the responsibility of getting John to be clean and nonviolent. I hardly listened to Glen's explanation that he was just reminding John to shower "for his own good" because community acceptance depended on John's behaving in normal ways. Instead, I cut him short with the only words that made sense to me:

"You're not his boss."

Within a few weeks, I was acting case manager as well as director. John, his team, and I were gathered for my first experience with a team meeting. I wasn't surprised when John started the meeting with his constantly offered assertion, "Not my boss"; but he was startled by my response.

"You're right. I'm not your boss. You are your own boss. You tell us what you want to do."

I don't remember the course of the conversation at that team meeting, but I remember clearly that it was Glen who knew that John wanted to live in his own apartment. Moving to an apartment had been delayed because John was "out of control." Past teams had decided that he needed to control his temper and improve his appearance before being allowed to live more independently.

After that meeting, John moved to his own apartment, and his aggressive episodes immediately dropped to one per week. He also didn't take a shower for the first 4 months. Choosing not to shower, the team hypothesized, was a test to determine who had the power to control his actions and was neither a skill deficit nor a reflection of his values on cleanliness or social acceptance. Therefore, another part of the plan for supporting John's independence was the team's decision to stop trying to get him to shower regularly and to focus instead on helping him to understand the consequences of his decisions. When people didn't want to sit next to John at work, staff would calmly say to John that it was because he smelled but that it was his choice whether to take a shower. There were, however, many debates at staff meetings about how long we should wait for him to choose to take a shower.

Some staff members argued that he ought to be encouraged to shower because it was unhealthy to be that dirty and people in the community would shun him. If positive reinforcement didn't bring about the needed results, then John ought to be placed on a behavior intervention program to ensure that he bathed on a more regular basis. We needed to step in at some point because he'd made an unacceptable choice, one that would cause him to fail in his attempt to live more independently.

Others recognized that, for John, daily showering was a symbol of staff control. If he was ever to believe that his relationship with staff had changed, they reasoned, then we were going to have to wait him out on this issue. Not only would forcing him to shower prove to him that, ultimately, staff really did have control, but it would also demonstrate that eventually he would be saved from the consequences of his decisions. They argued that not showering was not as dangerous or as unhealthy as refusing to take his seizure medication or peeling skin off his arms, two other regularly occurring actions that appeared to be responses to his lack of independence.

Usually, it is only if some plan works and therefore justifies our strategies that we begin to say we made the right decision. Even then, other plans might also have increased the regularity of John's showering and decreased his violence but have achieved those results using unacceptable methods, such as aversives or time out. Using immediate positive reinforcement might be more acceptable to many professionals and might have more quickly increased how often John showered. Our task, however, was not only to encourage John to shower but also to help him address the deeper question of who controlled his life.

INTERPRETING CONTROL

Professionals analyze the behavior of people with developmental disabilities within the framework provided by schemas available in their culture to interpret human actions (Ford, Mongon, & Whelan, 1982). One American schema is that mature adults choose socially appropriate behavior by exercising self-control (Feldman, 1997). An alternate view is that people are controlled by others because of an unequal distribution of power in American society (Urbinati, 1998). Each schema suggests different behavioral analyses and interventions.

An American Schema of Self-Control

Most Americans view society as curtailing personal autonomy through social controls (Paul, 1990). Some people believe that chaos, violence, and anarchy would ensue without those controls (Rosaldo, 1989). According to one American schema, harmonious social life is possible because individuals exercise self-control and become responsible, yet independent, members of society (Errington, 1987) who are able to choose mature and moral actions because they have internalized proper ways of behaving (Chong, 1996). This belief leads to the proposition that individuals who are either mentally ill or too young to have learned self-control are dependent on control provided by others (Hsu, 1975), with dependency (Stiver, 1991a) and lack of self-control (Brannigan, 1997) being evaluated negatively. Gaines claimed that this self-control schema structured the classifications in the *Diagnostic and Statistical Manual of Mental Disorders* (DSM) published by the American Psychiatric Association because his analysis of the first four editions of the DSM showed them to be "culturally meaningful etiologies that explain the absence of 'self control' " (1992, p. 3).

Another belief in this schema is that people with developmental disabilities are unable to learn self-control, leading some Americans to fear that if people with developmental disabilities are not governed by others, then they are not governed at all (Mackelprang & Salsgiver, 1996). Professionals are not immune to seeing people with developmental disabilities through the self-control schema. For example, in their research on self-injury, aggression, and functional communication, Bird, Dores, Moniz, and Robinson found that when people were given control of taking breaks from work, they continued to work most of the time, although the researchers suggested that it was "reasonable to be concerned that" people would "take advantage of that control and avoid work all of the time" (1989, p. 46). Some of the people working with Margaret identified her unwillingness to make decisions as an inability to exercise self-control. Even a simple action, such as Bobby's using 10 teaspoons of creamer in a cup of coffee, was sometimes seen as evidence of his needing control rather than as his love of creamer. Describing John as "out of control" was probably an unintended double entendre meaning both that he was perceived as having no self-control and that he had escaped the control of others by intimidating them through aggression.

In this schema, conforming to prescribed social norms (i.e., normalization) is evidence of self-control, maturity, and mental health. However, nonconforming behavior is rated as immature or abnormal and is used as evidence of the absence of self-control. This interrelated cluster of beliefs and values accounts for Glen's equating normalization and normal behavior. Causes of problem behavior, as well as solutions (Furnham & Hayward, 1997), are firmly located within the individual. Using this schema led John's earlier team to suggest that the solution to John's problem of aggression was for him to learn self-control.

An Alternative Interpretation of Control

Another American schema provides an alternative analysis of control as the unequal distribution of power in society. In this perspective, the power to control certain categories of people, such as women, children, African Americans, and the working class, is an unearned privilege conferred by cultural beliefs and values on other categories of people, that is, on men, adults, whites, and the middle class, respectively (Bourdieu, 1991; Lacombe, 1996; Urbinati, 1998). Because social order ensures the rights of some people at the expense of others (Scott, 1990), protesting social inequalities is synonymous with disorder (Sangren, 1995), and accepting the social order means acquiescing to one's own oppression, although people do not necessarily recognize that they have done so because they have been "subtly indoctrinated" through normalization (Nader et al., 1997, p. 717).

Lutz (1988, 1990) used this schema of inequality to analyze how the self-control schema subjugates certain categories of people by defining a mature adult as a rational and emotionally self-controlled person. When women and the working class protest their powerlessness, they are often dismissed as being overly emotional. Other groups that have been stereotyped as being very emotionally expressive are African Americans, Latinos, and people with developmental disabilities. According to Lutz's argument, these characterizations are not a reflection of their actual emotional state but a consequence of their powerlessness. "Control yourself" really means "Don't try to change the status quo of power relations."

Reason and emotion are defined in the inequality schema as opposites (thinking versus feeling). Because other meanings of reason link it to qualities attributed to intelligence (e.g., reasonable, logical, rational), a presumed increase in emotionality is linked to a presumed decrease in intelligence (Levy, 1984). People who protest their powerlessness are therefore not only emotional but also unreasonable, illogical, irrational, and unintelligent. Pejorative epithets ("dumb broad") and negative stereotypes (e.g., Polish jokes) further justify the power of the controlling group because only they have the rationality and intelligence to direct, for "their own good" and in "their own best interests" the actions of those characterized as less endowed (Edelman, 1974).

Most emotions, with the exception of anger, are disapproved of in men and expected of women and powerless groups (Lutz, 1990). Men are allowed to be angry because their anger is a "moral emotion" (Middleton, 1989), which is the consequence of an offensive or frustrating event or situation (Solomon, 1984). Bosses, ministers, army generals, and husbands are justified in becoming angry when reacting to another person's contravention of the standards or disobedience to the rules (Miller & Sperry, 1987). It is assumed by those in power that there is only one set of standards and rules and that the groups to which they are applied accept and agree with them (Goodenough, 1997). Women and powerless groups are not supposed to be offended or frustrated by the protection provided for them by those in power. Thus, their anger, which often is demonstrated in exaggerated form when finally expressed, is classified as aggression (Miller, 1991).

Challenging the Schema of Self-Control

During a discussion of problem behavior, an in-service participant once asked me what to do about a woman he was working with who cut up all her clothes. I asked him why the woman was angry, assuming that acts of property destruction usually are acts of anger.

"She doesn't want to live in a group home."

I was not surprised that he understood the woman's reason for her action, just as Glen had known that John's refusal to shower was related to his lack of independence. I asked him what the woman had learned, hoping to lead him into seeing this woman's actions as a protest of her powerlessness rather than as a failure in self-control.

"She learned that if she cuts up her clothes, she won't have any clothes and it will cost her a lot of money to buy more because she had to pay for new clothes."

Well, yes, she would learn that, if she didn't already know it. She also learned, however, that she has no control over where she lives *and* is punished for even being angry about it.

Service providers in the field of developmental disabilities often say, "She is aggressive" rather than "She is angry" or, even, "I made her angry." There is recognition that violent actions may be a way to control situations or demands made by others; however, the actions are identified as aggression and categorized as unacceptable behavior resulting from the lack of self-control, not as a political protest about the oppression of inequality. Using a self-control schema rather than an inequality schema leads to solutions geared toward changing the person's behavior rather than supporting her right to protest her powerlessness. As Trent pointed out about mental retardation, "by restricting the gaze to the person with 'it,' issues of the maldistribution of resources, status, and power . . . remain muted" (1994, p. 274). When John's new team changed their focus from self-control to inequality, they were able to plan an intervention that decreased his anger because it addressed the imbalance of power in his relationships with staff.

People usually are not conscious of the system of inequality that created their powerlessness (Linger, 1993) and, consequently, direct their anger inward through depression and self-hatred (Miller, 1991) or outward at the perpetrators of oppression (Pickett, 1996). From the point of view of the disenfranchised, whether they are women, African Americans, people living in poverty, or people with developmental disabilities, the only way they can assert their power and demonstrate their independence is by acting in ways contrary to the ways in which those in control want them to act. Therefore, the inequality schema leads to behavioral analysis that is focused on the person's environment, including relationships with others and their beliefs and values.

CONTROLLING RELATIONSHIPS

"You can either buy the camera or pay for your ride home to see your family. You can choose one. You don't have enough money to do both."

Gloria's community living coach, Donna, was unhappy with providing the financial supports the team had designed for Gloria;

nonetheless, she conscientiously balanced Gloria's checkbook and doled out money in carefully controlled amounts after Gloria chose one of the limited options offered to her each day.

The team had decided that this control was necessary to protect Gloria while she learned about monetary amounts. She could not yet determine whether $10 was more or less than $100 nor could she recognize bill denominations. Even having her carry all her money in $1 bills hadn't helped. There was some suspicion that Gloria had been shortchanged more than once by clerks who knew she couldn't tell a $10 bill from a $1 bill.

At least there had been a discussion as to whether to allow Gloria to control her money, and there was a plan in place to teach Gloria the necessary skills to decrease the control others had. At the time I was convinced that this plan was better than the thoughtless control I had observed applied by some providers in their interactions with the people they were assisting.

Random Acts of Control

Many acts of control are automatic and out of awareness. For example, I once heard a staff member explain different options to one young man to help him make a choice. The staff member's voice was light, cheerful, and quick when explaining some options but low, slow, and dark when describing others. It was fairly obvious which options the staff member thought were acceptable. In this same vein, Smull cautioned that service providers need to learn "when encouragement stops and coercion begins" (1995, p. 5).

Control is also maintained by what service providers choose to comment on and to ignore and in how to define problems (Charonko, 1992; Jenkinson, 1993). Powell and Andersen (1994) described the ways in which teachers in classrooms control student behavior by using pseudoquestions, such as "Is that where you're supposed to put that book?" A study by Kuder and Bryen (1993) showed that the highest percentage of comments by service providers to people with developmental disabilities were control statements rather than instructions, social comments, or idiosyncratic small talk. "Eat your vegetables or no dessert" is not stating a natural consequence but is saying, "Do what I want you to do" (Sidman & Ishaq, 1991, p. 61).

An environment of control is created when service providers set the tone, define the rules, and resist having their actions determined by the people they serve. When staff members assume the role of negotiator in disputes among people who share group homes or work together, then they are in control (Levy, Levy, & Samowitz, 1994). One person I knew was regularly transferred from her wheelchair to a stationary chair because it would be "more comfortable for her" rather than because she went places in her wheelchair that staff did not want her to go. A professional telling a person to make an appointment instead of talking to him when he spontaneously drops by is the act of a powerful person controlling the actions of a powerless person (LeVine, 1987). A similar interruption by the police or the President of the United States would probably be handled differently.

The American self-control schema, because it includes the belief that people with developmental disabilities need control, creates an environment in which it is difficult for service providers to interact with individuals with disabilities in noncontrolling ways. Even staff members who genuinely want to empower people to be independent inadvertently perpetuate a controlling environment; having to provide control in some instances often fosters an increase in unnecessary acts of control at other times. The service environment is also not immune to the subtle, and sometimes not so subtle, power differentials between men and women, middle class and working class, or white and non-white in the United States (Skinner, Bryant, Coffman, & Campbell, 1998). Still, service providers must find ways within this environment to create helping relationships that empower rather than impede, encourage rather than coerce, and liberate rather than limit the people whom they support (Hasenfeld & Chesler, 1989).

Assessing Relationship Schemas

What empowers one person limits another, just as what impedes one person gives needed structure to another. It is not a question of being controlled by others or having self-control, of being independent or being dependent, or of being safe or being free. When the person providing help is doing so in a way that is not valued by the person receiving it, there is a strong possibility that the recipient will interpret the relationship to be controlling rather than helpful (Cohen, 1998). It is the match between the type of help a particular person wants and the type of help another thinks is the best kind of help to provide that determines whether the relationship is evaluated as oppressive or empowering (Kaplan, 1991).

Assessment Tools   There are many sources of power in helping relationships: ability to withdraw assistance (Cohen, 1998), authority to apply sanctions (Gitterman, 1989) or confer rewards (Rodrigues, 1995), employment of distancing procedures and terminology (Stiver, 1991b), unequal access to specialized knowledge (Swigonski, 1996), one partner's acquiescence to (Atwater, 1995) or protest of the other's actions (Gerris, Dekovic, & Janssens, 1997), and the right to define the problem and available solutions (Saunders, Resnick, Hoberman, & Blum, 1994). A critical factor in understanding schemas about helping relationships is the attribution of responsibility for problems and solutions because "[r]esponsibility and power are often considered synonymous as determinants of behavior" (Mass, 1997, p. 244). Therefore, one can "identify the presence of power through the ascription of responsibility" (Kernohan, 1989, p. 725). For example, assigning responsibility for the solution of a problem to the service provider gives her the power to impose her solutions on the service receiver.

The type of help offered depends on whether the person providing help feels responsible for the problem and on who he feels is responsible for the solution (Furnham & Hayward, 1997). The type of help sought depends on whether the person seeking help feels responsible for the problem and who she feels is responsible for the solution (Wehmeyer & Palmer, 1998). Possible combinations of attributions of responsibility for problems and solutions form the basis of the assessment tools in Figures 8.1 and 8.2.

Construction   The previous assessments were constructed by five volunteers who varied in age, gender, ethnicity, and class. They rated 40 propositions on whether the statement showed that the helper felt that he, the recipient, both, or neither were responsible for the problem and whether he, the recipient, both, or neither were responsible for the solution. The 40 statements were reworded to reflect the help recipient's point of view and rated by the five volunteers on whether the statement showed that the recipient felt that he, the helper, both, or neither were responsible for the solution.

Statements that described problems that were rated as no one's responsibility (e.g., genetically or environmentally caused problems) were removed from the assessment because, according to the volunteers, including them would make the assessment too complex. Statements that generated disagreement among volunteers were removed. The remaining 20 statements for each tool were then clustered and

Assessment of Values Guiding Type of Help Offered

Read each statement, and check whether you agree or disagree with it.

Agree Disagree

_____ _____ 1. I think that motivating people to figure out for themselves what work they need to do is better than just telling them what work they need to do.

_____ _____ 2. I am not responsible if someone I am helping gets into trouble.

_____ _____ 3. People should not be held accountable for things they do not know or do not understand.

_____ _____ 4. Sometimes other people just need consoling; therefore, I should empathize with them rather than try to change things.

_____ _____ 5. It is my responsibility to help people to obtain correct information so they can make good decisions.

_____ _____ 6. I have the responsibility to stop the people I supervise from making mistakes that have the potential to hurt them or others.

_____ _____ 7. It is important for me to determine what activities the people I am helping can learn to do for themselves and what activities I need to help them with.

_____ _____ 8. I only provide information; getting people to use the information to make particular choices is not my responsibility.

_____ _____ 9. It is my responsibility to help the people I supervise to understand and be responsible for their own actions.

_____ _____ 10. It is all right for me to do things for others that they are unable to do for themselves.

_____ _____ 11. Helping people to identify their own values so they can make their own choices is more important than helping them to learn skills that I know they need.

_____ _____ 12. It is more important for me to help people who are discriminated against to understand and deal with others' attitudes than it is for me to change laws or reform social practices to decrease discrimination.

Your Values, My Values, Pengra, ©2000 Paul H. Brookes Publishing Co.

Figure 8.1.   Assessment of values guiding type of help offered.

Figure 8.1.   (*continued*)

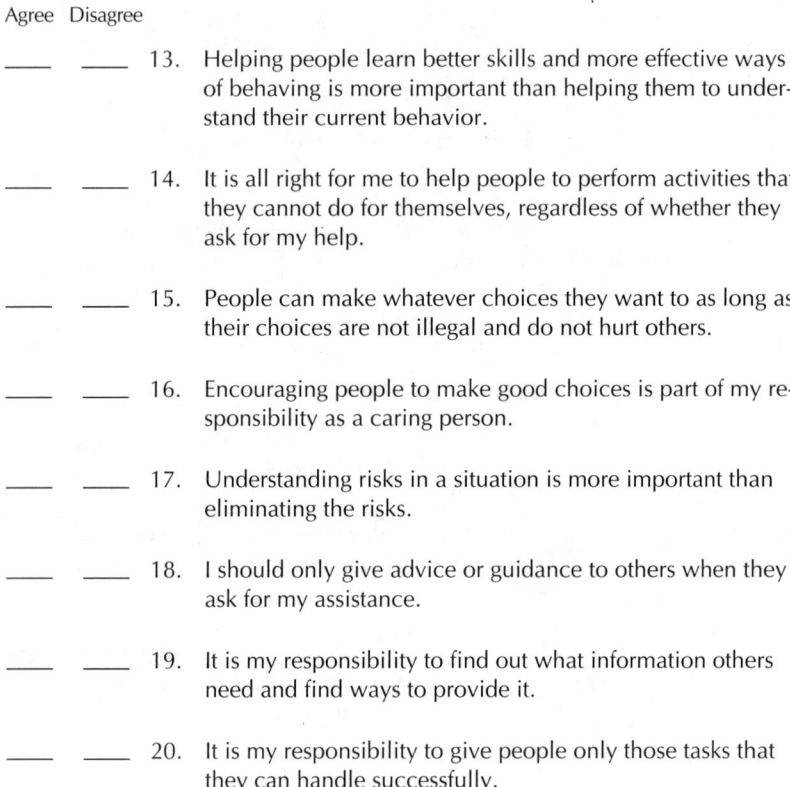

Agree   Disagree

____   ____   13.   Helping people learn better skills and more effective ways of behaving is more important than helping them to understand their current behavior.

____   ____   14.   It is all right for me to help people to perform activities that they cannot do for themselves, regardless of whether they ask for my help.

____   ____   15.   People can make whatever choices they want to as long as their choices are not illegal and do not hurt others.

____   ____   16.   Encouraging people to make good choices is part of my responsibility as a caring person.

____   ____   17.   Understanding risks in a situation is more important than eliminating the risks.

____   ____   18.   I should only give advice or guidance to others when they ask for my assistance.

____   ____   19.   It is my responsibility to find out what information others need and find ways to provide it.

____   ____   20.   It is my responsibility to give people only those tasks that they can handle successfully.

form the basis of the two profile sheets shown in Figures 8.3 and 8.4. Respondents may have high scores in more than one profile because different kinds of help may be offered or sought in different situations, and people do not have perfectly consistent, noncontradictory values. There is no claim that these propositions or groupings are the most salient or predictive, only that they have the greatest face validity for the five volunteers who sorted them.

Interpretation   The names of the help-provider and help-recipient profiles and the descriptions of them given in Tables 8.1 and 8.2 were generated by the five volunteers during discussion of the sorting of the original 40 propositions. Several names were suggested and rejected, for example, "moral helper" and "caretaker" for types A and D,

Assessment of Values Guiding Type of Help Sought

Read each statement, and check whether you agree or disagree with it.

Agree   Disagree

____ ____ 1. I want people to understand why I act the way I do.

____ ____ 2. I am responsible for whatever trouble I get into, even when someone else did not give me enough information to make a better decision.

____ ____ 3. It is not my fault when there are things I do not know or do not understand.

____ ____ 4. Sometimes I just need consoling; I want people to empathize with me, not change things.

____ ____ 5. Other people should explain things to me so that I can make good decisions.

____ ____ 6. Sometimes others do know better than I what the consequences of my behavior will be, so they should stop me from making mistakes.

____ ____ 7. I am the one who determines what I want others to teach me and what things I want to learn on my own.

____ ____ 8. I only want information from others; I do not want them to tell me what to do with that information.

____ ____ 9. I think that other people can help me to understand and be responsible for my own actions.

____ ____ 10. It is all right for others to help me to do things that I cannot do for myself.

____ ____ 11. I want others to help me identify my values so that I can make my own choices about what to learn; this is more important than having others actually teach me things I need to know.

____ ____ 12. I want to learn to cope with how people treat me instead of changing how they treat me.

____ ____ 13. Learning new skills is more important to me than learning how my attitudes affect my performance.

(continued)

Your Values, My Values, Pengra, ©2000 Paul H. Brookes Publishing Co.

Figure 8.2.   Assessment of values guiding type of help sought.

Figure 8.2.   (*continued*)

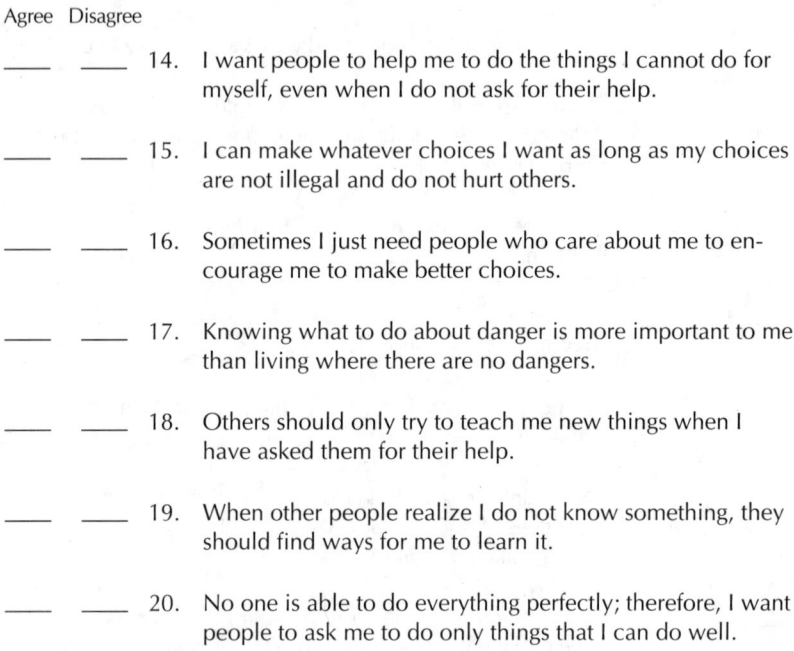

Agree Disagree

_____   _____   14.   I want people to help me to do the things I cannot do for myself, even when I do not ask for their help.

_____   _____   15.   I can make whatever choices I want as long as my choices are not illegal and do not hurt others.

_____   _____   16.   Sometimes I just need people who care about me to encourage me to make better choices.

_____   _____   17.   Knowing what to do about danger is more important to me than living where there are no dangers.

_____   _____   18.   Others should only try to teach me new things when I have asked them for their help.

_____   _____   19.   When other people realize I do not know something, they should find ways for me to learn it.

_____   _____   20.   No one is able to do everything perfectly; therefore, I want people to ask me to do only things that I can do well.

Table 8.1, because those names had negative connotations for some people.

The profiles do not define universally right and wrong ways of behaving; however, they do describe approaches differently valued by particular individuals. Conflicts are reduced and better support relationships are possible when the service receiver is matched with a service provider who gives the type of help the service receiver prefers. For example, Margaret scored very high on Self-Acceptance Seeker (profile A, Table 8.2) and, thus, did well when she was matched with a staff member who had a high response as a Values Helper (profile A, Table 8.1). Gloria scored high as an Advice Seeker (profile C, Table 8.2) and preferred staff who scored high as Advice Helpers (profile C, Table 8.1). Matching service providers and receivers according to their help provider and help recipient profiles reduces the inequality between the two people in the service relationship; both agree on what is appropriate rather than the service provider requiring the service receiver to accept the type of help that is offered.

Help Provider Profiles

Directions: Score one point for agreeing or disagreeing with each statement in Figure 8.1, as indicated here. For example, if you answered *agree* on statement 1, then score one point on the first line under profile A, Values Helper. However, if you answered *disagree* on statement 1, then score one point on the first line under profile D, Support Helper. Total your points in each profile. Read the descriptions in Table 8.1 for the two or three profiles with your highest totals.

A. **Values Helper**

1.	agree	_____
9.	agree	_____
12.	agree	_____
13.	disagree	_____
14.	disagree	_____
15.	disagree	_____
16.	agree	_____
19.	disagree	_____
	Total:	_____

B. **Teaching Helper**

3.	agree	_____
5.	agree	_____
7.	disagree	_____
10.	disagree	_____
11.	disagree	_____
13.	agree	_____
17.	agree	_____
18.	disagree	_____
	Total:	_____

C. **Advice Helper**

2.	agree	_____
3.	disagree	_____
5.	disagree	_____
8.	agree	_____
9.	disagree	_____
15.	agree	_____
16.	disagree	_____
18.	agree	_____
	Total:	_____

D. **Support Helper**

1.	disagree	_____
2.	disagree	_____
4.	agree	_____
6.	agree	_____
8.	disagree	_____
14.	agree	_____
17.	disagree	_____
20.	agree	_____
	Total:	_____

Your Values, My Values, Pengra, ©2000 Paul H. Brookes Publishing Co.

Figure 8.3.   Help provider profiles.

Figure 8.3.   (*continued*)

E.   **Advocate Helper**

    4.   disagree   _____

    6.   disagree   _____

    7.   agree   _____

    10.   agree   _____

    11.   agree   _____

    12.   disagree   _____

    19.   agree   _____

    20.   disagree   _____

        Total: _____

Use   In addition to matching service receiver and provider, the assessment can be used by having the parents of a person with a disability respond to the Assessment of Values Guiding Type of Help Sought (Figure 8.2) by thinking about what type of help they want their child to receive. Comparing those results with the results obtained from their child and other team members may clarify different points of view. Parents and other team members can also take both assessments by thinking about what type of help they think they ought to give and receive themselves. Comparing both the help provider and help recipient profiles for parents, direct support staff, and other team members is useful as a basis for discussing what they want and expect from each other and for identifying potential areas of conflict, whether between supervisor and direct support staff, professional staff and parent, or any other combination of team members. For example, in my experience, direct support staff usually score high in the skills or advice seeker profiles (B and C) for how they want to receive help, but supervisory and management staff tend to score high in the values or advocate profiles (A and E) for how they think they ought to give help, a finding that possibly accounts for why some team members feel powerless and evaluate other team members as pushy or incompetent.

Help Recipient Profiles

Directions: Score one point for agreeing or disagreeing with each statement in Figure 8.2, as indicated here. For example, if you answered *agree* on statement 1, then score one point on the first line under profile A, Self-Acceptance Seeker. However, if you answered *disagree* on statement 1, then score one point on the first line under profile D, Support Seeker. Total your points in each profile. Read the descriptions in Table 8.2 for the two or three profiles with your highest totals.

A.	**Self-Acceptance Seeker**		B.	**Skill Seeker**	
1.	agree	_____	3.	agree	_____
9.	agree	_____	5.	agree	_____
12.	agree	_____	7.	disagree	_____
13.	disagree	_____	10.	disagree	_____
14.	disagree	_____	11.	disagree	_____
15.	disagree	_____	13.	agree	_____
16.	agree	_____	17.	agree	_____
19.	disagree	_____	18.	disagree	_____
	Total:	_____		Total:	_____

C.	**Advice Seeker**		D.	**Support Seeker**	
2.	agree	_____	1.	disagree	_____
3.	disagree	_____	2.	disagree	_____
5.	disagree	_____	4.	agree	_____
8.	agree	_____	6.	agree	_____
9.	disagree	_____	8.	disagree	_____
15.	agree	_____	14.	agree	_____
16.	disagree	_____	17.	disagree	_____
18.	agree	_____	20.	agree	_____
	Total:	_____		Total:	_____

(*continued*)

Your Values, My Values, Pengra, ©2000 Paul H. Brookes Publishing Co.

Figure 8.4. Help recipient profiles.

Figure 8.4.   *(continued)*

E.   **Cooperation Seeker**

4.   disagree   _____

6.   disagree   _____

7.   agree   _____

10.   agree   _____

11.   agree   _____

12.   disagree   _____

19.   agree   _____

20.   disagree   _____

Total: _____

Evaluating Relationships

The most direct way, however, to find out if people receiving services are being helped in the way they think they ought to be helped is by having them evaluate the staff members who work with them. The staff evaluation form in Figure 8.5 also touches on the issues of privacy discussed in Chapter 7.

A New Relationship for Gloria and Donna   When Gloria gave Donna a poor evaluation and Donna was increasingly unhappy with having to "nag" Gloria to stay on her budget, the team decided to reevaluate their earlier decision concerning how much financial control was necessary to ensure Gloria's safety. After deciding that the only real risk to giving Gloria more control over her finances was Gloria's losing her apartment if she didn't pay her rent, the team designed an envelope system that met their goals of decreasing risks and honoring Gloria's preference for being responsible for solutions.

Now, when her checks come, Gloria and Donna pay the rent and the heat bill together. Then, following a discussion of needs, choices, outstanding bills, and other commitments, Gloria's remaining cash and her food stamps are apportioned into four or five different envelopes, each colored to match a week on a color-coded calendar. Each envelope

Table 8.1.   Help provider profiles

A. Values Helper

1. The values helper is the "know why" helper. He often uses strategies of motivation and encouragement, choosing strategies he thinks will work with that person. He recognizes that people have different values and, therefore, need different kinds of encouragement.

2. The values helper often feels responsible for others' problems but not for providing solutions. He thinks that only the recipient of help is responsible for solutions; choices must be made by the recipient in terms of his own values.

B. Teaching Helper

1. The teaching helper is the "know how" helper. She commonly provides training and education. She recognizes that people have different learning styles and skill levels and, therefore, need different kinds of instruction.

2. The teaching helper does not feel responsible for the recipient's lack of knowledge or skill but does feel responsible for finding ways to teach needed skills. She thinks that the recipient is not responsible for wrong answers but that the teacher is responsible for helping her to learn the right answers.

C. Advice Helper

1. The advice helper is the "know what" helper. He gives information and advice when asked but does not feel responsible for telling people what is going on. He recognizes the importance of information as the basis of making choices and decisions.

2. The advice helper does not feel responsible for others' problems or for finding solutions. He feels that the recipient is responsible for determining his own course of action, has the responsibility to seek information from others, and has the choice to accept or reject information and advice from others.

D. Support Helper

1. The support helper is the "know for" helper. She offers comfort, support, and empathy. She often suggests strategies for adaptation of the environment or does other things for the recipient to facilitate the efforts of the recipient.

2. The support helper feels responsible for problems and for the recipient's well-being. She also feels responsible for helping the recipient think through the consequences of her choices because no one can know all the answers.

(continued)

Table 8.1. (*continued*)

E.   Advocate Helper

   1.   The advocate helper is the "know with" helper. He suggests strategies for self-determination but does not think people have to make all of their own decisions. He thinks that people can be interdependent, are involved with each other, and should look for mutually satisfying solutions.

   2.   The advocate helper does not feel that either he or the recipient is responsible for problems but that they are equally responsible for finding solutions together. Those solutions might involve changing others' attitudes and values.

is also stamped with a picture of the grocery store, television, telephone, taxi, clothing, and so on, that matches pictures on her calendar. For example, there are four envelopes (one of each color to match each week on the calendar), each containing the amount of cash and food stamps budgeted for a week's worth of groceries. The same picture is stamped on four successive Mondays on the calendar. Gloria keeps all envelopes in a locked cash box to which only she has the key. Each day, Gloria checks off one square on her calendar. When she checks off a day that is green with a picture of the grocery store, she knows to retrieve the green envelope with the picture of the grocery store and go grocery shopping that day. The red envelope with a picture of her television matches the corresponding picture and color on her calendar and indicates that her cable payment is due that day, and so on for each color and picture. There is no further intervention in Gloria's business that month unless she requests information or advice.

Gloria often takes money out of the laundry, telephone, taxi, and grocery envelopes and spends it on other choices. She sometimes goes without food the week before her food stamps arrive and occasionally has her telephone disconnected for nonpayment. However, Gloria, who had never been able to stay on a budget, even with close supervision by a staff member, is now able to independently accomplish this feat for months at a time. She also is making progress in learning to identify bill denominations and their relative values, especially now that learning is separated from control. Donna is happier because she received an improved performance rating from Gloria, and their interactions are cooperative and mutually satisfying.

Table 8.2. Help recipient profiles

A. Self-Acceptance Seeker

    1.   The self-acceptance seeker wants to "know why" she does things. She likes to take the initiative in trying things for herself but sometimes wants moral support from others for doing so. She seeks to identify her own goals and values and strives to live in terms of them. She often is a thinker rather than a doer.

    2.   The self-acceptance seeker takes responsibility for her actions, although she sees where others' actions have affected her. She wants to make her own choices and decisions in terms of her goals and values, although she is aware that her choices affect others.

B. Skill Seeker

    1.   The skill seeker wants to "know how" to do things. He commonly seeks training and education. He seeks to improve himself through self-help programs and books. If he has difficulty learning a particular skill, then he looks for a better teacher. He is often more task oriented than people oriented.

    2.   The skill seeker does not feel responsible for things not yet learned but does feel responsible for continuing to learn new skills. He believes that there is a correct or best way of doing things and wants to learn it. He generally respects people who have more skills than he does and accepts their advice and guidance.

C. Advice Seeker

    1.   The advice seeker wants to "know what" she should do. She actively seeks information and advice from others. She recognizes the importance of information as the basis for making choices and decisions. She believes that "ignorance of the law is no excuse."

    2.   The advice seeker thinks that she is responsible for determining her own course of action and that she has the responsibility to seek information from others. She may shop for several opinions and seek many sources of information, even when those sources give conflicting advice. She feels she has the choice to accept or reject information and advice from others.

D. Support Seeker

    1.   The support seeker wants someone else to "know (things) for" or about himself. He wants comfort, support, and empathy. He does not believe that he has to do everything for himself and expects assistance from others. He sometimes thinks that others should change how they work with him rather than seeking to change how he works with others.

(continued)

Table 8.2.   (*continued*)

---

2.   The support seeker takes responsibility for his own problems but recognizes how others' actions have contributed to these problems. He sometimes needs to have others help him think through his own options. He is more now oriented than future oriented and people oriented rather than task oriented.

E.   Cooperation Seeker

1.   The cooperation seeker wants to "know (things) with" others in order to work together to achieve joint goals. She is willing to share decision making, although she wants to take an active role in determining the goals. She thinks that people can be interdependent, are involved with each other, and should look for mutually satisfying solutions. She is a superb team player who sees herself as being equal to others rather than being a follower.

2.   The cooperation seeker does not worry about who caused problems but is focused on finding solutions that work for everyone in the group. Those solutions might involve changing others' attitudes and values because "no man is an island."

Evaluations of staff by service receivers should be taken very seriously; in a trusting atmosphere, these evaluations can pinpoint problems accurately (Fiske, Morling, & Stevens, 1996). When services are adjusted to meet the expectations and recommendations of service receivers, service providers may find that they have to provide help in ways that are not part of their Help Provider Profiles. Using these strategies may not feel very natural and may require conscious effort, but it can be done. People who were not Lakota learned to work effectively with Gloria. People who were not Norwegian farmers adapted to Bobby's values. However, not all people learned to work equally well with every person. Matching service providers and receivers in terms of their values on giving and receiving help is a reasonable place to start. Then, evaluations of staff can guide improvements in services or indicate the need for a different match.

THE MEANING OF INDEPENDENCE

"Biiiig boss."

John said this while pointing at me, smiling at our secret, shared joke. He had first made the pun several months before, noting both my

Staff Evaluation

Staff evaluation by _____ Date _____

If someone helps you answer these questions, ask him or her to sign here:

_____

Signature   Title   Date

For each question, fill in the name of the staff person being evaluated. For yes/no questions, give an example if you want to.

1. How does _____ help you?

2. Does _____ treat you fairly?

3. Does _____ tell other people things you do not want them to know about you?

4. When you need to talk, does _____ take time to listen?

5. Has _____ ever been mad at you or made you feel bad?

6. Does _____ help you make your own choices and decisions?

7. What do you like best about _____ ?

8. Is there something you want to change about _____?

9. Is there anything else you want to say about _____ ?

10. Do you want to continue working with _____ ?

11. If yes, what other ways could _____ help you?

12. If no, is there someone else you would rather have help you? Who?

Your Values, My Values, Pengra, ©2000 Paul H. Brookes Publishing Co.

Figure 8.5.   Staff evaluation.

physical size and work status as director. Because John had refused to take his seizure medications several times during the previous week, on this particular day I was trying to explain to John that everyone, even the "big boss," has a boss over some part of her life. I had brought with me a newspaper picture of the local television weatherman, a bottle of my own medication, a picture of me with my family, and minutes from the Board of Directors' meeting. I wanted to talk to John about decisions and events a person cannot control (the weather and the necessity of some medications) and shared decisions (family discussions and team meetings). John pointed at my pills and then at me.

"You boss."

He again pointed at the pill bottle and then pointed at himself.

"No boss."

His message finally sank in. I was so concerned about the consequences of John's refusal to take his medication that I hadn't really listened to him. He hadn't said, "No pills," asserting his right to refuse his medication. He'd said, "No boss," meaning that others' telling him it was time to take his medication was not helpful advice; instead, it was control.

Self-Reliance and Autonomy

When we listened more closely to John, we learned that he did not think independence meant that he needed to make many choices. He preferred to choose from a very limited range of meals and activities and was unconcerned when the alternatives were determined by someone else. He was equally content to choose from a very small wardrobe and follow an unvarying routine, as long as he was the one who took care of himself. For John, independence did not mean having the autonomy to determine what to do but, instead, meant being self-reliant by controlling how and when to do it, an interpretation of independence he shares with other working-class people. Many of John's service providers, however, are middle class and, like others with middle-class values, define independence as autonomy. Some misunderstandings among service providers and receivers revolve around the difference in values embedded in the distinction between self-reliance and autonomy.

Class-Based Differences   Generalizations describing class-based cultural differences are difficult to formulate because class identity is discounted as the source of differences (Cotton, 1994), confounded with other identities such as gender (Pyke, 1996) and ethnicity (Chen, 1992), based on simplistic divisions between higher and lower classes (Reay, 1997), mistakenly equated with income levels (Lee, 1994), and too often considered without regard to environmental factors (Gonzales, Cauce, Friedman, & Mason, 1996). Ignoring class differences, however, allows class conflicts to be misinterpreted as interpersonal problems (Ross, 1995), supports the power of the middle class to define social norms by denying the existence of working-class norms (Reay, 1998), and permits stereotypes to go unchallenged (McDermott & Schaefer, 1996).

A simplistic but useful contrast between the working and middle classes is that their values are based on the "manual or mental" (Willis & Corrigan, 1985) requirements of their work tasks because values help people to cope with the opportunities and limitations of their environments (Hughes & Perry-Jenkins, 1996). For the working class, job tasks are often manual and involve physical skills, strength, and endurance (Sacks & Remy, 1984). The dangers and everyday requirements of the job are managed through self-reliance by valuing "taking care of oneself" and "getting the job done" (Paules, 1992). For the middle class, work responsibilities are mental: planning market strategies, using quantitative business skills, and applying personnel policies (Preissle & Grant, 1998). These tasks are supported by and enable autonomy and self-actualization (Kohn, 1969).

Autonomy is also accentuated in middle-class families when authority is established by reference to rules, using the "Do it because that's the family rule" approach. Questioning the validity of a rule is an acceptable way to handle interpersonal conflict and does not make the disagreement a personal attack (Gos, 1995). However, in many working-class families, authority is embedded in relationships by using the "Do it because I said so" approach. Therefore, questioning a rule is challenging the power of the person (Ritchie, 1997).

Outside the home, working-class disputants also interpret conflicts as affronts to the person and believe that they must counter them to maintain their independence (Knights & Willmott, 1989). People interviewed in a Polish/Czech working-class community near Chicago declared that a person ought to employ a "physical response to those who impugn one's honor" (Schwartz, 1981, p. 103). Miller and Moore's study of child-rearing philosophies of women in a mixed German/Irish/Appalachian working-class neighborhood in south Baltimore showed how mothers taught their children through teasing routines not to be "sissies," to be able to stand up for themselves to handle "the harsh realities of life" (1989, p. 434). Strauss' interviews with working-class men in an Italian neighborhood in Cranston, Rhode Island, revealed a value on "not being afraid to fight" (1990, p. 321) and on standing up to neighborhood punks and factory bosses.

To say that working-class people value physical aggression is inaccurate. People may act a certain way because it is a necessary survival strategy in their particular environment, not because they value the particular behavior. (Wilkinson, 1996). Valuing taking care of yourself in an environment where many avenues of doing so are blocked because of lower status and unequal access to resources may result in behavior that looks aggressive (Lears, 1985); however, the behavior can be interpreted as defensive rather than antisocial (McDermott & Schaefer, 1996). On the one hand, some middle-class professionals have argued that people should be assisted in learning to take control of their lives through autonomous decision making because defining independence as physical self-reliance results in violence (Martinek & Hellison, 1998). On the other hand, when "having a high sense of control would lead to disappointment and frustration" because the environment does "not afford opportunities for taking control" (Lachman & Weaver, 1998, p. 763), self-reliance is probably the more adaptive response. For example, self-reliance has been credited with maintaining lower levels of mental illness for people faced with chronic unemployment (Biegel, Cunningham, Yamatani, & Martz, 1989).

Supporting John's Independence   Part of John's anger came from interpreting staff reminders as evidence that they thought that he was unable to take care of himself. Finding a way that helped him remember when to take his pills and that also accentuated his self-reliance was a critical factor in his eventual success. The system that was designed for him involved painting each lid of his three-compartment daily pill box a different color to match the color of a Christmas tree light bulb. The bulbs were plugged into individual timers to go on for 2 hours at the correct time of day so that John could take the pills in the compartment that matched the light. The length of time the light was on allowed him to check several times to reassure himself that he had taken his pills and provided flexibility in when he needed to be home. Each morning, he showed the empty pill dispenser to his community living coach and filled the compartments again himself. His coach could then compliment John on being his own boss and monitor his compliance unobtrusively.

Although John's violent behavior decreased when people treated him as capable of managing his own care, some staff members still categorized some of his behavior as aggressive rather than as defensive. As with the schema of theft in Chapter 4, people of different social categories often vary in their definitions of the boundaries of specific types of behavior, despite a shared basic schema. Staff members agreed that certain behaviors qualify as "aggressive" if less harmful, equally effective, responses are available (Tulloch, 1995); however, there was some disagreement as to the effectiveness of those alternatives. A second point of disagreement was whether anger directed at a person because of conflict over a rule was justified (Weisinger, 1995). The compromise negotiated by John and his team was to separate the issues of when to be angry and how to be angry. Together they developed a behavior intervention plan that focused on nonaggressive ways to be angry on those occasions when John decided that anger was justified.

Responding to Intent

John's behavior clearly signaled a problem, although the analysis of what the problem was and how to address it changed as his team adopted different schemas for understanding it. A more difficult situation is when a person is so compliant that there are few independent actions to interpret. Ted, for example, ate what was placed in front of him, bathed when directed to the bathroom, and went to bed when urged toward his bedroom.

Ted's team wanted to help him make choices because many researchers have reported increased motivation, interest, and involvement when people make choices about their work tasks, personal care, and recreation (Dattilo & Rusch, 1985; Parsons, Reid, Reynolds, & Bumgarner, 1990; Realon, Favell, & Lowerre, 1990). Other researchers have noted increases in self-esteem (O'Brien, 1987; West & Parent, 1992) and positive self-identity (Lim & Browder, 1994). Satisfaction with services and an increased quality of life have also been found to correlate with increased involvement in making choices (Schloss, Alper, & Jayne, 1993).

Glen, a staff member who took a special interest in Ted, suggested that Ted might learn to indicate choices if he had an opportunity to select a place to go out to eat once per week. Pictures of restaurants didn't elicit a response, but Glen found that driving to several places allowed

Ted to choose where to eat that day, although he often was unsure as to whether Ted was making a choice or was just tired of driving around.

Ted's behavior was unchanged—until one night when he simply would not go to bed. This, in itself, was very unusual. Then he went to the closet and put on his coat. Because all the restaurants were closed, Glen and Ted took a snack with them and ate it parked in front of the restaurant chosen by Ted that night.

Glen said later that it was the first time that Ted had ever really asked for something. He believed that ignoring Ted's request because it was the wrong time and wrong day would mean that Ted might never ask for anything again. Ted might also have missed the chance to learn that he could control some aspects of his environment, including the actions of others.

Low service provider response to expressions of intent (Houghton, Bronicki, & Guess, 1987) may impede people from learning that they have control of their choices (Foxx, Faw, Taylor, Davis, & Fulia, 1993; Parmenter, Cummins, Shaddock, & Stancliff, 1994). Ferguson (1994) and O'Brien (1994) both suggested that responding to the intention of people to communicate is a crucial part of supporting people because it helps them to develop a perception of control and a sense of self. Wehmeyer, Kelchner, and Richards (1996) and Zimmerman (1990) identified two dimensions of perceived control: people need to believe that they have the capacity to perform behaviors needed to influence outcomes, and they need to believe that, if they perform those behaviors, the anticipated outcome will result.

Early in Margaret's struggle to see herself as able to make decisions, Brenda, her case manager, helped her make yes-and-no sticks. They cut a tongue depressor in half, painted one half red, and wrote "no" on it. The other half of the tongue depressor was painted green and labeled with "yes." The idea was that the pieces of tongue depressor were small enough for Margaret to conceal them in the palm of her hand. During her team meetings, she could pass one under the table to Brenda if she wanted help with saying "yes" or "no" to plans that were being made. Even then, Brenda told me later, Margaret would often simply twist the sticks, unable to select one or assert herself by passing it to Brenda. Brenda, however, interpreted the nervous twisting as an intent to communicate and interceded on Margaret's behalf. It was a happy day when Margaret threw the sticks away; she finally learned that others would not be angry if she exercised her autonomy and no longer needed extra support to do so.

Ted and Margaret needed to learn that they were capable of independent actions and could control some actions of others. Staff members who provided supports to John and Gloria, however, needed to learn when they were being too controlling as defined in different schemas of independence. There is no single method for enhancing independence because it does not depend on how much self-control a particular person is said to have or how much external control he is said to need. Enhancing independence is dependent on becoming aware of different values, designing assistive devices that support those values, carefully matching service providers and receivers based on their values, and challenging the limitations of the social environment when possible. This requires careful listening and good responses, like Glen's and Brenda's, and a willingness to learn other schemas, such as John's and Gloria's teams did.

POINTS TO REMEMBER

To enhance independence, we need to embrace the following four viewpoints:

1. *See anger as evidence of oppression, not as a lack of self-control.* Enhancing independence means not locating problems in the person but relating them to the limitations imposed by an environment of inequality. For example, the woman who cut up her clothes may not have used the best technique for expressing her anger, but her action can be interpreted as a protest of her powerlessness rather than as a loss of self-control.

2. *Look for a match between service providers and receivers in attributions of responsibility for problems and solutions.* Whether a person sees a helping relationship as controlling depends on the way in which she defines a good relationship. For example, Gloria thought that staff ought to provide advice but were not responsible for her actions. Her evaluation of Donna's assistance changed when Donna was enabled by the team to provide advice without being required to control outcomes.

3. *Discern different definitions of independence such as self-reliance or autonomy.* Accepting the middle-class schema of independence as autonomy may interfere with the perception of other actions that signal independence for working-class people. For example, de-

signing an assistive device that allows John to be in charge of his own medication routine enhanced his independence because it accentuated his self-reliance.

4. *Notice and respond to a person's attempts to control the actions of others.* Learning appropriate ways to control the actions of others requires understanding that this kind of control works and is acceptable. For example, if Glen had not responded to Ted's attempt to communicate that he wanted Glen to take him out to eat, he might never again have initiated an independent action.

Rejecting Schemas About People with Developmental Disabilities

"Some people might say I have a disability."

I was interested in this comment from Margaret because she is the only person I've known who had actually at one time called herself mentally retarded. So I asked:

"What do you say?"

Her answer was a reflection of a new philosophy and her vastly improved self-esteem.

"Nothing. I don't say I'm fat. I don't say I'm female. What you see is what you get. I'm just me. It's nobody's business if I need help sometimes."

In fact, Margaret was like her neighbors in most ways. She attended a weight loss group with other women who were worried about their weight, went to church with other Christians who struggled with temptations, and held a job she chose but wished paid more. She worked hard, went to an occasional party with friends, and looked forward to marrying her boyfriend some day just as other women her age in this small town did. The fact that she had been labeled as having a developmental disability no longer overshadowed her whole life.

Margaret had discovered for herself that in most ways she is no different from anyone else. She transcended the categorization of herself as first and foremost a person with a disability and became Margaret, a multi-faceted person. Because her goal was to help others share this perspective, she had just given a presentation at a local grade school about the rights of people with disabilities and had eloquently argued that all people, regardless of whether they have a disability, are equal and should be treated respectfully.

I agree with Margaret, but I often doubt that her vision will be easily achieved in the United States because a devalued and marginal existence for people with developmental disabilities is predetermined by values about intelligence implied in a capitalist schema of social class (Fischer et al., 1996). These values are so pervasive throughout American culture that they are encapsulated in proverbs and figures of speech, making them seem like common sense rather than opprobrious judgments. Because inequality does not result from any actual personal characteristic or from how much people with developmental disabilities do or do not act like others, efforts to reduce oppression might be most effective if directed toward replacing the language and counteracting the schemas that perpetuate prejudice and discrimination (Abberley, 1993).

INTELLIGENCE AND SOCIAL CLASS SCHEMAS

Proverbs are "familiar, fixed, sentential expressions that express well-known truths, social norms, or moral concerns" (Gibbs & Beitel, 1995, p. 134) and supply evidence of implicit beliefs and values common in a particular culture (White, 1987). American proverbs clearly connect intelligence with social class (e.g., smart, rich owners versus poor, foolish workers) by sayings such as "Fools build houses for wise men to live in," and "Fools are never prosperous, smart men are never poor." Proverbs also link intelligence with personal responsibility for success through observations such as "A fool says, 'I can't.' A wise man says, 'I'll try,' " and "Early to bed and early to rise, makes a man healthy, wealthy, and wise" (Bledstein, 1994; Fergusson, 1983; Mieder, 1992).

These proverbs succinctly present the judgment that people who have not risen in the class system are personally responsible for their poverty, poor health, and low status, a pithy kernel of illogic that confuses consequence with cause and that has plagued social scientists' analyses of social problems for years (Wilkinson, 1996). That there is a correlation between IQ and class is not contested (Wolfe, 1995); however, whether it is proof that individuals' traits and actions collectively cause social problems depends on how the analyst envisions the direction of causality in correlations. For example, being born into dysfunctional and abusive families may correlate with babies' "failure to thrive" but might be caused by families' "failure to nurture." The inadequacy of a capitalist class system to provide equally for all its members is overlooked by those who attribute low status to lack of motivation and intellectual impairment (Curtis & Tepperman, 1994).

A peculiarity of reasoning in the class schema is that hard work alone does not account for successful entry into the upper reaches of the class system. Together, intelligence and hard work enable a person to earn higher status (and respect, prestige, value, etc.); however, because hard physical labor is too closely associated with the working class (Baron, 1991), intelligence becomes the critical factor in advancement, as in the proverb, "Wisdom is better than strength." Whether intelligence, with or without hard work, actually does result in moving up or down is irrelevant (Weakliem, McQuillan, & Schauer, 1995). Once people believe that it is the key, then intelligence is valued and intellectual deficits are devalued because, in an individualist person schema, "deficiency is not tolerated because it challenges the principle of personal fulfillment through competition between equal individuals by recognizing that some are more equal than others" (Calvez, 1993, p. 422). Therefore, "social exclusion of people with disabilities" results "from the rise of capitalism with its emphasis upon individualism, achievement and independence" (Westbrook, Legge, & Pennay, 1993, p. 615).

COMMUNICATING VALUES ABOUT INTELLIGENCE

Clinicians claim that terms identifying a person's intelligence are merely diagnostic tools (Gill & Maynard, 1995) that must be used for people to receive needed services (Szymanski & Trueba, 1994). Applying these terms, however, is not simply a descriptive act having only scientific functions, but automatically becomes political (Edelman,

1974) because the trait of intelligence is valued in the American class schema. It is not the act of labeling but the meaning of the label that devalues or elevates category members because, according to Mumby, humans are "enmeshed in meaning-laden cultural webs," where terms are understood "within a particular ideological formation which articulates a whole chain of connotations" (1989, pp. 292, 297). Changing attitudes toward people with developmental disabilities requires understanding how connotations associated with particular labels are conveyed through linguistic patterns such as euphemisms, dichotomies, metaphors, and colloquialisms.

Euphemisms

Some researchers believe that changing the names of social categories based on intelligence will change the image of the people in those categories. "The hope is," according to Fernald, "that 'words with dignity' [will] help communication, reduce stigma, and transcend boundaries of time and place" (1995, p. 99). There have been many changes in terms of reference from moron and idiot, to mental defective or mentally deficient, to trainable retarded or educable retarded, to mentally retarded or developmentally disabled, to people with developmental disabilities or intellectual disabilities, and recently, for some, simply to people with disabilities.

Using a word currently believed to be nicer (i.e., substituting a euphemism) is "a compensating strategy in language to skirt the taboo word" (Farb, 1974, p. 87). "The trouble with all euphemisms," according to Follett, "is that they wear out. They become 'indecent' from association with the object or idea that they cloak and a new screen has to be erected" (1966, pp. 160–161) because word choice is an indicator that something is wrong "rather than . . . the problem itself" (Lakoff, 1975, p. 21).

Greater anxiety is indicated by how many euphemisms are available and by how fast they deteriorate to be replaced by ever more distancing euphemisms (Murphy, 1996). Thus, *developmental* disability dilutes the reference to mental retardation by combining it with other types of developmental problems, although people who use the term still understand that mental retardation is included. Developmental *delay* replaces the idea of disability. The term *people with disabilities* leaves out the connection to development and potentially expands the category to include all types of disabilities, most of which are less negatively judged than mental retardation (Westbrook et al., 1993).

None of these terms has received unqualified acceptance or alleviated the anxiety associated with differences in intelligence, forcing mental retardation to be signaled in increasingly subtle ways. Schnorr (1990) observed a teacher referring to some children as "the little guys," which marked them as "special" education students, main-streamed for some activities but not really "in our class." As Carabello (quoted in Dybwad, 1996, p. 12 [emphasis in original]) asked, "How long do I have to be a *self-advocate* before I can become an *advocate*?" In visiting "sheltered workshops," I often noted that staff referred to their work locations as their "desks," but assisted people with developmental disabilities at their "workstations"; in most cases, the actual furniture was indistinguishable.

Possible Solutions   Farb (1974) advocated simply using ugly and bad words rather than euphemisms for the denoted objects or ideas as a method for exposing anxiety-producing concepts. Trent agreed with this strategy for mental retardation because "[w]hile our contemporary phrases appear more benign, too often we use them to hide from the offense in ways that the old terms did not permit" (1994, p. 5). For the same reason, the definitions introduced in 1992 by the American Association on Mental Retardation continued to use "mental retardation" as the main label in addition to the modifiers of mild, moderate, severe, and profound (Luckasson et al., 1992).

Because people who have been labeled have protested the use of certain terms, most notably "retarded," Goldfarb suggested finding another term and proposed that "any name, label or phrase designed to free the oppressed [should] be simpler, shorter, and easier to say than its predecessor" (1990, p. vi). However, because euphemisms, especially efficient ones (Mumby, 1989), eventually take on the same values that caused anxiety with the original term, attitude change might be more effectively produced by replacing oppressive words with long, unwieldy phrases. Doing so would draw attention to the problem of implied evaluation, make the speaker's politics explicit, and potentially force listeners to question their assumptions and anxieties (Greenwald & Banaji, 1995). For example, when Greenbaum referred to her son as a person who "just happens to be mentally challenged" (1996, p. 129), she put the person before the condition and also communicated her interpretation that the feature of intelligence is sometimes relevant, sometimes irrelevant, but not totally encompassing or devaluing.

Countersuggestion   If intelligence were not considered an important personal trait by most Americans, then terms would not have to be found to refer to the "amount" a person had nor would euphemisms need to· be created to prettify the presumed awfulness of not having "enough" of it. Instead, the difficulties associated with having various kinds of intelligence could be attributed to the social causes of disability (Liachowitz, 1988). Efforts could then be directed toward naming and reforming the social structures that cause disability and eliminating all terms that categorize individuals by intelligence rather than toward finding uglier, more accurate labels or more awkward euphemisms.

One problem with this alternative approach is that people with shared interests can wield political power if they organize, but, as Deveaux asked, "[h]ow does a group or an individual simultaneously resist an identity and mobilize around it for the purposes of empowerment and political action?" (1994, p. 240). A second problem is that this change would involve challenging two of the most widespread schemas in the United States, the individualist person schema (see Chapter 3) and the class schema, because they promulgate individual rather than structural views of the social world (Edwards, 1997). Eliminating anxiety about intelligence, and thus the need for euphemisms, would require radically changing the American world view of what people are and how society works, a somewhat more daunting task than simply getting Americans to see people with disabilities in a more positive way.

Dichotomies

Categories are constructed not only by choosing to notice certain features, such as intelligence or color, but also by determining where the boundaries are among variations of that feature. There are no absolute boundaries or obvious discontinuities available in nature. The point at which something is red rather than orange or orange rather than yellow, at which a person is of average intelligence rather than of borderline intelligence, or at which a person has severe rather than profound mental retardation can be set at different places, or ignored, by different people or languages. Discrete, discontinuous categories are being arbitrarily created from continuous variation.

In American English, however, there is a tendency toward dichotomization, that is, naming the opposite poles of a continuum but not the intervening points. This makes it difficult to see an array of equally weighted choices because objects are either mine or yours, expectations are either high or low, and sermons are either short or long. Dichotomization also identifies the positive pole in the contrast pair when questions are asked (Stewart & Bennett, 1991). Although speakers can ask, "What is his height?" they usually inquire, "How tall is he?" and instead of "How much does she earn?" they ask, "How rich is she?" A question is phrased from the negative pole when humor is implied or when the answer is already known. For example, a person might inquire about the quality of hospital food by asking, "How bad was it?" because it is widely assumed that it is not very good.

Speakers of American English intuitively know, because of the way questions are phrased, that tall, rich, and smart are good things to be. They also know that if someone is not tall, he's short rather than medium and that if she's not smart, she's stupid rather than average. Middle points can be talked about regardless of whether they are labeled, but dichotomies draw attention away from an array of diverse possibilities and toward the evaluative poles (e.g., black-and-white issues rather than shades of gray).

Language shapes and reflects values in very subtle ways, making it quite difficult to override the automatic evaluation implied in morphological and lexical choices (Sweetser, 1991). For example, English speakers also intuitively know that an adjective plus "dis-," "un-," "in-," or "im-" is the negative label in a contrast set (e.g., harmony/disharmony, loved/unloved, moral/immoral, complete/incomplete). Therefore, labeling a task as unskilled or a person as unwed makes a description into a judgment (Langacker, 1987). No English speaker is in any doubt about whether being disadvantaged, disabled, unfit, immature, incapacitated, incompetent, or insane is at the positive or negative pole of the implied dichotomies. There also are no single-word labels for naming any of the intervening points in the continuum; there is little linguistic recognition that a person could be partly advantaged, partly abled, or partly fit.

Possible Solutions   One obvious solution is not to use descriptive terms with the prefixes of "dis-," "un-," "in-," or "im-," which is a difficult task, as "disability" currently has fairly wide acceptance. A second obvious, and also not easy, solution is to resist dichotomization. For example, after having eliminated the clearly evaluative dichotomy of high- and low-functioning individuals as terms of reference, the same judgment is conveyed by collapsing the four levels of support to a dichotomy of mild/moderate versus severe/profound.

Lister, who identified a similar difficulty with dichotomies for feminist theories, remarked that it is "easier to state the problems with dualistic thinking than to find a way to move beyond it" (1997, p. 21) and recommended overturning "false dichotomies" by accentuating "pluralist" solutions. In the field of developmental disabilities, pluralism might be enhanced by using specific labels when appropriate, such as person with Down syndrome or person with Rubella syndrome, as these terms do not automatically place the person at a particular pole of the retardation dichotomy, although they do place the person at the negative pole of the intelligence dichotomy. Finally, a term that refers to a trait other than intelligence, for example, service receiver, should be used when possible. This strategy would be more effective if services in the United States were not segregated by entitlement category; if people received services regardless of whether they were elderly, mentally ill, poor, mentally retarded, or none of the foregoing but simply because they needed services, then *service receiver, client,* or *consumer* may not eventually become three more euphemisms for people with developmental disabilities.

Metaphors

Metaphors are figures of speech constructed by using objects and ideas that literally denote one thing to figuratively refer to something else to suggest an analogy between them. Although metaphors may be spontaneously created to illustrate a speaker's point more creatively, certain metaphors in the English language, called "cognitive metaphors," provide templates for reasoning (Lakoff & Johnson, 1980). For example, English speakers use the metaphor "anger is heat" (i.e., burning with anger, being hot under the collar, boiling over) and then reason how to deal with the anger by comparing it to how one deals with heat (i.e., blowing off steam, cooling down, fighting fire with fire, turning down the heat to decrease the pressure) (Lakoff & Kövecses, 1987).

Cognitive metaphors operate unconsciously (Lakoff, 1995), but their effect on reasoning and judgment is measurable (Allbritton, McKoon, & Gerrig, 1995). Metaphor-based schemas are particularly effective in structuring how "information is processed and represented in memory" (Buzzanell & Burrell, 1997, p. 112), with single words from metaphor-based schemas capable of "effortless activation" of attitudes and stereotypes (Greenwald & Banaji, 1995, p. 6). Metaphors in English surreptitiously lead speakers into one-word judgments, according to Shweder (1984), by applying the evaluative contrast of dichotomies from a sensory modality. For example, a "sweet vision" is understood to be good because sweet is the positive pole in the contrast between sweet and sour in the sensory modality of taste.

Spatial Orientation Metaphors   A sensory dichotomy metaphor, although not consciously recognized as a metaphor, structures one of the most pervasive cognitive metaphors used in American English. The sensory modality of proprioception—that is, the ability to sense the body's orientation in space—provides a global spatial orientation metaphor that evaluates actions or objects. "Up," "high," "ahead," and "in" or "central" are at the good pole of the dichotomy in contrast to "down," "low," "behind," and "out" or "edge" (Buzzanell & Burrell, 1997). Being described as marginal is bad because it implies that a person is at the edge rather than in the middle of the action—an outsider rather than an insider. The spatial orientation metaphor shows up when a morally good person is described as upright and an immoral person as low-down (Lakoff, 1995).

Although numbers are large or small, or greater than or less than other numbers, numeric intelligence measures are translated into a spatial orientation metaphor by calling them high or low scores, and coincidentally alluding to a competition metaphor because high scores (i.e., good ones) win games. Describing intelligence as high or low not only predetermines evaluative ratings about it, but also strengthens the link with social class. Using the spatial metaphor for both classes and intelligence cements the proverbial set of high intelligence/high class/high status.

The spatial orientation metaphor also connects directly to a control metaphor, in which "control is up, lack of control is down" (Gibbs, 1992, p. 574). Thus, supervisors (from Latin "supra" for above), heads of state (head is at the top of the body), top dogs, and overseers are in control. By using the same metaphor, the figurative premises are linked: Control is up, and up is good; therefore, control is good. It also suggests actions needed when considering intelligence and control (see Chapter 8). If low intelligence is down and down is lack of control, then people with low intelligence scores must lack control and therefore need to be controlled by others.

Possible Solution   Creating an alternative metaphor not based on a dichotomy might challenge assumptions about intelligence in relation to control and social class and impede the automatic devaluation of people with developmental disabilities implied in the high/low dichotomy. Although a consciously created metaphor will not produce as effective a template for reasoning as a cognitive metaphor (Clausner &

Croft, 1997), it might generate "alternative ways of looking at things" (Mühlhäusler, 1995, p. 282) but only if introduced to children before they have completely learned the cognitive metaphor used by adult speakers.

The metaphor "community is a chocolate chip cookie" has been successfully used to explore the idea of diversity with grade school children. The raw ingredients for the cookies are used to help the children discuss how some things are similar (e.g., flour, sugar, and chocolate chips all come in bags; nuts and chocolate chips are little, chunky objects), some things are very similar yet have differences (e.g., brown and white sugar differ in color and texture but are more similar to each other than to any of the other ingredients), and other things are completely different (e.g., an egg is like no other ingredient). After the children make the cookies, the teacher continues to explore the metaphor with them by asking whether the cookies would be as tasty without one or more of the ingredients. The idea that the ingredients blend together but others remain identifiable is then related to diversity in the classroom and the community. Although the metaphor facilitates good discussion, it is not a particularly powerful template for reasoning, does not directly challenge the high/low dichotomy, and reinforces an individualist person schema.

Colloquialisms

Colloquialisms are idioms, slang, and word combinations that occur in familiar, informal speech but are unacceptable for formal or elite contexts. Colloquial expressions that refer to wisdom and common sense or foolishness and stupidity are widespread (Bohlken, 1996; Casselman, 1998). Distasteful as it is to review colloquialisms that defame and devalue, listening to the "vernacular disdains of everyday life" is a way to explore the "cultural . . . importance of the mind" (Webb, 1998, pp. 541, 544).

Although there are degrading terms that use animal and vegetable references (e.g., dumb ox, dumb bunny, harebrained, peabrain, cabbagehead), most colloquialisms for less than average intelligence are derived by using a contrast with one of the multiple meanings of power, as the following six definitions from *The New Shorter Oxford English Dictionary* (Brown, 1993, pp. 2315–2316) demonstrate.

- *Power* **meaning "control or authority over others"** accounts for the use of contrasting terms, such as *idiot*, from Greek for private citizen; *simple,* for a person of humble birth; and *foolish,* originally meaning "humble, insignificant." These synonyms for a person with less than average intelligence convey the idea of powerlessness because they contrast with public officials and aristocratic rulers who have control, and thus power, over others. Original meanings are sometimes further transformed; for example, *moron* is Greek for "foolish."

- *Power* **meaning "strength, might"** contributes colloquialisms using the opposite of strength and its synonyms "strong" and "hard" to denote people with less than average intelligence, such as in *weak-minded, feeble-minded,* and *soft in the head. Lame* means "a weak limb" and contributes to "lame brain." *Imbecile* literally means "without support, weak."

- *Power* **meaning "a particular . . . physical faculty"** such as the powers of perception, described as "keen" or "acute" (sense of smell or hearing) and "sharp," "clear," or "penetrating" (sense of sight), contributes the contrast for sensory metaphors of powerlessness such as the colloquialisms of *dull, obtuse, thick-headed,* and *dense.*

- *Power meaning* **"supply of energy, especially electricity"** provides the contrast for conveying powerlessness through such idioms as *dim bulb* and *dim-witted* versus *bright* or *brilliant.*

- *Power* **meaning "an abundance of, a great deal of"** is itself a colloquialism (he has a powerful lot of money) and leads to expressions that imply powerlessness by incorporating the idea of not being complete or not having enough, such as *not playing with a full deck, one brick short of a full load, half-witted,* and *nothing upstairs.* The original meaning of *vacuous* is "lacking content" and of *addled* is "a spoiled egg, empty inside." Both are similar to the contemporary colloquialisms of *airhead, bubblehead,* and *empty-headed.*

- *Power* **meaning "a form or source of energy or force applied . . . to produce motion"** relates to the idea of speed versus slowness and provides adjectives and synonyms currently most often used in vernacular speech for people with less than average intelligence: being *delayed, retarded, slow witted,* and being a *slow thinker* or *slow learner.*

Speakers of American English learn that a person who "thinks quickly" or is "brilliant" also has power, and being a "slow learner" and "dull" means one is not powerful because fusing unrelated multiple meanings of a single word is one way that idiomatic meaning is created (Levorato, 1993). The subtle attributions conveyed by idioms and other colloquialisms are more harmful than overt prejudice because they are difficult to identify and thus hard to dispute (Leets & Giles, 1997).

Constantly referring to people with developmental disabilities as powerless gives power to people without a labeled deficiency not because they are innately powerful but because they are at the opposite pole of the power dichotomy. Their power is not removed by proverbs that relegate them to the powerless bottom layer of a class system or by metaphors that define them as having low status and needing control. It is not necessary to use euphemisms to create distance from the mere thought of their average intelligence. Unlabeled people, therefore, do not have to earn the power conferred on them (McIntosh, 1988). Because language shapes perception (Hill & Mannheim, 1992), they are able to exercise power as long as their right to do so remains unchallenged.

By the same argument, people who are labeled are powerless because they are defined to be so, not because they are unable to exercise power. In fact, to overcome the unearned attribution of powerlessness, they have to prove their abilities and, even then, that proof can be ignored or misinterpreted by others who expect to see powerlessness and, therefore, see it. Their right and ability to exercise power is constantly denied, both implicitly and explicitly, by the connotations of language as well as by how others' actions, and even labeled people's own actions, are guided by that language.

Traditional Solution   Normalization (Wolfensberger, 1980) has successfully improved the lives of people with developmental disabilities, for example, by abolishing dehumanizing living conditions and improving attitudes toward them (Rees, Spreen, & Harnadek, 1991), and might also provide the guidelines for additional reforms. Normalization theory hypothesizes that powerlessness (marginalization) is the result of traits and behaviors that are devalued (stigmatized) by others. Helping people with developmental disabilities live within those community norms and changing some of those norms and values will result, according to the principle of normalization, in less marginalization. People with developmental disabilities might, therefore, gain more power if society's values changed.

Alternative Solutions   An alternative view is that normalization theory depends on "the assumption . . . [that] there is consensus between providers and users" (Chappell, 1992, p. 41) about what is a normalized activity or a stigmatizing trait. If a person with a disability embraces different norms (e.g., rejecting society's norms of how he should be treated and how he should behave), then having to act in terms of others' norms so as not to be marginalized and devalued by them is oppression. When powerlessness is seen as being created by the language people use rather than as being the consequence of a trait of a person, then attention can be focused on questions of power rather than of value. That is, the root of the problem is not that certain behaviors are unacceptable and particular traits stigmatizing but that others have been granted the power to enforce behavior and define stigma (Abberley, 1987). Further improvement in the lives of people with developmental disabilities in this conceptualization requires asking who has power and determining how their power to define stigma can be rejected, rather than asking who is stigmatized and how can their stigma be reduced.

Separate Power and Intelligence   Service providers can challenge the unearned power of people who are not labeled by not using any colloquial expression that connects intelligence with power. Rather than focusing efforts on changing language used to refer to people with developmental disabilities, they can question terms applied to people without labeled disabilities. Is an idea voiced by a particular person an acute insight or simply interesting? Does an unlabeled person have an electric personality and bright ideas, or is she just provocative? Does another person think fast on her feet or just make relevant rejoinders?

Not using colloquialisms that draw on one of the meanings of power might, at a minimum, stop reinforcing the implicit connection between intelligence and power. It has never been demonstrated, however, that attitudes can be changed by not using certain terms; that is, naming things confers the power to shape attitudes, but the "unnaming process" does not necessarily reverse or preclude those attitudes (Zola, 1993, p. 167). Therefore, unnaming must be combined with other strategies.

Assist People to Reject the Power of Others to Define Them   According to Breton, subjective empowerment "refers to a way of thinking about oneself, a way of defining oneself and one's situation" (1994, p. 28), similar to what Wehmeyer and Palmer (1998) called *learned hopefulness*. Service providers can support activities that build pride in the identity a particular person has chosen and solidarity with others who share that identity. Embracing the power to define and value one's own identity (e.g., "Black is beautiful") decreases internalized oppression (Pheterson, 1986) by rejecting others' rights to control one's feelings, a lesson learned in both the civil rights and women's movements.

For many people, empowerment has occurred because of their participation in People First. No amount or kind of euphemisms, alternative metaphors, normalization strategies, or system advocacy by service providers can match the effectiveness of the People First organization; "self-developed empowerment . . . [rather than] empowerment bestowed from others" is real social power (Mackelprang & Salsgiver, 1996, p. 12).

Counteract Powerlessness   When the problem of disability is defined as social exclusion rather than as a shortcoming of the individual, remedies can be sought through legal and political efforts (Hahn, 1993). Providing the supports that enable people to exercise their personal and political power not only increases their civil rights and access to better goods and services, but also neutralizes the image of powerlessness conveyed in colloquialisms. For Ted, after he discovered the joy of choosing what to wear each morning, empowerment meant changing staff schedules and adding a later bus instead of getting him up earlier when making choices took longer than his former morning routine. For John, empowerment was getting the city to install a pedestrian crosswalk where it was needed so he could walk to his place of employment and receiving the supports he needed to be president of the local People First chapter. Anna exercised her power one day at the meals program she attended; she refused, quite emphatically, to sit at the "needs help" table and sat instead at a regular table. For Gloria, it meant receiving the support needed to be part of the steering committee for a community powwow. Bobby chose to participate on the committee that interviewed and selected new staff for the group home where he lived. Margaret requested assistance with transportation to pursue her advocacy activities in local schools.

Eliminate the Power Differentials in Service Provision   Quality-of-life improvements within the service environment can also be the basis for empowerment by basing needed improvements on the values of the individuals receiving services and facilitating their participation in implementing change. For example, the staff evaluation form suggested in Chapter 8 can be used to measure a person's level of satisfaction with services and as a tool for the team to provide better services. It can also be used to impart real social power by having the results, by policy, determine staffing patterns, promotions, and merit increases.

At a minimum, service receivers need to wield power and feel empowered at team meetings. Choosing the time and place for the meeting, having the power to choose team members and veto the participation of particular people, determining who will chair the meeting, stopping the meeting at any time, and even being in control of assigning seats at the meeting can be empowering. The agency's policy manual, residence rules, and bill of rights can empower people if they are available in several forms (including sign language videotapes and videotapes of vignettes that demonstrate the rules and rights, as well as several levels of accessible language in printed materials) because then people can use them to their advantage or challenge their fairness. Service receivers can form an advisory board to solve internal problems (Boggs, 1992) or actually serve on the board of directors. Both service receivers and providers can participate in collaborative relationships to plan agency training programs (Heller, Pederson, & Miller, 1996) and research projects (Pederson, Chaikin, Koehler, Campbell, & Arcand, 1993). Ultimately, real social power will be transferred to people with developmental disabilities when they control their funding dollars and own, rather than rent, their homes (Racino, Walker, O'Connor, & Taylor, 1993).

Some service providers may argue that these activities take a lot of time (they do) and are not bread-and-butter services, only frosting on the cake. But who has the power to determine what is a basic service and what is a frill? If we want people with developmental disabilities to have equal power in society at large, then they must become equals within the service environment. They should have the right and the power to shape services in terms of their own values. What service this is and how it is offered can only be determined with reference to each person's own values and goals. There is no single answer to any question about what services are basic or appropriate because "people with developmental disabilities" are only similar in that they have a developmental disability; that is, they only share the feature that defines them as a member of the category. Providing values-based services to people who have their own values, choices, and visions for the future is a powerful way, and possibly the only way, to create equality.

POINTS TO REMEMBER

To empower people with developmental disabilities, we need to adopt a new conceptualization of disability by employing the following four strategies:

1. *Reject the conceptualization of disability as a personal character-istic that leads to low status and, instead, locate the problem in the American social class and individualist person schemas.* Seeing intelligence as the key to personal success in the class system and, therefore, assuming that intellectual deficits will result in fewer achievements, places responsibility on the individual and limits in-tervention to supports designed to help the person live up to his or her full potential. Shifting to a conceptualization of disability as the inability of American society to provide equally for all its members encourages interventions that support the exercise of power, challenge inequality, and reject the cloak of oppression.

2. *Assist people to reject the power of others to define them or the rules of acceptability.* Rather than helping people to be more like others so as not to be devalued and marginalized, encourage others to accept them as they already are. Margaret, for example, gained pride in who she was and rejected the right of others to determine how she viewed herself or how she was going to live her life.

3. *Resist using schemas and language that define disability as neces-sarily resulting in powerlessness or the lack of a labeled disability as automatically conferring power.* Describing one person as "thinking quickly" and another as "thinking slowly" also conveys the idea that one is powerful and the other is not. Rather than attributing power to some and denying it to others, learn to see power as equally possible, although not equivalently exercised, by various individuals. One per-son may choose to run for political office and another may choose to accept direction from others, regardless of whether either has been labeled as having a developmental disability.

4. *Affirm the personal power of all people by assisting them in receiv-ing services and supports in terms of their values.* Support those activities that empower people to act on their values, whether that is by assigning seats at a team meeting or serving on the board of directors. What is a basic service to one person may be a frill for another and vice versa; all people have their own values.

Part IV

"MY OWN VALUES"

My memories have captured and crystallized special moments, meaningful to me because each moment combined a piece of theory with a bit of practice and evolved into the main themes of this book. Therefore, I can think of no better way to close than to share one last story of each person you have met in these pages.

10

Last Thoughts

The real people who shared their lives with me and helped me to formulate my ideas about values-based services have moved on, some to other towns and cities, some to new homes or jobs, and all to new stages of their lives. I hope that knowing them through my eyes will help others to understand not just values-based services but how these services can be applied one person at a time, to understand not just schema theory but how this theory can expand applied behavior analysis, and to understand not just category construction but how meanings attached to the label of developmental disability affect our services.

VALUES-BASED SERVICES

Every day I could hear Trudy, John's job coach, buy a soda for her morning shot of caffeine; the soda machine and a park bench were located just outside my office window. One time, I heard the quarters drop but no rattle and thump of the descending can, and then I heard a few choice expletives and the sound of a fist banging on the machine. I was just getting up to get the machine key when I heard John's voice.

"You mad. Okay. No hit. No yell."

John was telling Trudy exactly what she told him whenever he started to get angry. His behavior intervention plan stressed that he had the right to be angry but not the right to hit people or things or to intimidate others with violent, loud swearing. The person intervening would then ask him to remember the other ways to handle anger that he himself had suggested when he and his team had made this plan.

I was filled with admiration for Trudy when I heard her respond:

"You're right. I'm mad. I'll sit here and cool off."

A few minutes later, I heard John make the same offer to Trudy that she had made on many occasions in the past to him.

"Wanna talk?"

Trudy told John about the argument she'd had with a friend the day before and the pressure she was feeling because of all the work that she had to do today. John listened and agreed how upset that could make a person. Their exchange made me realize that Trudy and John had transcended the service provider–service receiver relationship and were friends. She saw him as her equal because his disability was irrelevant to her. John now saw Trudy as his equal because her support was not in the form of telling him what to do but helping him do what he knew he needed to do.

They transcended the power differential built into language by daily interactions based on respect for each other's values. They had come to know they were alike in many ways. They both liked to lift weights and shoot pool because they valued fitness and physical skills. They both were fiercely independent but easily hurt by unkind words. They were also aware of their differences. For example, John liked regularity and predictability in his life, whereas Trudy sought change and excitement.

Even though I support the idea of values-based services because my theoretical orientation as an anthropologist is toward cultural relativism when studying groups, I am still occasionally amazed at how successful an approach it is in practice with a single person. Many authors have recommended that service providers and service receivers and their families should respect each other. The methods of values-based services are an effective way to build that respect.

CAUSES AND REASONS

Ted, at irregular times and in different environments and circumstances, would jump up and begin doing calisthenics. After 10 or 15 seconds, he would just as suddenly stop and direct his attention elsewhere. His team didn't particularly worry about the behavior, as it was not life threatening. Yet, they continued to speculate about it, partly because it drew attention in public but mostly because they suspected that Ted might be communicating discomfort or unease.

Team members wondered whether Ted did not like crowds or whether he had another reason, perhaps a sudden desire to break out of the confines of this time and place. No one, however, suggested that he did it "for no reason." The phrase that I heard most often was that he did it "for a reason we don't understand yet." Nor did anyone expect it to be related only to Ted's values.

Seeing Ted burst into activity is similar to watching a football game without knowing either the rules or the values underlying the rules. However, behavior can be analyzed with both the tools of the behaviorist and the cognitivist. Finding the pattern in specific sequences of stimulus and response and identifying the meaning of his actions from Ted's point of view are both important sources of information in the struggle to understand Ted or any human.

THE MIDDLE GROUND

Several years after Anna's team found ways for her to control her own access to food, I was visiting the institution where she had formerly lived. One staff member there approached me, knowing that Anna now received services at the agency where I was employed, and wistfully asked:

"Does Anna get crackers with every meal now?"

She went on to tell me how angry it used to make her when Anna asked for crackers but she couldn't give them to her because the dietician wouldn't allow the extra calories. When Anna is as old as she is, she asked me, what difference does it make if she gains a little weight?

I could only see myself in this staff member and think how many times over the years I had argued with the state inspector, a nice person whose underwear condition still is unknown to me. There is no single right answer for every situation. Too often, the alternatives are forced into a needlessly divisive contrast between supporting individual uniqueness or supporting universal human rights; that is, Anna is a totally unique individual whose choice of crackers with every meal should be honored, versus Anna, like all humans, has the right to a nutritious diet and good health, therefore she cannot have crackers with every meal.

Her comment, however, set bells off in my head. We had only seen Anna as wanting access to snacks or wanting to control when and what she ate. We hadn't found the middle ground that situated her actions in context. Anna was from a German background and, being a fourth-generation German American myself, I knew from direct experience that a meal isn't a meal unless there is bread or crackers on the table. They do not have to be eaten, but they need to be there in order for it to be a proper meal.

Anna is unique in some ways and like all other humans in some ways. But she is most similar to other Midwestern, small-town, German American women who share the meaning she gives to her actions. Professionals can find the middle ground with each other by looking for answers from the service receiver's point of view, relative to the values she shares with others in the same social categories.

EVERYONE HAS VALUES

"I should have gotten here earlier. I wasn't thinking about how much time it would take Margaret to pack and say goodbye. I guess I'm just not a very good planner."

Margaret's sister continued on about needing to get gas before they started the trip to their hometown where she lived and where Margaret was moving. She said that she did not really like to drive this far by herself because she was always afraid of getting a flat tire and not being able to fix it. However, her husband had given her a cell phone for the trip so maybe she could call for help. . . . I let the words wash over me as I marveled at how much she was like Margaret—older, heavier, and more talkative maybe, but there was no mistaking that they were sisters. Even if they hadn't looked alike, just the content of her concerns was familiar. They were both, perhaps, closer than most to the stereotype of a worrywart, but the themes were clearly reflective of a rights-based, individualist world view. For example, failure is due to something in the person rather than in the situation; choices are personally controlled; time stretches into the future in a line, so there will be future consequences to current actions; getting assistance from others is help-ful; and risk can be averted by planning ahead.

Margaret and her sister were just as much part of a social category with regular and patterned ways of behaving as Gloria, Bobby, Anna, or John. Everyone has his or her own values, not just recent immigrants, ethnically or racially distinct people, or speakers of a language other than English. Identifying Margaret's middle-class values and tradi-tional gender role expectations was just as important as helping her cope with grief and mental illness.

In retrospect, after meeting Margaret's sister, I wondered if we had assumed too quickly that her father protected her because she has a de-velopmental disability. How easy it is to allow the label of developmen-tal disability to overshadow other explanations. Margaret and her sister are very similar to each other because they both have middle-class val-ues, rather than different because Margaret has a disability and her sis-ter does not. Together they remind me that the phrase "everyone has values" has two meanings. Everyone has values, regardless of whether they are middle class or working class; African American, Native American, or Norwegian American; young or old; or English-speaking or Spanish-speaking. Furthermore, regardless of whether they have a developmental disability and despite the severity of that disability, everyone has values.

FOCAL POINTS AND BOUNDARIES

My favorite memory of Bobby is through the eyes of Glen, the staff member with whom I argued most often and who was the least like me in so many ways. He was very grounded in the practical realities of helping people eat, shower, get to work, have friends, and be happy. I saw him as having no sense of humor, no flexibility, and no insight into the creative possibilities of life. He saw me, I suspect, as having no sense of responsibility, too much flexibility, and no understanding of the pragmatic necessities of life. Therefore, I remember with particular relish the day he told me about Bobby's last visit to the doctor to check that all the infection was gone after his toenail surgery. Glen was laugh-ing so hard he could hardly relate the story.

"Bobby said this to the doctor."

Then he proceeded to demonstrate a glaring face and a finger pointed at an imaginary doctor, followed by Bobby's sign for pain, and then a hip thrust to the side with the pointed finger now tapping on his right buttock.

"What did the doctor say?"

Between gusts of laughter, he managed to reply.

"She said, 'Well, yeah, Bobby, you're a pain in the butt sometimes, too.'"

I am sure there are things the doctor might find funny that I don't or vice versa. I know there are things Bobby and I find funny that Glen doesn't. Maybe, Glen finds things funny that none of the rest of us do. But it was clear that Bobby, Glen, the doctor, and I all thought Bobby's comment and the doctor's rejoinder were funny.

Sharing the focal points of categories, that is, knowing when something is really red, really abuse, really theft, or really funny, is why we can talk about *American* culture and an *American* world view. Shared focal points allow us to feel that there are overarching values in American society—on truth, justice, freedom, and equality—yet find many differences among ourselves because we do not share the boundaries for when a particular situation is no longer just or equal.

It's why we cannot know how to teach someone else an acceptable way to act just by thinking about our own values. Finding where people in a particular social category draw the boundary between acceptable and unacceptable behavior takes a lot of hard work. Analyzing an image schema like the one of theft in Chapter 4 or a proposition schema like the one for decision making in Chapter 5 is a major task. But it is well worth the effort, in my opinion, because it allows us to discover very subtle differences that may be creating very major problems.

MAKING VALUES EXPLICIT

Over the years, I talked often about values with many people, including staff members and the people using our support services and their families, and people in the community. At first we only worked at understanding the differences between Indian and non-Indian because it was the most obvious variation and because not understanding it well enough is why we failed to provide adequate supports for Delbert. Eventually, staff members became more aware of their own values, found that not all staff had the same values, and realized that the people they supported had their own values, too. We learned that our support services were far more satisfactory if we found the right values match between service providers and receivers. We discovered that teaching new behavior was easier and generalized more quickly when it was approached in terms of the person's specific values. We also taught "know why" as well as "know how" to help people regulate their own behavior more effectively.

So, the final memory I am going to share is of Gloria on the day she took me to see her house, which was being renovated with funding from a housing authority grant. Because she was very involved in choosing paint colors, the location for appliances, and other modifications, she wanted to show me how the work was progressing. As I entered, I exclaimed over the beautiful oak floors, one of the few things in the house that didn't need to be replaced. Shaking her head in disagreement, Gloria explained her choice to me.

"Carpet. That wood floor cold."

I was lost in my own reverie about a home of one's own, making decisions, wood floors, and different values, when Gloria, impatient with my long hesitation and not wanting to discuss this issue further, repeated very firmly:

"Carpet, Lilah."

Then she paused, to emphasize the finality of this decision and to deliver the justification that she knew—from our many discussions about her values as a woman, a Lakota, and an American citizen—would convince me. With a smile, she said:

"My own values."

References

Aamodt, A. (1981). Neighboring: Discovering support systems among Norwegian-American women. In D. Messerschmidt (Ed.), *Anthropologists at home: Toward an anthropology of issues in America* (pp. 133–149). New York: Cambridge University Press.

Abberley, P. (1987). The concept of oppression and the development of a social theory of disability. *Disability, Handicap & Society, 2,* 5–19.

Abberley, P. (1993). Disabled people and normality. In J. Swaim, V. Finkelstein, S. French, & M. Oliver (Eds.), *Disabling barriers—Enabling environments* (pp. 107–115). Newbury Park, CA: Sage.

Abu-Lughod, L., & Lutz, C. (1990). Introduction: Emotion, discourse, and the politics of everyday life. In C. Lutz & L. Abu-Lughod (Eds.), *Language and the politics of emotion* (pp. 1–23). New York: Cambridge University Press.

Alba, R. (1990). *Ethnic identity: The transformation of white America.* New Haven, CT: Yale University Press.

Albers, P. (1979). Freedom and responsibility in scientific research. In M. Leininger (Ed.), *Transcultural nursing* (pp. 569–578). New York: Masson International Nursing Publications.

Allbritton, D., McKoon, G., & Gerrig, R. (1995). Metaphor-based schemas and text representations: Making connections through conceptual metaphors. *Journal of Experimental Psychology, 21,* 612–625.

Allen, B., & Allen, A. (1994). Looking past the logic of dichotomy. *Journal of The Association for People with Severe Handicaps, 19,* 233–234.

Althen, G. (1988). *American ways: A guide for foreigners in the United States.* Yarmouth, ME: Intercultural Press.

Amado, A. (1993). *Friendships and community connections between people with and without developmental disabilities.* Baltimore: Paul H. Brookes Publishing Co.

Angrosino, M. (1976). The evolution of the new applied anthropology. In M. Angrosino (Ed.), *Do applied anthropologists apply anthropology?* (pp. 1–9). Athens: University of Georgia Press.

Aponte, J., Rivers, R., & Wohl, J. (1995). *Psychological interventions and cultural diversity.* Needham Heights, MA: Allyn & Bacon.

Atwater, L. (1995). The relationship between supervisory power and organizational characteristics. *Group and Organization Management, 20,* 460–485.

Bader, G., & Nyce, J. (1993). When freedom of choice fails: Ideology and action in a secondary school hypermedia project. *National Association for the Practice of Anthropology, 12,* 66–72.

Balshem, M. (1991). Cancer, control, and causality: Talking about cancer in a working-class community. *American Ethnologist, 18,* 152–172.

Bannerman, D., Sheldon, J., Sherman, J., & Harchik, A. (1991). Balancing the right to personal liberties: The rights of people with developmental disabilities to eat too many doughnuts and take a nap. *Journal of Applied Behavior Analysis, 23,* 79–89.

Baron, A. (1991). *Work engendered: Toward a new history of American labor.* Ithaca: Cornell University Press.

Barrett, R. (1984). *Culture and conduct.* Belmont, CA: Wadsworth.

Beatty, J. (1994). Language and communication. In L. Adler & U. Gielen (Eds.), *Cross-cultural topics in psychology* (pp. 41–51). Westport, CT: Praeger.

Berlin, B., & Kay, P. (1969). *Basic color terms: Their universality and evolution.* Berkeley: University of California Press.

Bernheimer, L., Gallimore, R., & Weisner, T. (1990). Ecocultural theory as a context for the individual family service plan. *Journal of Early Intervention, 14,* 219–233.

Bersani, H. (1996). Leadership in developmental disabilities: Where we've been, where we are, and where we're going. In G. Dybwad & H. Bersani (Eds.), *New voices: Self-advocacy by people with disabilities* (pp. 258–269). Cambridge, MA: Brookline Books.

Biegel, D., Cunningham, J., Yamatani, H., & Martz, P. (1989). Self-reliance and blue-collar unemployment in a steel town. *Social Work, 34,* 399–407.

Biersdorff, K. (1991). Pain insensitivity and indifference: Alternative explanations for some medical catastrophes. *Mental Retardation, 29,* 359–362.

Biklen, D., & Duchan, J. (1994). "I am intelligent": The social construction of mental retardation. *Journal of The Association for Persons with Severe Handicaps, 19,* 173–184.

Bird, F., Dores, P., Moniz, D., & Robinson, J. (1989). Reducing severe aggressive and self-injurious behaviors with functional communication training. *American Journal on Mental Retardation, 94,* 37–48.

Black, M. (1973). Belief systems. In J. Honigmann (Ed.), *Handbook of social and cultural anthropology* (pp. 509–577). Chicago: Rand McNally.

Blatt, S. (1990). Interpersonal relatedness and self-definition: Two personality configurations and their implications for psychopathology and psychotherapy. In J. Singer (Ed.), *Repression and dissociation* (pp. 299–335). Chicago: University of Chicago Press.

Bledstein, B. (1994). The definition of a profession: The authority of metaphor in the history of intelligence testing, 1890–1930. *Reviews in American History, 22,* 113–119.

Bloch, M. (1994). Language, anthropolgy, and cognitive science. In R. Borofsky (Ed.), *Assessing cultural anthropology* (pp. 276–283). New York: McGraw-Hill.

Blotzer, M., & Ruth, R. (1995). On sitting with uncertainty: Treatment considerations for persons with disabilities. In M. Blotzer & R. Ruth (Eds.), *Sometimes you just want to feel like a human being* (pp. 15–24). Baltimore: Paul H. Brookes Publishing Co.

Blustein, J. (1991). *Care and commitment: Taking the personal point of view.* New York: Oxford University Press.

Bogdan, R., & Taylor, S. (1992). The social construction of humanness: Relationships with severely disabled people. In P. Ferguson, D. Ferguson, & S. Taylor (Eds.), *Interpreting disability: A qualitative reader* (pp. 275–293). New York: Teachers College Press.

Boggs, E. (1992). Getting into the jet stream. *Mental Retardation, 30,* 178–182.

Bohlken, B. (1996). The idiom experience. *ETC.: A Review of General Semantics, 53,* 218–221.

Boone, M. (1991). Policy and praxis in the 1990s: Anthropology and the domestic health policy arena. In C. Hill (Ed.), *Training manual in applied medical anthropology, special publication #27* (pp. 23–53). Washington, DC: American Anthropology Association.

Borofsky, R. (1994). On the knowledge and knowing of cultural activities. In R. Borofsky (Ed.), *Assessing cultural anthropology* (pp. 331–348). New York: McGraw-Hill.

Bourdieu, P. (1991). *Language and symbolic power* (G. Raymond & M. Adamson, trans.). Cambridge, MA: Harvard University Press.

Bower, B. (1997). My culture, my self. *Science News, 152,* 248–249.

Brannigan, A. (1997). Self control, social control and evolutionary psychology: Towards an integrated perspective on crime. *Canadian Journal of Criminology, 39,* 403–431.

Brave Bird, M., & Erdoes, R. (1993). *Ohitika woman.* New York: Harper-Perennial.

Breton, M. (1994). Relating competence-promotion and empowerment. *Journal of Progressive Human Services, 5,* 27–44.

Brislin, R., Cushner, K., Cherrie, C., & Yong, M. (1986). *Intercultural interactions: A practical guide.* Newbury Park, CA: Sage.

Brown, F. (1991). Creative daily scheduling: A nonintrusive approach to challenging behaviors in community residences. *Journal of The Association for Persons with Severe Handicaps, 16,* 75–84.

Brown, L. (1993). *The new shorter Oxford English dictionary.* Oxford, England: Clarendon Press.

Burgess, D., Kempton, W., & MacLaury, R. (1985). Tarahumara color modifiers: Individual variation and evolutionary change. In J. Dougherty (Ed.), *Directions in cognitive anthropology* (pp. 49–72). Urbana: University of Illinois Press.

Burgest, D. (1982). *Social work practice with minorities.* Metuchen, NJ: The Scarecrow Press.

Burke, J. (1989). *Contemporary approaches to psychotherapy and counseling: The self regulation and maturity model.* Pacific Grove, CA: Brooks/Cole.

Buzzanell, P., & Burrell, N. (1997). Family and workplace conflict: Examining metaphorical conflict schemas and expressions across context and sex. *Human Communication Research, 24,* 109–147.

Calvez, M. (1993). Social interactions in the neighborhood: Cultural approach to social integration of individuals with mental retardation. *Mental Retardation, 31,* 418–423.

Carr, E., Levin, L., McConnachie, G., Carlson, J., Kemp, D., & Smith, C. (Eds.). (1994). *Communication-based intervention for problem behavior.* Baltimore: Paul H. Brookes Publishing Co.

Casselman, B. (1998). Dissing the weather and the dim-witted. *Canadian Geographic, 118,* 33.

Cerroni-Long, E. (1993). Life and cultures: The test of real participant observation. In P. DeVita & J. Armstrong (Eds.), *Distant mirrors: America as a foreign culture* (pp. 77–92). Belmont, CA: Wadsworth.

Chambers, E. (1985). *Applied anthropology: A practical guide.* Englewood Cliffs, NJ: Prentice Hall.

Chappell, A. (1992). Towards a sociological critique of the normalisation principle. *Disability, Handicap and Society, 7,* 35–51.

Charonko, C. (1992). Cultural influences in "noncompliant" behavior and decision making. *Holistic Nursing Practice, 6,* 73–78.

Chen, H. (1992). *Chinatown no more.* Ithaca, NY: Cornell University Press.

Chock, P. (1987). The irony of stereotypes: Toward an anthropology of ethnicity. *Cultural Anthropology, 2,* 347–368.

Chong, D. (1996). Values versus interests in the explanation of social conflict. *University of Pennsylvania Law Review, 5,* 2079–2134.

Chrisman, N., & Johnson, T. (1990). Clinically applied anthropology. In T. Johnson & C. Sargent (Eds.), Medical anthropology: Contemporary theory and method (pp. 93–113). New York: Praeger.

Christopherson, V. (1966). *Sociocultural correlates of pain response.* Tucson: University of Arizona Press.

Clausner, T., & Croft, W. (1997). Productivity and schematicity in metaphors. *Cognitive Science, 21,* 247–282.

Cohen, M. (1998). Perceptions of power in client/worker relationships. *Families in Society: The Journal of Contemporary Human Services, 79,* 433–443.

Cohen, R. (1981). Evolutionary epistemology and human values. *Current Anthropology, 22,* 201–218.

Cohler, B. (1992). Intent and meaning in psychoanalysis and cultural study. In T. Schwartz, G. White, & C. Lutz (Eds.), *New directions in psychological anthropology* (pp. 269–293). Cambridge, England: Cambridge University Press.

Cole, M. (1985). The zone of proximal development: Where culture and cognition create each other. In J. Wertsch (Ed.), *Culture, communication, and cognition: Vygotskian perspectives* (pp. 146–161). New York: Cambridge University Press.

Cotton, C. (1994). Social class as a neglected variable in organizational behavior. *The Journal of Psychology, 128,* 409–418.

Crimmins, D. (1994). Quality of life for persons with challenging behaviors: Intervention goal, contradiction in terms or both? In D. Goode (Ed.), *Quality of life for persons with disabilities: International perspectives and issues* (pp. 208–217). Cambridge, MA: Brookline Books.

Curtis, J., & Tepperman, L. (1994). *Haves and have-nots.* Englewood Cliffs, NJ: Prentice Hall.

D'Andrade, R. (1984). Cultural meaning systems. In R. Shweder & R. LeVine (Eds.), *Culture theory: Essays on mind, self, and emotion* (pp. 88–119). Cambridge, England: Cambridge University Press.

D'Andrade, R. (1987). A folk model of the mind. In D. Holland & N. Quinn (Eds.), *Cultural models in language and thought* (pp. 112–150). Cambridge, England: Cambridge University Press.

D'Andrade, R. (1991). The identification of schemas in naturalistic data. In M. Horowitz (Ed.), *Person schemas and maladaptive interpersonal behavior patterns* (pp. 279–302). Chicago: University of Chicago Press.

D'Andrade, R. (1992). Schemas and motivation. In R. D'Andrade & C. Strauss (Eds.), *Human motives and cultural models* (pp. 23–44). Cambridge, England: Cambridge University Press.

D'Andrade, R., & Strauss, C. (Eds.). (1992). *Human motives and cultural models.* Cambridge, England: Cambridge University Press.

Daniels, R. (1970). Cultural identities among the Oglala Sioux. In E. Nurge (Ed.), *The modern Sioux* (pp. 198–245). Lincoln: University of Nebraska Press.

Dattilo, J., & Rusch, F. (1985). Effects of choice on leisure participation for persons with severe handicaps. *Journal of The Association for Persons with Severe Handicaps, 10,* 194–199.

deCraemer, W. (1983). A cross-cultural perspective on personhood. *Milbank Memorial Fund Quarterly, 61,* 19–34.

Demchak, M., & Bossert, K. (1995). *Assessing problem behaviors.* Washington, DC: American Association on Mental Retardation.

DeMott, B. (1990). *The imperial middle: Why Americans can't think straight about class.* New York: William Morrow & Co.

Denzin, N. (1989). *Interpretive interactionism.* Newbury Park, CA: Sage.

DeVault, G., Krug, C., & Fake, S. (1996). Why does Samantha act that way? *Exceptional Parent, 26,* 43–47.

Deveaux, M. (1994). Feminism and empowerment: A critical reading of Foucault. *Feminist Studies, 20,* 223–247.

Devereux, G. (1991). Ethnopsychological aspects of the terms "deaf" and "dumb". In D. Howes (Ed.), *The varieties of sensory experience: A source-*

book in the anthropology of the senses (pp. 43–46). Toronto: University of Toronto Press.

DeVita, P., & Armstrong, J. (1993). *Distant mirrors: America as a foreign culture.* Belmont, CA: Wadsworth.

Dinerstein, R. (1994). Revising the consent handbook—From consent to choice. *AAMR News & Notes, 7,* 1, 5.

Dombeck, M. (1991). *Dreams and professional personhood: The context of dream telling and dream interpretation among American psychotherapists.* Albany: State University of New York Press.

Domínguez, V. (1986). *White by definition: Social classification in Creole Louisiana.* New Brunswick, NJ: Rutgers University Press.

Dougherty, J. (1985). *Directions in cognitive anthropology.* Urbana: University of Illinois Press.

Douglas, M. (1973). *Natural symbols: Explorations in cosmology.* New York: Vintage Books.

Downing, C., & Cobb, A. (1990). Value orientations of homeless men. *Western Journal of Nursing Research, 12,* 619–628.

Drews, E., & Lipson, L. (1978). *Values and humanity.* New York: John Wiley & Sons.

Dundes, A. (1968). The number three in American culture. In A. Dundes (Ed.), *Every man his way* (pp. 401–424). Englewood Cliffs, NJ: Prentice Hall.

Duran, E. (1988). *Teaching the moderately and severely handicapped student and autistic adult.* Springfield, IL: Charles C. Thomas.

Durand, V., Crimmins, D., Caulfield, M., & Taylor, J. (1989). Reinforcer assessment: Using problem behavior to select reinforcers. *Journal of The Association for Persons with Severe Handicaps, 14,* 113–126.

Dussart, F. (1993). First impressions: Diary of a French anthropologist in New York City. In P. DeVita & J. Armstrong (Eds.), *Distant mirrors: America as a foreign culture* (pp. 66–76). Belmont, CA: Wadsworth.

Dybwad, G. (1996). Setting the stage historically. In G. Dybwad & H. Bersani (Eds.), *New voices: Self-advocacy by people with disabilities* (pp. 1–17). Cambridge, MA: Brookline Books.

Dybwad, G., & Bersani, H. (1996). *New voices: Self-advocacy by people with disabilities.* Cambridge, MA: Brookline Books.

Eddy, E., & Partridge, W. (Eds.). (1987). *Applied anthropology in America* (2nd ed.). New York: Columbia University Press.

Edelman, M. (1974). The political language of the helping professions. *Politics & Society, 4,* 295–310.

Edwards, S. (1997). The moral status of intellectually disabled individuals. *The Journal of Medicine and Philosophy, 22,* 29–42.

Erdoes, R. (1990). *Crying for a dream: The world through Native American eyes.* Sante Fe, NM: Bear & Co. Publishers.

Errington, F. (1987). Reflexivity deflected: The festival of nations as an American cultural performance. *American Ethnologist, 14,* 654–667.

Esber, G. (1979). Designing Apache homes with Apaches. In R. Wulff & S. Fiske (Eds.), *Anthropological praxis: Translating knowledge into action* (pp. 187–196). Boulder, CO: Westview Press.

Evans, I., & Meyer, L. (1985). *An educative approach to behavior problems: A practical decision model for intervention with severely handicapped learners.* Baltimore: Paul H. Brookes Publishing Co.

Ewing, K. (1990). The illusion of wholeness: Culture, self, and the experience of inconsistency. *Ethos, 18,* 251–278.

Fahey, T. (1995). Privacy and the family: Conceptual and empirical reflections. *Sociology, 29,* 687–702.

Farb, P. (1974). *Word play: What happens when people talk.* New York: Bantam Books.

Feldman, J., & Lynch, J. (1988). Self-generated validity and other effects of measurement on belief, attitude, intention, and behavior. *Journal of Applied Psychology, 73,* 421–435.

Feldman, S. (1997). The revolt against cultural authority: Power/knowledge as an assumption in organization theory. *Human Relations, 50,* 937–955.

Feraca, S. (1990). *Why don't they give them guns?: The great American Indian myth.* New York: University Press of America.

Ferguson, D. (1994). Is communication really the point?: Some thoughts on interventions and membership. *Mental Retardation, 32,* 7–18.

Ferguson, D., Meyer, G., Jeanchild, L., Juniper, L., & Zingo, J. (1992). Figuring out what to do with the grownups: How teachers make inclusion "work" for students with disabilities. *Journal of The Association for Persons with Severe Handicaps, 17,* 218–226.

Ferguson, P., Ferguson, D., & Taylor, S. (Eds.). (1992). *Interpreting disability: A qualitative reader.* New York: Teachers College Press.

Fergusson, R. (1983). *The facts on file dictionary of proverbs.* New York: Market House Books, Ltd.

Fernald, C. (1995). When in London . . . : Differences in disability language preferences among English-speaking cultures. *Mental Retardation, 33,* 99–103.

Fetterman, D. (1987). The ethnographic evaluator. In E. Eddy & W. Partridge (Eds.), *Applied anthropology in America* (2nd ed., pp. 340–365). New York: Columbia University Press.

Fischer, C., Hout, M., Jankowski, M., Lucas, S., Swidler, A., & Voss, K. (1996). *Inequality by design: Cracking the bell curve myth.* Princeton, NJ: Princeton University Press.

Fiske, S., Morling, B., & Stevens, L. (1996). Controlling self and others: A theory of anxiety, mental control, and social control. *Personality and Social Psychology Bulletin, 22,* 115–123.

Foley, D. (1989). Does the working class have a culture in the anthropological sense? *Cultural Anthropology, 4,* 137–162.

Follett, W. (1966). *Modern American usage.* New York: Hill & Wang.

Ford, J., Mongon, D., & Whelan, M. (1982). *Special education and social control: Invisible disasters.* London: Routledge & Kegan Paul.

Foster, M. (1994). Symbolism: The foundation of culture. In T. Ingold (Ed.), *Companion encyclopedia of anthropology* (pp. 366–393). London: Routledge.

Fouquier, E. (1981). On the interpretation of other people's dress. *Diogenes, 113,* 177–193.

Fox, W. (1982). Why we should abandon Maslow's need hierarchy theory. *Journal of Humanist Education and Development, 21,* 29–32.

Foxx, R., Faw, G., Taylor, S., Davis, P., & Fulia, R. (1993). "Would I be able to . . .?": Teaching clients to assess the availability of their community living style preferences. *American Journal on Mental Retardation, 98,* 235–248.

Fried, C. (1980). Privacy: A rational context. In R. Wasserstrom (Ed.), *Today's moral problems* (pp. 351–370). New York: Macmillan.

Friedman, M. (1979). Confirmation and the community of otherness. In M. Leininger. (Ed.), *Transcultural nursing* (pp. 341–350). New York: Masson International Nursing Publications.

Fullwood, D. (1990). *Chances and choices.* Baltimore: Paul H. Brookes Publishing Co.

Furnham, A., & Hayward, R. (1997). A study and meta-analysis of lay attributions of cures for overcoming specific psychological problems. *Journal of Genetic Psychology, 158,* 315–332.

Gaines, A. (1982). Cultural definitions, behavior and the person in American psychiatry. In A. Marsella & G. White (Eds.), *Cultural conceptions of mental health and therapy* (pp. 167–192). Dordrecht: Reidel.

Gaines, A. (1992). From DSM-I to DSM III-R: Voices of self, mastery and the other: A cultural constructivist reading of United States psychiatric classification. *Social Science & Medicine, 25,* 3–24.

Gallimore, R., Goldenberg, C., & Weisner, T. (1993). The social construction and subjective reality of activity settings: Implications for community psychology. *American Journal of Community Psychology, 21,* 537–560.

Garbarino, J., & Kostelny, K. (1992). Cultural diversity and identity formation. In J. Garbarino (Ed.), *Children and families in the social environment* (2nd ed., pp. 179–199). New York: Aldine de Gruyter.

Gardiner, H. (1994). Child development. In L. Adler & U. Gielen (Eds.), *Cross-cultural topics in psychology* (pp. 61–72). Westport, CT: Praeger.

Gardner, W., & Cole, C. (1989). Self-management approaches. In E. Cipani (Ed.), *The treatment of severe behavior disorders* (pp. 19–36). Washington, DC: American Association on Mental Retardation.

Gaventa, B. (1993). Gift and call: Recovering the spiritual foundations of friendships. In A. Amado (Ed.), *Friendships and community connections between people with and without developmental disabilities* (pp. 41–66). Baltimore: Paul H. Brookes Publishing Co.

Gaylord-Ross, R. (1980). A decision model for the treatment of aberrant behavior in applied settings. In W. Sailor, B. Wilcox, & L. Brown (Eds.), *Methods of instruction for severely handicapped students* (pp. 135–158). Baltimore: Paul H. Brookes Publishing Co.

Geertz, C. (1973). *The interpretation of cultures.* New York: Basic Books.

Geertz, C. (1983). *Local knowledge: Further essays in interpretive anthropology.* New York: Basic Books.

Gelb, S. (1997). The problem of typological thinking in mental retardation. *Mental Retardation, 35,* 448–457.

Gerber, D. (1990). Listening to disabled people: The problem of voice and authority in Robert B. Edgerton's *The Cloak of Competence. Disability, Handicap & Society, 5,* 3–23.

Gerety, T. (1977). Redefining privacy. *Harvard Civil Rights-Civil Liberties Law Review, 12,* 233–296.

Gergen, K., & Davis, K. (1985). *The social construction of the person.* New York: Springer-Verlag.

Gerris, J., Dekovic, M., & Janssens, J. (1997). The relationship between social class and childrearing behaviors: Parents' perspective taking and value orientations. *Journal of Marriage and Family, 59,* 834–847.

Gibbs, R. (1992). Categorization and metaphor understanding. *Psychological Review, 99,* 572–577.

Gibbs, R., & Beitel, D. (1995). What proverb understanding reveals about how people think. *Psychological Bulletin, 118,* 133–154.

Gill, V., & Maynard, D. (1995). On labeling in actual interaction: Delivering and receiving diagnoses of developmental disabilities. *Social Problems, 42,* 11–37.

Gitterman, A. (1989). Testing professional authority and boundaries. *Social Casework: The Journal of Contemporary Social Work, 70,* 165–172.

Goldfarb, M. (1990). Guest editorial. *American Journal on Mental Retardation, 95,* v–vi.

Goldschmidt, W. (1974). Social class and the dynamics of status in America. In J. Jorgenson & M. Truzzi (Eds.), *Anthropology and American life* (pp. 36–46). Englewood Cliffs, NJ: Prentice Hall.

Gonzales, N., Cauce, A., Friedman, R., & Mason, C. (1996). Family, peer, and neighborhood influences on academic achievement among African-American adolescents: One year prospective effects. *American Journal of Community Psychology, 24,* 365–388.

Good Tracks, J. (1976). Native American non-interference. *Social Work, 18,* 30–34.

Goode, D. (1994). *A world without words: The social construction of children born deaf and blind.* Philadelphia: Temple University Press.

Goodenough, W. (1987). Multiculturalism as the normal human experience. In E. Eddy & W. Partridge (Eds.), *Applied anthropology in America* (2nd ed., pp. 89–96). New York: Columbia University Press.

Goodenough, W. (1990). Evolution of the human capacity for beliefs. *American Anthropologist, 92,* 597–612.

Goodenough, W. (1994). Toward a working theory of culture. In R. Borofsky (Ed.), *Assessing cultural anthropology* (pp. 262–275). New York: McGraw-Hill.

Goodenough, W. (1997). Moral outrage: Territoriality in human guise. *Zygon, 32,* 5–28.

Gos, M. (1995). Overcoming social class markers: Preparing working class students for college. *The Clearing House, 69,* 30–35.

Gowans, C. (1996). Intimacy, freedom, and unique value: A "Kantian" account of the irreplaceable and incomparable value of persons. *American Philosophical Quarterly, 33,* 75–89.

Green, J. (1982). *Cultural awareness in the human services.* Englewood Cliffs, NJ: Prentice Hall.

Greenbaum, E. (1996). Forrest Gump and his box of chocolates. *Mental Retardation, 34,* 128–129.

Greenhouse, C. (1985). Anthropology at home: Whose home? *Human Organization, 44,* 261–264.

Greenspan, S., & Granfield, J. (1992). Reconsidering the construct of mental retardation: Implications of a model of social competence. *American Journal on Mental Retardation, 96,* 442–453.

Greenwald, A., & Banaji, M. (1995). Implicit social cognition: Attitudes, self-esteem, and stereotypes. *Psychological Review, 102,* 4–27.

Greenwood, J. (1987). Scientific psychology and hermeneutical psychology: Causal explanation and the meaning of human action. *Human Studies, 10,* 171–204.

Grella, C. (1990). Irreconcilable differences: Women defining class after divorce and downward mobility. *Gender & Society, 4,* 41–55.

Grobsmith, E. (1981). Lakota of the Rosebud: A contemporary ethnography. New York: Holt, Rinehart and Winston.

Groce, N. (1981). Growing up rural: Children in the 4-H and the Junior Grange. In R. Sieber & A. Gordon (Eds.), *Children and their organizations: Investigations in American culture* (pp. 106–121). Boston: G.K. Hall.

Guess, D., & Carr, E. (1991). Emergence and maintenance of stereotypy and self-injury. *American Journal on Mental Retardation, 96,* 299–319.

Guess, D., Turnbull, H., & Helmstetter, E. (1990). Science, paradigms, and values: A response to Mulick. *American Journal on Mental Retardation, 95,* 157–163.

Gwaltney, J. (1980). *Drylongso: A self-portrait of Black America.* New York: Random House.

Hahn, H. (1993). The potential impact of disability studies on political science (as well as vice-versa). *Policy Studies Journal, 21,* 740–752.

Hahn, R. (1973). Understanding beliefs: An essay on the methodology of the statement and analysis of belief systems. *Current Anthropology, 14,* 207–227.

Hall, E. (1959). *The silent language.* Greenwich, CT: Fawcett Premier.

Halperin, R. (1990). *The livelihood of kin: Making ends meet "the Kentucky way."* Austin: University of Texas Press.

Hanson, M. (1998). Ethnic, cultural, and language diversity in intervention settings. In E. Lynch & M. Hanson (Eds.), *Developing cross-cultural competence: A guide for working with children and their families* (2nd ed., pp. 3–22). Baltimore: Paul H. Brookes Publishing Co.

Harding, S. (1994). Is science multicultural?: Challenges, resources, opportunities, uncertainties. *Configurations, 2,* 301–330.

Harkness, S., & Super, C. (1985). Child–environment interactions in the socialization of affect. In M. Lewis & C. Saarni (Eds.), *The socialization of emotions* (pp. 21–36). New York: Plenum.

Harris, G. (1989). Concepts of individual, self, and person in description and analysis. *American Anthropologist, 91,* 599–612.

Hasenfeld, Y., & Chesler, M. (1989). Client empowerment in the human services: Personal and professional agenda. *Journal of Applied Behavioral Science, 25,* 499–522.

Hawthorne, N. (1960). The scarlet letter. In H. Levin (Ed.), *The scarlet letter and other tales of the Puritans* (p. 123). Boston: Houghton Mifflen Co.

Heath, S. (1986). What no bedtime story means: Narrative skills at home and school. In B. Schieffelin & E. Ochs (Eds.), *Language socialization across cultures* (pp. 97–126). Cambridge, England: Cambridge University Press.

Heelas, P. (1984). Emotions across cultures: Objectivity and cultural divergence. In S. Brown (Ed.), *Objectivity and cultural divergence* (pp. 21–42). Cambridge, England: Cambridge University Press.

Helander, B. (1995). Disability as an incurable illness: Health, process, and personhood in Southern Somalia. In B. Ingstad & S. Whyte (Eds.), *Disability and culture* (pp. 73–93). Berkeley: University of California Press.

Heller, T., Pederson, E., & Miller, A. (1996). Guidelines from the consumer: Improving consumer involvement in research and training for persons with mental retardation. *Mental Retardation, 34,* 141–148.

Hill, J., & Mannheim, B. (1992). Language and world view. *Annual Review of Anthropology, 21,* 381–406.

Hill-Burnett, J. (1987). Developing anthropological knowledge through application. In E. Eddy & W. Partridge (Eds.), *Applied anthropology in America* (2nd ed., pp. 123–139). New York: Columbia University Press.

Hinde, R. (1987). *Individuals, relationships, and culture: Links between ethology and the social sciences.* Cambridge, England: Cambridge University Press.

Hofstede, G. (1980). *Culture's consequences: International differences in work-related values.* Beverly Hills, CA: Sage.

Holland, D. (1985). From situation to impression: How Americans get to know themselves and one another. In J. Dougherty (Ed.), *Directions in cognitive anthropology* (pp. 389–412). Urbana: University of Illinois Press.

Holland, D. (1992). The woman who climbed up the house: Some limitations of schema theory. In T. Schwartz, G. White, & C. Lutz (Eds.), *New directions in psychological anthropology* (pp. 68–82). Cambridge, England: Cambridge University Press.

Holland, D., & Quinn, N. (Eds.). (1987). *Cultural models in language and thought.* Cambridge, England: Cambridge University Press.

Hornstein, B. (1997). How the religious community can support the transition to adulthood: A parent's perspective. *Mental Retardation, 35,* 485–487.

Horowitz, M. (1991). Person schemas. In M. Horowitz (Ed.), *Person schemas and maladaptive interpersonal behavior patterns* (pp. 1–13). Chicago: University of Chicago Press.

Houghton, J., Bronicki, G., & Guess, D. (1987). Opportunities to express preferences and make choices among students with severe disabilities in classroom settings. *Journal of The Association for Persons with Severe Handicaps, 10,* 79–86.

Hsu, F. (1975). American core value and national character. In J. Spradley & M. Rynkiewich (Eds.), *The nacirema* (pp. 378–394). Boston: Little, Brown.

Hughes, C., Hwang, B., Kim, J., Eisenman, L., & Killian, D. (1995). Quality of life in applied research: A review and analysis of empirical measures. *American Journal on Mental Retardation, 99,* 623–641.

Hughes, R., & Perry-Jenkins, M. (1996). Social class issues in family life education. *Family Relations, 45,* 175–182.

Ingstad, B., & Whyte, S. (Eds.). (1995). *Disability and culture.* Berkeley: University of California Press.

Jacobson, J., Burchard, S., Ackerman, L., & Yoe, J. (1991). Assessing community environmental effects upon people with developmental disabilities: Satisfaction as an outcome measure. *Adult Residential Care Journal, 5,* 147–164.

Jenkinson, J. (1993). Who shall decide? The relevance of theory and research to decision-making by people with an intellectual disability. *Disability, Handicap & Society, 8,* 361–375.

Johnson, T., Heimerl, S., Lanpher, J., Olsen, P., Rossiter, H., & Thies, D. (1995). Contributions and limitations of human services. *Mental Retardation, 33,* 332–333.

Kaplan, A. (1991). Female or male psychotherapists for women: New formulations. In J. Jordan, A. Kaplan, J. Miller, I. Stiver, & J. Surrey (Eds.), *Women's growth in connection: Writings from the Stone Center* (pp. 268–282). New York: Guilford Press.

Kaufman, S. (1999). *Retarded isn't stupid, mom!* (rev. ed.). Baltimore: Paul H. Brookes Publishing Co.

Kennedy, M. (1994). The disability blanket. *Mental Retardation, 32,* 74–76.

Kernohan, A. (1989). Social power and human agency. *The Journal of Philosophy, 86,* 712–727.

Kleinman, A. (1980). *Patients and healers in the context of culture.* Berkeley: University of California Press.

Knights, D., & Willmott, H. (1989). Power and subjectivity at work: From degradation to subjugation in social relations. *Sociology, 23,* 535–558.

Kohn, M. (1969). *Class and conformity: A study in values* (2nd ed.). Chicago: University of Chicago Press.

Kuder, S., & Bryen, D. (1993). Conversational topics of staff members and institutional individuals with mental retardation. *Mental Retardation, 31,* 148–153.

Lachman, M., & Weaver, S. (1998). The sense of control as a moderator of social class differences in health and well-being. *Journal of Personality and Social Psychology, 74,* 763–773.

Lacombe, D. (1996). Reforming Foucault: A critique of the social control thesis. *British Journal of Sociology, 47,* 330–353.

Lakin, K., Bruininks, R., Chen, T.-H., Hill, B., & Anderson, D. (1993). Personal characteristics and competence of people with mental retardation living in foster homes and small group homes. *American Journal on Mental Retardation, 97,* 616–627.

Lakoff, G. (1995). Metaphor, morality, and politics, or, why conservatives have left liberals in the dust. *Social Research, 62,* 177–213.

Lakoff, G., & Johnson, M. (1980). *Metaphors we live by.* Chicago: University of Chicago Press.

Lakoff, G., & Kövecses, Z. (1987). The cognitive model of anger inherent in American English. In D. Holland & N. Quinn (Eds.), *Cultural models in language and thought* (pp. 195–221). Cambridge, England: Cambridge University Press.

Lakoff, R. (1975). *Language and woman's place.* New York: Harper Colophon Books.

Lane, J., & Wegner, D. (1994). Secret relationships: The back alley to love. In R. Erber & R. Gilmour (Eds.), *Theoretical frameworks for personal relationships* (pp. 67–86). Hillsdale, NJ: Lawrence Erlbaum Associates.

Langacker, R. (1987). *Foundations of cognitive grammar: Vol. I. Theoretical perspectives.* Stanford, CA: Stanford University Press.

LaPointe, J. (1976). *Legends of the Lakota.* San Francisco: The Indian Historian Press.

Laurenceau, J., & Barrett, L. (1998). Intimacy as an interpersonal process: The importance of self-disclosure, partner disclosure, and perceived partner responsiveness in interpersonal exchanges. *Journal of Personality and Social Psychology, 74,* 1238–1251.

Leach, E. (1964). Anthropological aspects of language: Animal categories and verbal abuse. In E. Lenneberg (Ed.), *New directions in the study of language* (pp. 23–63). Cambridge: M.I.T. Press.

Lear, J. (1984). Moral objectivity. In S. Brown, *Objectivity and cultural divergence* (pp. 135-170). Cambridge: Cambridge University Press.

Lears, T. (1985). The concept of cultural hegemony: problems and prospects. *American History Review, 90,* 567–593.

Lee, D. (1959). *Freedom and culture.* New York: Prentice Hall, Spectrum Books.

Lee, D. (1994). Class as a social fact. *Sociology, 28,* 397–415.

Leets, L., & Giles, H. (1997). Words as weapons—When do they wound? Investigations of harmful speech. *Human Communication Research, 24,* 260–302.

Leininger, M. (1970). *Nursing and anthropology: Two worlds to blend.* New York: John Wiley & Sons.

Leininger, M. (1979). *Transcultural nursing.* New York: Masson International Nursing Publications.

LeVine, H., & Langness, L. (1986). Conclusions: Themes in an anthropology of mild mental retardation. In L. Langness & H. LeVine (Eds.), *Culture and retardation: Life histories of mildly mentally retarded persons in American society* (pp. 191–206). Boston: D. Reidel.

LeVine, R. (1984). Properties of culture: An ethnographic view. In R. Shweder & R. LeVine (Eds.), *Culture theory: Essays on mind, self, and emotion* (pp. 67–87). Cambridge, England: Cambridge University Press.

LeVine, R. (1987). Waiting is a power game. *Psychology Today, 21,* 24–32.

Levorato, M. (1993). The acquisition of idioms and the development of figurative competence. In C. Cacciari & P. Tabossi (Eds.), *Idioms: Processing, structure, and interpretation* (pp. 101–128). Hillsdale, NJ: Lawrence Erlbaum Associates.

Levy, P., Levy, J., & Samowitz, P. (1994). Training staff on quality of life issues. In D. Goode (Ed.), *Quality of life for persons with disabilities: International perspectives and issues* (pp. 250–259). Cambridge, MA: Brookline Books.

Levy, R. (1984). Emotion, knowing, and culture. In R. Shweder & R. LeVine (Eds.), *Culture theory: Essays on mind, self, and emotion* (pp. 214–237). Cambridge, England: Cambridge University Press.

Levy, R. (1994). Person-centered anthropology. In R. Borofsky (Ed.), *Assessing cultural anthropology* (pp. 179–188). New York: McGraw-Hill.

Lewis, H. (1990). *A question of values: Six ways we make the personal choices that shape our lives.* San Francisco: Harper & Row.

Liachowitz, C. (1988). *Disability as a social construct.* Philadelphia: University of Pennsylvania Press.

Lieberman, D. (1994). Ethnocognitivism, problem solving and hemisphericity. In L. Samovar & R. Porter (Eds.), *Intercultural communication: A reader* (pp. 178–193). Belmont, CA: Wadsworth.

Lim, L., & Browder, D. (1994). Multicultural life skills assessment of individuals with severe disabilities. *Journal of The Association of Persons with Severe Handicaps, 19,* 130–138.

Linde, C. (1987). Explanatory systems in oral life stories. In D. Holland & N. Quinn (Eds.), *Cultural models in language and thought* (pp. 343–368). Cambridge, England: Cambridge University Press.

Linger, D. (1993). The hegemony of discontent. *American Ethnologist, 20,* 3–24.

Lister, R. (1997). Dialectics of citizenship. *Hypatia, 212,* 6–27.

Lovett, H. (1985). *Cognitive counseling and persons with special needs.* New York: Praeger.

Luckasson, R., Coulter, D., Polloway, E., Reiss, S., Schalock, R., Snell, M., Spitalnik, D., & Stark, J. (1992). *Mental retardation: Definition, classification, and systems of supports.* Washington, DC: American Association on Mental Retardation.

Lutfiyya, Z. (1991). "A feeling of being connected": Friendships between people with and without learning difficulties. *Disability, Handicap, & Society, 6,* 233–245.

Lutfiyya, Z. (1993). When "staff" and "clients" become friends. In A. Amado (Ed.), *Friendships and community connections between people with and without developmental disabilities* (pp. 97–108). Baltimore: Paul H. Brookes Publishing Co.

Lutz, C. (1988). *Unnatural emotions.* Chicago: University of Chicago Press.

Lutz, C. (1990). Engendered emotion: Gender, power, and the rhetoric of emotional control in American discourse. In C. Lutz & L. Abu-Lughod (Eds.), *Language and the politics of emotion* (pp. 69–91). New York: Cambridge University Press.

Lutz, C., & Abu-Lughod, L. (Eds.). (1990). *Language and the politics of emotion.* New York: Cambridge University Press.

Lynch, E., & Hanson, M. (Eds.). (1998). *Developing cross-cultural competence: A guide for working with children and their families* (2nd. ed.). Baltimore: Paul H. Brookes Publishing Co.

Lynch, E., & Stein, R. (1987). Parent participation by ethnicity: A comparison of Hispanic, Black, and Anglo families. *Exceptional Children, 54,* 105–111.

MacGregor, F. (1990). Uncooperative patients: Some cultural interpretations. In P. Brink (Ed.), *Transcultural nursing: A book of readings* (pp. 36–43). Prospect Heights, IL: Waveland Press.

Mackelprang, R., & Salsgiver, R. (1996). People with disabilities and social work: Historical and contemporary issues. *Social Work, 41,* 7–15.

Mageo, J. (1995). The reconfiguring self. *American Anthropology, 97,* 282–297.

Manion, M., & Bersani, H. (1987). Mental retardation as a western sociological construct: A cross-cultural analysis. *Disability, Handicap, & Society, 2,* 231–245.

Mann, L., Harmoni, R., & Power, C. (1989). Adolescent decision-making: The development of competence. *Journal of Adolescence, 12,* 265–278.

Markus, H., & Nurius, P. (1986). Possible selves. *American Psychologist, 41,* 954–969.

Marsella, A., DeVos, G., & Hsu, F. (1985). *Culture and self: Asian and western perspectives.* New York: Tavistock.

Martinek, T., & Hellison, D. (1998). Values and goal-setting with underserved youth. *The Journal of Physical Education, Recreation & Dance, 69,* 47–53.

Maslow, A. (1968). *Toward a psychology of being* (2nd ed.). Princeton, NJ: D. Van Nostrand.

Mass, M. (1997). The determinants of parenthood: Power and responsibility. *Human Relations, 50,* 241–260.

Maxwell, J. (1992). Understanding and validity in qualitative research. *Harvard Educational Review, 62,* 279–299.

McCaul, K., Veltum, L., Boyechko, V., & Crawford, J. (1990). Understanding attributes of victim blame for rape: Sex, violence, and foreseeability. *Journal of Applied Social Psychology, 20,* 1–26.

McDermott, P., & Schaefer, B. (1996). A demographic survey of rare and common problem behaviors among American students. *Journal of Clinical Child Psychology, 25,* 352–362.

McGrew, K., & Bruininks, R. (1990). Defining adaptive and maladaptive behavior within a model of personal competence. *School Psychology Review, 19,* 53–73.

McIntosh, P. (1988). *White privilege and male privilege: A personal account of coming to see correspondences through work in women's studies.* Unpublished manuscript, Center for Research on Women, Wellesley, MA.

McNair, J., & Smith, H. (1998). Community-based natural support through local churches. *Mental Retardation, 36,* 237–241.

Medicine, B. (1987). Learning to be an anthropologist and remaining "native." In E. Eddy & W. Partridge (Eds.), *Applied anthropology in America* (2nd ed., pp. 282–296). New York: Columbia University Press.

Merriam-Webster. (1993). *Merriam-Webster's collegiate dictionary* (10th ed.). Springfield, MA: Merriam-Webster.

Mest, G. (1988). With a little help from their friends: Use of social support systems by persons with retardation. *Journal of Social Issues, 44,* 117–125.

Meyer, L., Peck, C., & Brown, L. (1991). *Critical issues in the lives of people with severe disabilities.* Baltimore: Paul H. Brookes Publishing Co.

Michael, W. (1995). *Our America: Nativism, modernism, and pluralism.* Durham, NC: Duke University Press.

Middleton, D. (1989). Emotional style: The cultural ordering of emotions. *Ethos, 17,* 187–201.

Mieder, W. (1992). *A dictionary of American proverbs*. New York: Oxford University Press.

Miller, J. (1991). The construction of anger in women and men. In J. Jordan, A. Kaplan, J. Miller, I. Stiver, & J. Surrey (Eds.), *Women's growth in connection: Writings from the Stone Center* (pp. 181–196). New York: Guilford Press.

Miller, P., & Moore, B. (1989). Narrative conjunctions of caregiver and child: A comparative perspective on socialization through stories. *Ethos, 17,* 428–449.

Miller, P., Potts, R., Fung, H., Hoogstra, L., & Mintz, J. (1990). Narrative practices and the social construction of self in childhood. *American Ethnologist, 17,* 292–311.

Miller, P., & Sperry, L. (1987). The socialization of anger and aggression. *Merrill-Palmer Quarterly, 33,* 1–31.

Monroe, T. (1996). We need to educate the professionals. *Mental Retardation, 34,* 122–123.

Moore, B. (1984). *Privacy: Studies in social and cultural history*. Armonk, NY: M.E. Sharpe.

Mühlhäusler, P. (1995). Metaphors others live by. *Language & Communication, 15,* 281–288.

Mumby, D. (1989). Ideology and the social construction of meaning: A communication perspective. *Communication Quarterly, 37,* 291–304.

Murillo, N. (1978). The Mexican American family. In R. Martinez (Ed.), *Hispanic culture and health care: Fact, fiction, folklore* (pp. 3–18). St. Louis: Mosby.

Murphy, C. (1996). The e word. *The Atlantic Monthly, 273,* 16–18.

Murphy, R. (1987). *The body silent*. New York: Henry Holt and Company.

Muyskens, J. (1992). Equality vs. individuality: American values in conflict. *Scholarly Inquiry for Nursing Practice, 6,* 235–239.

Mwaria, C. (1990). The concept of self in the context of crisis: A study of families of the severely brain-injured. *Social Science & Medicine, 30,* 889–894.

Nader, L., Barabas, A., Bartolome, M., Bodley, J., Debert, G., Drucker-Brown, S., Gusterson, H., Hertz, E., Lock, M., Nash, J., & Pinxten, R. (1997). Controlling processes: Tracing the dynamic components of power. *Current Anthropology, 38,* 711–739.

Nagel, J. (1994). Constructing ethnicity: Creating and recreating ethnic identity and culture. *Social Problems, 41,* 152–176.

Nagel, J. (1996). *American Indian ethnic renewal: Red power and the resurgence of identity and culture*. New York: Oxford University Press.

Neisser, U. (1968). Cultural and cognitive discontinuity. In R. Manners & D. Kaplan (Eds.), *Theory in anthropology* (pp. 354–364). Chicago: Aldine-Atherton.

Nichter, M. (1991). Preface. In C. Hill (Ed.), *Training manual in applied medical anthropology, special publication #27* (pp. 1–13). Washington, DC: American Anthropology Association.

Nicolaisen, I. (1995). Persons and nonpersons: Disability and personhood among the Punan Bah of Central Borneo. In B. Ingstad & S. Whyte (Eds.), *Disability and culture* (pp. 38–55). Berkeley: University of California Press.

O'Brien, J. (1987). A guide to life-style planning: Using the activity catalog to integrate services and natural support systems. In B. Wilcox & G. Bellamy (Eds.), *A comprehensive guide to the activities catalog: An alternative curriculum for youth and adults with severe disabilities* (pp. 175–189). Baltimore: Paul H. Brookes Publishing Co.

O'Brien, J. (1994). Down stairs that are never your own: Supporting people with developmental disabilities in their own homes. *Mental Retardation, 32,* 1–6.

O'Connor, S. (1993). "I'm not Indian anymore": The challenge of providing culturally sensitive services to American Indians. In J. Racino, P. Walker, S. O'Connor, & S. Taylor (Eds.), *Housing, support, and community* (pp. 313–332). Baltimore: Paul H. Brookes Publishing Co.

Ogbu, J. (1987). Variability in minority school performance: A problem in search of an explanation. *Anthropology & Education Quarterly, 18,* 312–334.

Ortner, S. (1984). Theory in anthropology since the sixties. *Comparative Studies in Society & History, 26,* 126–166.

Ortner, S. (1991). Reading America: Preliminary notes on class and culture. In R. Fox (Ed.), *Recapturing anthropology: Working in the present* (pp. 163–190). Santa Fe, NM: School of American Research Press.

Paine, R. (1989). High-wire culture: Comparing two agonistic systems of self-esteem. *Man, 24,* 657–672.

Pargament, K., & Park, C. (1995). Merely a defense? The variety of religious means and ends. *Journal of Social Issues, 51,* 13–33.

Parmenter, T., Cummins, R., Shaddock, A., & Stancliff, R. (1994). The view from Australia: Australian legislation, service delivery, and quality of life. In D. Goode (Ed.), *Quality of life for persons with disabilities: International perspectives and issues* (pp. 75–102). Cambridge, MA: Brookline Books.

Parsons, M., Reid, D., Reynolds, J., & Bumgarner, M. (1990). Effects of chosen versus assigned jobs on the work performances of persons with severe handicaps. *Journal of Applied Behavior Analysis, 23,* 253–258.

Paul, R. (1990). What does anybody want? Desire, purpose, and the acting subject in the study of culture. *Cultural Anthropology, 5,* 431–451.

Paules, G. (1992). *Dishing it out: Power and resistance among waitresses in a New Jersey restaurant.* Philadelphia: Temple University Press.

Peacock, J., & Holland, D. (1993). The narrated self: Life stories in process. *Ethnos, 21,* 367–383.

Pedersen, P. (1982). Cross-cultural triad model. In E. Marshall & P. Kurtz (Eds.), *Interpersonal helping skills* (pp. 238–284). San Francisco: Jossey-Bass.

Pedersen, P. (1988). *A handbook for developing multicultural awareness.* Alexandria, VA: American Association for Counseling and Development.

Pederson, E., Chaikin, M., Koehler, D., Campbell, A., & Arcand, M. (1993). Strategies that close the gap between research, planning, and self-advocacy. In E. Sutton, A. Factor, B. Hawkins, T. Heller, & G. Seltzer (Eds.), *Older adults with developmental disabilities* (pp. 277–326). Baltimore: Paul H. Brookes Publishing Co.

Pelto, P., & Schensul, J. (1987). Toward a framework for policy research in anthropology. In E. Eddy & W. Partridge (Eds.), *Applied anthropology in America* (2nd ed., pp. 505–527). New York: Columbia University Press.

Pepitone, A. (1994). Beliefs and cultural social psychology. In L. Adler & U. Gielen (Eds.), *Cross-cultural topics in psychology* (pp. 139–152). Westport, CT: Praeger.

Perring, C. (1997). Degrees of personhood. *The Journal of Medicine and Philosophy, 22,* 173–197.

Pheterson, G. (1986). Alliances between women: Overcoming internalized oppression and internalized domination. *Signs: Journal of Women in Culture and Society, 12,* 146–160.

Pickett, B. (1996). Foucault and the politics of resistance. *Polity, 28,* 445–466.

Pill, R., & Stott, N. (1987). The stereotype of "working-class fatalism" and the challenge for primary care health promotion. *Health Education Research, 2,* 105–114.

Poole, F. (1994). Socialization, enculturation and the development of personal identity. In T. Ingold (Ed.), *Companion encyclopedia of anthropology* (pp. 831–860). London: Routledge.

Powell, R., & Andersen, J. (1994). Culture and classroom communication. In L. Samovar & R. Porter (Eds.), *Intercultural communication: A reader* (pp. 322–329). Belmont, CA: Wadsworth.

Powers, M. (1986). *Oglala women: Myth, ritual, and reality.* Chicago: University of Chicago Press.

Powers, W. (1985). Counting your blessings: Sacred numbers and the structure of reality. *Zygon, 21,* 75–94.

Powers, W. (1987). Dual religious participation: Stratagems of conversion among the Lakota. In W. Powers (Ed.), *Beyond the vision: Essays on American Indian culture* (pp. 94–125). Norman: University of Oklahoma Press.

Powers, W., & Powers, M. (1984). Metaphysical aspects of an Oglala food system. In M. Douglas (Ed.), *Food in the social order: Studies of food and festivities in three American communities* (pp. 40-96). New York: Russell Sage Foundation.

Preissle, J., & Grant, L. (1998). Social class and parental attitudes toward education: Resistance and conformity to schooling in the family. *Journal of Contemporary Ethnography, 27,* 10–45.

Pyke, K. (1996). Class-based masculinities: The interdependence of gender, class, and interpersonal power. *Gender & Society, 10,* 527–549.

Quinn, N., & Holland, D. (1987). Culture and cognition. In D. Holland & N. Quinn (Eds.), *Cultural models in language and thought* (pp. 3–42). Cambridge, England: Cambridge University Press.

Racino, J., & Walker, P. (1993). "Whose life is it anyway?" In J. Racino, P. Walker, S. O'Connor, & S. Taylor (Eds.), *Housing, support, and community* (pp. 57–80). Baltimore: Paul H. Brookes Publishing Co.

Racino, J., Walker, P., O'Connor, S., & Taylor, S. (Eds.). (1993). *Housing, support, and community.* Baltimore: Paul H. Brookes Publishing Co.

Rapid City Journal (anonymous). (1994). Three S. Dakota counties among America's poorest. *Rapid City Journal,* September 7, p. C4.

Ray, N. (1995). From paper tigers to consumer-centered quality assurance tools: Reforming incident-reporting systems. *Mental Retardation, 33,* 239–247.

Realon, R., Favell, J., & Lowerre, A. (1990). The effects of making choices on engagement levels with persons who are profoundly multiply handicapped. *Education & Training in Mental Retardation, 25,* 299–305.

Reay, D. (1997). Feminist theory, habitus, and social class: Disrupting notions of classlessness. *Women's Studies International Forum, 20,* 225–233.

Reay, D. (1998). Surviving in dangerous places: Working-class women, women's studies and higher education. *Women's Studies International Forum, 21,* 11–19.

Reber, A., Walkenfeld, F., & Hernstadt, R. (1991). Implicit and explicit learning: Individual differences and IQ. *Journal of Experimental Psychology: Learning, Memory & Cognition, 17,* 888–896.

Reddy, W. (1997). Against constructionism: The historical ethnography of emotions. *Current Anthropology, 38,* 327–352.

Rees, L., Spreen, O., & Harnadek, M. (1991). Do attitudes towards persons with handicaps really shift over time? Comparison between 1975 and 1988. *Mental Retardation, 29,* 81–86.

Reichle, J., & Wacker, D. (1993). *Communicative alternatives to challenging behavior: Integrating functional assessment and intervention strategies.* Baltimore: Paul H. Brookes Publishing Co.

Reis, H. (1994). Domains of experiences: Investigating relationship processes from three perspectives. In R. Erber & R. Gilmour (Eds.), *Theoretical frameworks for personal relationships* (pp. 87–110). Hillsdale, NJ: Lawrence Erlbaum Associates.

Rhodes, L. (1992). The subject of power in medical/psychiatric anthropology. In A. Gaines (Ed.), *Ethnopsychiatry: The cultural construction of professional and folk psychiatries* (pp. 51–66). Albany: State University of New York Press.

Ritchie, L. (1997). Parents' workplace experiences and family communication patterns. *Communication Research, 24,* 175–187.

Rodrigues, A. (1995). Attribution and social influence. *Journal of Applied Social Psychology, 25,* 1567–1577.

Rogan, P., Hagner, D., & Murphy, S. (1993). Natural supports: Reconceptualizing job coach roles. *Journal of The Association for Persons with Severe Handicaps, 18,* 275–281.

Rokeach, M. (1979). *Understanding human values: Individual and societal.* New York: The Free Press.

Romanucci-Ross, L., Moerman, D., & Tancredi, L. (1983). Preface. In L. Romanucci-Ross, D. Moerman, & L. Tancredi (Eds.), *The anthropology of medicine: From culture to method* (2nd ed., pp. vii–xiii). New York: Praeger.

Rosaldo, M. (1984). Toward an anthropology of self and feeling. In R. Shweder & R. LeVine (Eds.), *Culture theory: Essays on mind, self, and emotion* (pp. 137–157). Cambridge, England: Cambridge University Press.

Rosaldo, R. (1989). *Culture and truth: The remaking of social analysis.* Boston: Beacon Press.

Rosenthal, R., & Jacobson, L. (1968). *Pygmalion in the classroom.* New York: Holt, Rinehart, & Winston.

Ross, A. (1989). *Mitakuye oyasin: "We are all related."* Ft. Yates, ND: Bear.

Ross, J. (1975). Social borders: Definitions of diversity. *Current Anthropology, 16,* 53–61.

Ross, J. (1995). Social class tensions within families. *The American Journal of Family Therapy, 23,* 338–350.

Ross-Gordon, J., Martin, L., & Briscoe, D. (Eds.). (1990). *Serving culturally diverse populations.* San Francisco: Jossey-Bass.

Rubin, I. (1987). Health care needs of adults with mental retardation. *Mental Retardation, 25,* 201–206.

Rubin, L. (1983). *Intimate strangers: Men and women together.* New York: Harper & Row.

Rueda, R., & Martinez, I. (1992). Fiesta Educativa: One community's approach to parent training in developmental disabilities for Latino families. *Journal of The Association for Persons with Severe Handicaps, 17,* 95–103.

Rusch, F. (1986). *Competitive employment issues and strategies.* Baltimore: Paul H. Brookes Publishing Co.

Ruth, R., & Blotzer, M. (1995). Toward basic principles. In M. Blotzer & R. Ruth (Eds.), *Sometimes you just want to feel like a human being* (pp. 1–14). Baltimore: Paul H. Brookes Publishing Co.

Rybarczyk, B., & Bellg, A. (1997). Listening to life stories. New York: Springer.

Sacks, K., & Remy, D. (Eds.). (1984). *My troubles are going to have trouble with me: Everyday trials and triumphs of women workers.* New Brunswick, NJ: Rutgers University Press.

Sacks, O. (1987). *The man who mistook his wife for a hat and other clinical tales.* New York: Harper & Row.

Samovar, L., & Porter, R. (1982). *Intercultural communication: A reader.* Belmont, CA: Wadsworth.

Sangren, P. (1995). "Power" against ideology: A critique of Foucaultian usage. *Cultural Anthropology, 10,* 3–40.

Saunders, S., Resnick, M., Hoberman, H., & Blum, R. (1994). Formal help-seeking behavior of adolescents identifying themselves as having mental health problems. *Journal of the American Academy of Child and Adolescent Psychiatry, 33,* 718–729.

Schalock, R. (1996). *Quality of life: Vol. I. Conceptualization and measurement.* Washington, DC: American Association on Mental Retardation.

Schalock, R. (1997). *Quality of life: Vol. II. Application to persons with disabilities.* Washington, DC: American Association on Mental Retardation.

Scheibe, K. (1970). *Beliefs and values.* New York: Holt, Rinehart & Winston.

Schloss, P., Alper, S., & Jayne, D. (1993). Self determination for persons with disabilities. *Exceptional Children, 60,* 215–225.

Schnorr, R. (1990). "Peter? He comes and goes . . .": First graders' perspectives on a part-time mainstream student. *Journal of The Association for Persons with Severe Handicaps, 15,* 231–240.

Schwartz, G. (1981). Badasses, freaks, and working-class culture: The politics of youth work in a suburban community. In R. Hall (Ed.), *Investigations in American culture* (pp. 85–105). Boston: G.K. Hall.

Schwartz, T., White, G., & Lutz, C. (Eds.). (1992). *New directions in psychological anthropology.* Cambridge, England: Cambridge University Press.

Scott, J. (1990). *Domination and the arts of resistance: Hidden transcripts.* New Haven, CT: Yale University Press.

Serpell, R. (1988). Assessment criteria for severe intellectual disability in various cultural settings. *International Journal of Behavioral Development, 1,* 117–144.

Sherman, J., Sheldon, J., Harchik, A., Edwards, K., & Quinn, J. (1992). Social evaluation of behaviors comprising three social skills and a comparison of the performance of people with and without mental retardation. *American Journal on Mental Retardation, 96,* 419–431.

Shore, B. (1990). Human ambivalence and the structuring of moral values. *Ethos, 18,* 165–179.

Shore, B. (1991). Twice-born, once conceived: Meaning construction and cultural cognition. *American Anthropologist, 93,* 9–27.

Shweder, R. (1980). Factors and fictions in person perception: A reply to Lamiell, Foss and Cavenee. *Journal of Personality, 48,* 74–81.

Shweder, R. (1984). Anthropology's romantic rebellion against the enlightenment, or there's more to thinking than reason and evidence. In R. Shweder & R. LeVine (Eds.), *Culture theory: Essays on mind, self, and emotion* (pp. 27–66). Cambridge, England: Cambridge University Press.

Shweder, R., & Bourne, E. (1984). Does the concept of the person vary cross-culturally? In R. Shweder & R. LeVine (Eds.), *Culture theory: Essays on mind, self, and emotion* (pp. 158–199). Cambridge, England: Cambridge University Press.

Shweder, R., & LeVine, R. (Eds.). (1984). *Culture theory: Essays on mind, self, and emotion.* Cambridge, England: Cambridge University Press.

Shweder, R., & Miller, J. (1985). The social construction of the person: How is it possible? In K. Gergen & K. Davis (Eds.), *The social construction of the person* (pp. 42–69). New York: Springer-Verlag.

Sidman, M., & Ishaq, W. (1991). Beware of coercion. In W. Ishaq (Ed.), *Human behavior in today's world* (pp. 52–69). New York: Praeger.

Siegel, S., Ford, J., Park, H.-S., Tappe, P., Gumpel, T., & Gaylord-Ross, R. (1990). Research in vocational special education. In R. Gaylord-Ross (Ed.), *Issues and research in special education* (Vol. 1, pp. 173–242). New York: Teachers College Press.

Sigafoos, J., Reichle, J., & Light-Shriner, C. (1994). Distinguishing between socially and nonsocially motivated challenging behavior. In M. Hayden & B. Abery (Eds.), *Challenges for service systems in transition* (pp. 147–169). Baltimore: Paul H. Brookes Publishing Co.

Simmel, A. (1968). Privacy. In D. Sills (Ed.), *International encyclopedia of the social sciences* (Vol. 12, pp. 480-487). New York: Macmillan.

Singer, J., & Salovey, P. (1991). Organized knowledge structures and personality. In M. Horowitz (Ed.), *Person schemas and maladaptive interpersonal behavior patterns* (pp. 33–52). Chicago: University of Chicago Press.

Skinner, D., Bryant, D., Coffman, J., & Campbell, F. (1998). Creating risk and promise: Children's and teacher's coconstructions in the cultural world of kindergarten. *The Elementary School Journal, 98,* 297–311.

Slobogin, C. (1998). Psychiatric evidence in criminal trials: To junk or not to junk? *William and Mary Law Review, 40,* 1–56.

Smith, T. (1980). Ethnic measurement and identification. *Ethnicity, 7,* 78–95.

Smull, M. (1995). Revisiting choice—Part 1. *AAMR News & Notes, 8*(4), 3–5.

Solomon, R. (1984). Getting angry: The Jamesian theory of emotion in anthropology. In R. Shweder & R. LeVine (Eds.), *Culture theory: Essays on mind, self, and emotion* (pp. 238–256). Cambridge, England: Cambridge University Press.

Soodak, L. (1990). Social behavior and knowledge of social "scripts" among mentally retarded adults. *American Journal on Mental Retardation, 94,* 515–521.

Spengler, P., Strohmer, D., & Prout, H. (1990). Testing the robustness of the diagnostic overshadowing bias. *American Journal on Mental Retardation, 95,* 204–214.

Spindler, G., & Spindler, L. (1982). Anthropologists view American culture. *Annual Review of Anthropology, 12,* 49–78.

Spindler, G., Spindler, L., Trueba, H., & Williams, M. (1991). *The American cultural dialogue and its transmission.* Bristol, PA: Falmer.

Spiro, M. (1955). The acculturation of American ethnic groups. *American Anthropologist, 57,* 1240–1252.

Spiro, M. (1993). Is the Western conception of the self "peculiar" within the context of the world cultures? *Ethos, 21,* 107–153.

St. Pierre, M. (1991). *Madonna Swan: A Lakota woman's story.* Norman: University of Oklahoma Press.

Stamatelos, T., & Mott, D. (1985). Creative potential among persons labeled developmentally delayed. *The Arts in Psychotherapy, 12,* 101–113.

Stewart, E., & Bennett, M. (1991). *American cultural patterns: A cross-cultural perspective, revised edition.* Yarmouth, ME: Intercultural Press.

Stiver, I. (1991a). Work inhibitions in women. In J. Jordan, A. Kaplan, J. Miller, I. Stiver, & J. Surrey (Eds.), *Women's growth in connection: Writings from the Stone Center* (pp. 223–236). New York: Guilford Press.

Stiver, I. (1991b). The meaning of care: Reframing treatment models. In J. Jordan, A. Kaplan, J. Miller, I. Stiver, & J. Surrey (Eds.), *Women's growth in connection: Writings from the Stone Center* (pp. 250–267). New York: Guilford Press.

Storl, H. (1995). The marks and masks of personhood: Investigations into the nature of the self. *Choice, 33,* 411–425.

Strauss, C. (1990). Who gets ahead?: Cognitive responses to heteroglossia in American political culture. *American Ethnologist, 17,* 312–328.

Strauss, C. (1992). Models and motives. In R. D'Andrade & C. Strauss (Eds.), *Human motives and cultural models* (pp. 1–20). Cambridge, England: Cambridge University Press.

Strauss, C., & Quinn, N. (1994). A cognitive/cultural anthropology. In R. Borofsky (Ed.), *Assessing cultural anthropology* (pp. 284–300). New York: McGraw-Hill.

Strenta, A., & Kleck, R. (1984). Physical disability and the perception of social interaction: It's not what you look at but how you look at it. *Personality and Social Psychology Bulletin, 10,* 279–288.

Strully, J., & Strully, C. (1993). That which binds us: Friendship as a safe harbor in a storm. In A. Amado (Ed.), *Friendships and community connections between people with and without developmental disabilities* (pp. 213–226). Baltimore: Paul H. Brookes Publishing Co.

Sue, D., & Sue, D. (1990). *Counseling the culturally different: Theory and practice.* New York: John Wiley & Sons.

Sundram, C. (1994). Quality assurance in an era of consumer empowerment and choice. *Mental Retardation, 32,* 371–374.

Sweetser, E. (1991). *From etymology to pragmatics: Metaphorical and cultural aspects of semantic structure.* Cambridge: Cambridge University Press.

Swigonski, M. (1996). Challenging privilege through Africentric social work. *Social Work, 41,* 153–162.

Szwed, J. (1975). Race and the embodiment of culture. *Ethnicity, 2,* 19–33.

Szymanski, E., & Trueba, H. (1994). Castification of people with disabilities: Potential disempowering aspects of classification in disability services. *The Journal of Rehabilitation, 60,* 12–21.

Taussig, M. (1980). Reification and the consciousness of the patient. *Social Science and Medicine, 14B,* 3–13.

Taussig, M. (1992). Tactility and distraction. In G. Marcus (Ed.), *Rereading cultural anthropology* (pp. 8–14). Durham, NC: Duke University Press.

Taylor, S. (1994). In support of research on quality of life, but against QOL. In D. Goode (Ed.), *Quality of life for persons with disabilities: International perspectives and issues* (pp. 260–265). Cambridge, MA: Brookline Books.

Taylor, S., Biklen, D., & Knoll, J. (1987). *Community integration for people with severe disabilities.* New York: Teachers College Press.

Thornton, R. (1992). Rhetoric of ethnographic holism. In G. Marcus (Ed.), *Rereading cultural anthropology* (pp. 15–33). Durham, NC: Duke University Press.

Trent, J. (1994). *Inventing the feeble mind: A history of mental retardation in the United States.* Berkeley: University of California Press.

Triandis, H. (1989). Cross-cultural studies of individualism and collectivism. In J. Berman (Ed.), *Nebraska symposium on motivation 1989: Cross-cultural perspectives* (Vol. 37, pp. 41–133). Lincoln: University of Nebraska Press.

Triandis, H., Bontempo, R., Villareal, M., Asai, M., & Lucca, N. (1987). Individualism and collectivism: Cross-cultural perspectives on self-group relationships. *Journal of Personality and Social Psychology, 54,* 323–338.

Trotter, R. (1991). Ethnographic research methods for applied medical anthropology. In C. Hill (Ed.), *Training manual in applied medical anthropology* (pp. 180–212). Washington, DC: American Anthropology Association.

Tulloch, M. (1995). Evaluating aggression: School students' responses to television portrayals of institutional violence. *Journal of Youth and Adolescence, 24,* 95–116.

Turnbull, A., & Ruef, M. (1996). Family perspectives on problem behavior. *Mental Retardation, 34*, 280–293.

Turner, V. (1967). *The forest of symbols*. Ithaca, NY: Cornell University Press.

Urbinati, N. (1998). From the periphery of modernity: Antonio Gramsci's theory of subordination and hegemony. *Political Theory, 26*, 370–392.

vanDijk, T. (1984). *Prejudice in discourse: An analysis of ethnic prejudice in cognition*. Amsterdam: John Benjamins.

Varenne, H. (1986). Doing the anthropology of America. In H. Varenne (Ed.), *Symbolizing America* (pp. 34–48). Lincoln: University of Nebraska Press.

Wahba, M., & Bridwell, L. (1976). Maslow reconsidered: A review of research on the need hierarchy theory. *Organizational Behavior and Human Performance, 15*, 212–240.

Walmsley, J. (1993). Talking to top people": Some issues relating to the citizenship of people with learning difficulties. In J. Swaim, V. Finkelstein, S. French, & M. Oliver (Eds.), *Disabling barriers—Enabling environments* (pp. 257–266). Newbury Park, CA: Sage.

Ward, N. (1996). Supporting self-advocacy in national organizations: Our role and yours. *Mental Retardation, 34*, 121–122.

Watson, G. (1991). Rewriting culture. In R. Fox (Ed.), *Recapturing anthropology: Working in the present* (pp. 73–92). Santa Fe, NM: School of American Research Press.

Weakliem, D., McQuillan, J., & Schauer, T. (1995). Toward meritocracy? Changing social-class differences in intellectual ability. *Sociology of Education, 88*, 271–286.

Webb, D. (1998). A "revenge" on modern times: Notes on traumatic brain injury. *Sociology, 32*, 541–556.

Wehmeyer, M. (1992a). Self-determination and the education of students with mental retardation. *Education and Training in Mental Retardation, 27*, 302–314.

Wehmeyer, M. (1992b). Self-determination: Critical skills for outcome-oriented transition services. *The Journal for Vocational Special Needs Education, 15*, 3–7.

Wehmeyer, M. (1995). A career education approach: Self-determination for youth with mild cognitive disabilities. *Intervention in School and Clinic, 30*, 157–163.

Wehmeyer, M., Kelchner, K., & Richards, S. (1996). Essential characteristics of self-determined behavior of individuals with mental retardation. *American Journal on Mental Retardation, 100*, 632–642.

Wehmeyer, M., & Palmer, S. (1998). Factor structure and construct validity of scores on the hopelessness scale for children with cognitive disabilities. *Educational and Psychological Measurement, 58*, 661–668.

Weidman, H. (1979). The transcultural view: Prerequisite to interethnic (intercultural) communication in medicine. *Social Science & Medicine, 13B*, 85–87.

Weisinger, H. (1995). *Anger at work*. New York: William Morrow and Co.

Weiss, N. (1990). Positive behavioral programming: An individualized functional approach. In J. Gardner & M. Chapman (Eds.), *Program issues in de-*

velopmental disabilities (2nd ed., pp. 59–77). Baltimore: Paul H. Brookes Publishing Co.

Weisz, J., Rothbaum, F., & Blackburn, T. (1984). Standing out and standing in: The psychology of control in America and Japan. *American Psychologist, 39*, 955–969.

Wells, J. (1993). Making it up as we go along: A story about friendship. In A. Amado (Ed.), *Friendships and community connections between people with and without developmental disabilities* (pp. 197–212). Baltimore: Paul H. Brookes Publishing Co.

West, M., & Parent, W. (1992). Consumer choice and empowerment in supported employment services: Issues and strategies. *Journal of The Association for Persons with Severe Handicaps, 17*, 47–52.

Westbrook, M., Legge, V., & Pennay, M. (1993). Attitudes towards disabilities in a multicultural society. *Social Science & Medicine, 36*, 615–623.

White, G. (1987). Proverbs and cultural models: An American psychology of problem solving. In D. Holland & N. Quinn (Eds.), *Cultural models in language and thought* (pp. 151–172). Cambridge, England: Cambridge University Press.

White, G. (1992). Ethnopsychology. In T. Schwartz, G. White, & C. Lutz (Eds.), *New directions in psychological anthropology* (pp. 21–46). Cambridge, England: Cambridge University Press.

White, R. (1970). The lower-class "culture of excitement" among the contemporary Sioux. In E. Nurge (Ed.), *The modern Sioux* (pp. 175–197). Lincoln: University of Nebraska Press.

Whitman, T. (1990a). Development of self-regulation in persons with mental retardation. *American Journal on Mental Retardation, 94*, 373—376.

Whitman, T. (1990b). Self-regulation and mental retardation. *American Journal on Mental Retardation, 94*, 347–362.

Wilkinson, R. (1996). *Unhealthy societies: The afflictions of inequality.* New York: Routledge.

Williams, G., & Asher, S. (1992). Assessment of loneliness at school among children with mild mental retardation. *American Journal on Mental Retardation, 96*, 373–385.

Willis, P., & Corrigan, P. (1985). Orders of experience: The differences of working class cultural forms. *Social Text, 4*, 95–103.

Wilson, R. (1997). Human rights, culture and context: An introduction. In R. Wilson (Ed.), *Human rights, culture and context: Anthropological perspectives* (pp. 1–27). Chicago: Pluto Press.

Wise, S. (1996). The legal thinghood of nonhuman animals. *Boston Law College Environmental Affairs Review, 23*, 471–525.

Wlodkowski, R., & Ginsberg, M. (1995). *Diversity and motivation.* San Francisco: Jossey-Bass.

Wohlfarth, T., & Van Den Brink, W. (1998). Social class and substance use disorders: The value of social class as distinct from socioeconomic status. *Social Science & Medicine, 47*, 51–58.

Wolfe, A. (1995). Has there been a cognitive revolution in America?: The flawed sociology of the bell curve. In S. Fraser (Ed.), *The bell curve wars:*

Race, intelligence, and the future of America (pp. 11–22). New York: Basic Books.

Wolfensberger, W. (1980). A brief overview of the principle of normalization. In R. Flynn & K. Nitsch (Eds.), *Normalization, social integration and community services* (pp. 7–30). Baltimore: University Park Press.

Wolfensberger, W. (1989). Bill F.: Signs of the times read from the life of one mentally retarded man. *Mental Retardation, 27,* 369–373.

Wolfensberger, W., & Thomas, S. (1983). *PASSING (Program analysis of service systems' implementation of normalization goals): Normalization criteria and ratings manual* (2nd ed.). Toronto: National Institute on Mental Retardation.

Wolff, B., & Langley, S. (1968). Cultural factors and response to pain: A review. *American Anthropologist, 70,* 494–501.

Wyatt, B., & Conners, F. (1998). Implicit and explicit memory in individuals with mental retardation. *American Journal on Mental Retardation, 102,* 511–526.

Zborowski, M. (1960). Cultural components in responses to pain. In D. Apple (Ed.), *Sociological studies of health and sickness* (pp. 118–133). New York: McGraw-Hill.

Zborowski, M. (1969). *People in pain.* San Francisco: Jossey-Bass.

Zimmerman, M. (1990). Toward a theory of learned hopefulness: A structural model analysis of participation and empowerment. *Journal of Research in Personality, 24,* 71–86.

Zola, I. (1966). Culture and symptoms: An analysis of patients' presenting complaints. *American Sociological Review, 31,* 615–630.

Zola, I. (1993). Self, identity and the naming question: Reflections on the language of disability. *Social Science & Medicine, 36,* 167–173.

Index

Page numbers followed by "f" indicate figures; those followed by "t" indicate tables.